Fascism on Trial

Also Available from Bloomsbury

Insurrections, Henry A. Giroux
Race, Politics, and Pandemic Pedagogy, Henry A. Giroux
Pedagogy of Resistance, Henry A. Giroux
On Critical Pedagogy, 2nd edition, Henry A. Giroux
Critical Pedagogy and the Covid-19 Pandemic, edited by Fatma Mizikaci and Eda Ata
Capitalism, Pedagogy, and the Politics of Being, Noah DeLissovoy
Ecopedagogy, Greg William Misiaszek
Transnational Feminist Politics, Education, and Social Justice, edited by Silvia Edling and Sheila Macrine
Education, Equality and Justice in the New Normal, edited by Inny Accioly and Donaldo Macedo
Education for Social Change, Douglas Bourn

Fascism on Trial

Education and the Possibility of Democracy

HENRY A. GIROUX AND
ANTHONY R. DIMAGGIO

BLOOMSBURY ACADEMIC
LONDON · NEW YORK · OXFORD · NEW DELHI · SYDNEY

BLOOMSBURY ACADEMIC
Bloomsbury Publishing Plc
50 Bedford Square, London, WC1B 3DP, UK
1385 Broadway, New York, NY 10018, USA
29 Earlsfort Terrace, Dublin 2, Ireland

BLOOMSBURY, BLOOMSBURY ACADEMIC and the Diana logo
are trademarks of Bloomsbury Publishing Plc

First published in Great Britain 2024

Copyright © Henry A. Giroux and Anthony R. DiMaggio, 2024

Henry A. Giroux and Anthony R. DiMaggio have asserted their right under the
Copyright, Designs and Patents Act, 1988, to be identified as Author of this work.

For legal purposes the Acknowledgments on p. x constitute an
extension of this copyright page.

Cover design: Grace Ridge
Cover image © Isaac Cordal. San Cristobal de las Casas.
Chiapas. Mexico. 2013

All rights reserved. No part of this publication may be reproduced or
transmitted in any form or by any means, electronic or mechanical,
including photocopying, recording, or any information storage or retrieval
system, without prior permission in writing from the publishers.

Bloomsbury Publishing Plc does not have any control over, or
responsibility for, any third-party websites referred to or in this book.
All internet addresses given in this book were correct at the time of
going to press. The author and publisher regret any inconvenience
caused if addresses have changed or sites have ceased to exist, but
can accept no responsibility for any such changes.

A catalogue record for this book is available from the British Library.

A catalog record for this book is available from the Library of Congress.

ISBN: HB: 978-1-3504-2167-7
PB: 978-1-3504-2168-4
ePDF: 978-1-3504-2171-4
eBook: 978-1-3504-2169-1

Typeset by Integra Software Services Pvt. Ltd.

To find out more about our authors and books visit www.bloomsbury.com
and sign up for our newsletters.

For Rania
Henry A. Giroux
For Mary, Frankie, Tommy, and Lizzy
Anthony DiMaggio

CONTENTS

Acknowledgments x

Introduction 1

PART ONE Fascist Nightmares and the Cult of Violence 15

1 America's Fascist Problem: Rethinking Education in an Age of Conspiracy Theories and Election Deniers 17
2 Vigilantes on Parade 29

PART TWO Neoliberal Fascism, Cruelty, and Street Politics 41

3 Neoliberal Fascism, Cruel Violence, and the Politics of Disposability 43
4 Street Fascism and the Politics of Denialism 59

PART THREE The Language of Fascism 71

5 Language and Violence as Spectacle in the New Age of Fascist Politics 73

6 Language and the Politics of Lying: The Big Lie and White Supremacy 87

PART FOUR Fascism's Fundamentalist Passions 99

7 Fascist Politics and the Scourge of Anti-Semitism in the Age of Disconnected Present 101
8 Fascism, White Christian Nationalism, and QAnon Rising 117

PART FIVE Fascism's Attack on Political Agency and Historical Memory 127

9 The Menace of American Authoritarianism and the Crisis of Political Agency 129
10 Politicizing January 6th, White Supremacy, and the Assault on Historical Memory 143

PART SIX American Society and the Turn Towards Fascism 155

11 The Nazification of American Society 157
12 What Fascism Is (and Isn't): The White Working Class and White Supremacy 173

PART SEVEN Education and the Mobilizing Passions of Fascism 185

13 The Nazification of American Education 187

14 Orwell, Totalitarian Politics, and the War on Anti-Racism in Education 197

Conclusion: Gangster Capitalism and the Politics of Fascism 209

Notes 220
Index 276

ACKNOWLEDGMENTS

We live in an age in which the mainstream and far-right media largely ignore important social problems, especially those considered critical of capitalism, neoliberalism, and the emerging fascist state in the U.S. and abroad. Our work does not align with the media of complicity and its unwavering support for existing political, economic, and cultural structures of inequality, oppression, and domination. We have chosen to write from the margins, to address the voices of the excluded, to include theorists often ignored, to combine theory with statistical evidence, and to make comparisons that connect rather than isolate issues. We have also chosen to address the ideal of democracy against its conservative and liberal renderings, which confuse the reality of democracy with its possibilities. Against those who believe hope is lost in an age of emerging fascism, we argue in the words of Ernst Bloch that hope is wounded but not lost. We are grateful for a range of courageous writers, educators, and cultural workers whose work inspires our own—who were and are willing to say the unthinkable, to think and write against the grain, and who demonstrate that power is not only about domination but also about resistance. We are grateful to Mark Richardson at Bloomsbury for continuing to support our work. A number of the ideas in this book appeared in different forms in *Truthout*, *CounterPunch*, *Salon*, *The Review of Education, Pedagogy, and Cultural Studies*, *Policy Studies*, *Fast Capitalism*, *Symploke*, *LA Progressive*, *Rise Up Times*, *Uncommon Thought*, and other online and scholarly sources.

Introduction

Henry A. Giroux and Anthony DiMaggio

Americans live in an era in which history is being erased and rewritten. The long shadow of domestic fascism, defined largely as a project of racial and genocidal cleansing, has made clear what the end of democracy, if not humanity, would look like.[1] As theorists such as Aimé Césaire and Frantz Fanon have reminded us, the legacy of fascism is evident in acts of savage colonialism, which long predated the European forms of fascist politics.[2] Colonial fascism was the driving force that slaughtered native Americans and legalized colonial dispossession and slavery. A distinctly American version emerged in full force in its white supremacy guise via the rise of the Ku Klux Klan, which inaugurated a period of lynching and intense racialized terror. W. E. B. Dubois echoed this, arguing that the white supremacy of Jim Crow was in fact a form of fascism. In its twentieth-century American form, fascism as a new site of politics rebranded itself and merged the materiality and violence of the carceral state and racial capitalism.[3]

In its current form, racialized state terror has returned as neoliberalism, and its global finance regime no longer covers over its crimes with the discourse of democracy. In fact, the economically privileged and their political cronies now view democracy as the enemy of markets and government as a defender of the wealth and power of the financial elites. As G. M. Tamas observes, a "cluster" of anti-democratic, anti-egalitarian practices "finds its niche easily in the new world of global capitalism without upsetting the dominant political forms of electoral democracy."[4] What results are rebranded forms of fascism that emerge "sans Führer, sans one-party rule, sans SA or SS."[5] What is left is a form of fascism hostile to universal citizenship in which the range of exclusion expands to include those "who are ethnically, racially, denominationally, or culturally 'alien,' [and who] do not really belong."[6]

Illiberal democracy, with its rabid nativism and hatred of racial mixing, is currently at the center of American politics. Aligning with illiberal democracies in Hungary, Poland, and elsewhere, far-right politicians and their followers in the United States are waging a war on those civic institutions crucial to a democracy. Traditional liberal values of equality, social justice, dissent, and freedom are considered a threat to a Republican Party supportive of staggering levels of inequality, white Christian nationalism, and racial purity. And yet, the lessons of history with its genocidal camps, horrors, torture, and embrace of murderous violence as a political tool are largely ignored—though its mobilizing fascist passions are once again on the horizon. As education collapses under racist forms of censorship, the banning of books, the cleansing of history, and a war on critical thought, the American public falls prey to a culture of violence, retribution, ignorance, repression, and the decline of civil society. As racist lies and a tsunami of right-wing cultural apparatuses wage war on truth, reason, and social responsibility, moments of infamy proliferate. These include the January 6th storming of the U.S. Capitol, the war on trans youth, the endless police violence waged against Black people, the elimination of women's reproductive rights, increasing acts of cultural genocide, and the naming of those who do not buy into the cult of the strongman as enemies of the state. Under such circumstances, much of the American public loses its connection to what should be lessons learned from the history of fascism.

Culture as an educational force has been poisoned and plays a key role in normalizing fascist politics in America and around the globe. The mass media have turned into flame throwers of hate and bigotry, stylized as spectacle. Alienating misery, social atomization, the death of the social contract, the militarization of public space, concentrations of wealth and power in the hands of the financial and ruling elite, all fuel a fascist politics. The signs of fascism no longer hide in the shadows. Against those politicians, pundits, and academics who falsely claim that fascism rests entirely in the past, we argue in the manner of Hannah Arendt, Sheldon Wolin, Ruth

Ben-Ghiat, Sarah Churchill, Robert O. Paxton, and others, that fascism is always present in history and can crystallize in different forms. Or as Jason Stanley observes, "Fascism [is] 'a political method' that can appear anytime, anywhere, if conditions are right."[7] The historical arc of fascism is not frozen in history and its attributes lurk in different forms in diverse societies, waiting to adapt to times favorable to its emergence. As Paul Gilroy notes, the "horrors [of fascism] are always much closer to us than we like to imagine," and our duty is not to look away but to make them visible.[8] The refusal by an array of politicians, scholars, and the mainstream media to acknowledge the scale of the fascist threat bearing down on American society is more than an act of refusal—it is an act of complicity. Fascism draws much of its energy from a culture of fear, resentment, blind faith, and a state of mind in which the distinction between true and false collapses into alternative realities. We believe that one cannot be silent in the face of such a dire threat. The conditions that produce fascism are with us once again and the threat along with the forces that produce it must be named so it can be understood and overcome.

We believe that the symptoms of rising fascism in America are all around us. What do you call someone who demands that his subordinates shoot Mexican immigrants at the border,[9] while calling on the military to shoot overwhelmingly non-violent Black Lives Matter activists in the streets?[10] What name would you use to describe a person and his accomplices who plot to overthrow a democratic election, demanding that members of their party in Congress and in state government ignore popular majorities based on non-existent mass voter fraud, and hand Trump an election he did not win? What term would best describe a person who indulges in severe egotism and anti-intellectualism, demonizing scientists during a pandemic and claiming they are lying to the public?[11]

What about someone who demands unquestioning loyalty from his subordinates and supporters in the public at large? What if he demanded that his political allies be thrown in prison based on paranoid and delusional claims that they are spying on him and trying to overthrow him in a coup?[12] What do you call someone who brags about assaulting women, while using dehumanizing language against people of color, comparing them to animals?[13] Let us say that same person valorizes extremist social movements like QAnon, which embraces violent rhetoric and politics calling for the overthrow of the two-party system and trafficking in antisemitic "blood libel" conspiracies?[14] And what about someone who indulges in white nationalism, romanticizing the confederate flag and confederate monuments,[15] and demanding an end to immigration from Latin America and the Middle East, while congratulating white Americans for their "good genes,"[16] and calling for more immigration from northern Europe?[17] There is a name for someone who fits all of these political traits—a fascist.

We live in a time defined by a rising fascist movement in America. No other explanation is logical when we consider that the head of one of the two major political parties in this country—Donald Trump—has indulged in all the rhetoric and actions above, while avoiding political or legal accountability throughout the entirety of his presidential term and for years afterwards. We argue throughout this book that this rising fascist movement includes many different political actors—the Republican Party and its leaders, right-wing media, far-right political activists, and most of the GOP base, which has been consistently willing to normalize Trump's fascism without question.

Fascism is a concept that is much talked about in western discourse but is seldom understood. We examine fascism in this text, in relation to some very specific features of this far-right political ideology. When we speak of fascism, we are talking about the following:

- A political system dominated by an authoritarian leader who valorizes masculinity as a source of authority and remains in power through a support base that indulges in the cult of patriarchal personality, eschewing evidence-based claims whenever they undermine the positions of *The Leader*. This is a political system marked by a contempt for weakness and a propensity for violence in the service of power.

- A political discourse and process that embraces militarism and the pursuit of a narrow version of national rebirth that elevates white nationalist ideology to the highest societal ideal. This is a discourse that trades in fear and uses white supremacy as a tool to enable Americans to accept if not normalize the unthinkable.

- A party system where one of the major parties identifies with eliminationist messaging and politics that dehumanizes opponents of *The Leader* and his political party, seeks to incarcerate their political critics, and assaults multi-party democracy by undermining the integrity of and trust in democratic elections. This is a politics of mass terror and a steady purging of the space of plurality and difference.

- A political system that assaults immigrants and people of color, while dominating women's bodies, demonizing and assaulting the poor, and marginalizing religious minorities, all in pursuit of a politics that elevates whites, and particularly affluent white men, to the highest positions of authority and power.

- A political system whose mobilizing passions and constants include the disappearance of a meaningful politics—one reduced to the mere circulation of propaganda; a politics of disposability marked by scapegoating and eliminating individuals and groups unworthy of occupying public space; a frenzied lawlessness and ideological certainty; a politics of resentment and denigration of those considered enemies of the state/leader; a reliance upon a culture of lies and agitation; a violent descent into a species of regression and anarchical modes of behavior; the outgrowth of a neoliberal capitalism that cannot live up to its promises, attacks historical memory and invents a mythic past, displays a hatred of critical thought and a hostility to intellectualism and an oppositional press, and assumes the posture of being grieved and victimhood.

Note that we are *not* arguing that the United States as we know it is a fully consolidated fascist republic, equivalent to the ones that existed in the interwar years in Italy and Germany and controlled by Benito Mussolini and Adolf Hitler. Such an argument makes it easier to think fascism cannot happen again in America and elsewhere. It is intellectually irresponsible to offer straw man arguments, suggesting that those of us warning about rising fascism in America are wrong because the current version of right-wing extremism in this country does not fully match that seen in the era of classical fascism of the 1930s. We are aware of no one who even offers up this position as a serious argument. It is unrealistic to expect that the specific social, political, and economic conditions that existed a century ago will replicate themselves today. We do believe, however, that there are enough substantive similarities and overlap between the conditions that existed a century ago and today to merit talking about an updated version of fascism for the twenty-first century. We argue that fascism can be observed as a series of patterns that can be examined both in the past and in the present. Learning from history is different from suggesting the present mindlessly repeats the past.

History is once again unleashing its crueler lessons amid a climate of denial and counterattacks. Ignoring the lessons of history comes at great peril since they provide a glimpse of not only the conditions that produce the terror and cruelty endemic to authoritarianism, but also serve as warning signs of what the end of morality, justice, and humanity might look like, and which are imperative to recognize. These include vengeful nationalism, a politics of disposability, nativism, the language of decline and resurrection, the appeal of the strong man, anti-intellectualism, a culture of lies, contempt for the rule of law and dissent, the elevation of instinct over reason, and hatred of the other. The historical conditions that have produced totalitarian forms have returned, and it is crucial to learn how they emerged in the past and how they take a different form in the present. In this book, we offer an approach that blends theoretical and critical exploration with social scientific evidence. Each section of the book includes two chapters—the first which explores broader concepts and ideas as related to the rise of authoritarian and fascist politics in America, and the second which follows it up with an application of these ideas, relying on qualitative case studies and empirical evidence.

Main Themes

This book represents an interrogation of rising fascism in America. It spotlights the major facets of fascism that increasingly characterize contemporary U.S. politics, in relation to political authoritarianism, the rise of anti-intellectualism and the mainstreaming of conspiracy theories and mass paranoia, the glorification of political street violence and state violence, rising white supremacy, and the militarization of U.S. political discourse, led chiefly by the U.S. right under Donald Trump and his acolytes.

It situates the January 6th insurrection within the context of these ascending traits of fascist ideology and politics, which have been embraced primarily by the Republican Party. In particular we challenge the commonly embraced notion that Trumpism is primarily a function of economic insecurity within his base, documenting how support for the former president predominantly centered on reactionary socio-cultural values and white supremacy. We also document how white supremacist values are central to the Trump base defending the January 6th insurrection, despite academics, journalists, and political officials in both major parties ignoring the threat of rising white nationalism. We examine the centrality of the assault on critical education and pedagogy to the fascist program, while stressing the vital importance of reprioritizing education as a public good to combating fascist politics and ideology.

I. Fascist Nightmares and the Cult of Violence

Chapter 1: America's Fascist Problem: Rethinking Education in an Age of Conspiracy Theories and Election Deniers

This chapter examines both the long-standing roots of American fascism and its current upgraded political formation. It stresses fascism's enactment of an existential crisis of identity, an economic crisis, and an educational crisis. It emphasizes the failure of progressives, leftists, and others to address the symbolic, structural, and pedagogical dimensions of fascist politics and how to name and resist it. It also emphasizes the need for a wider public to recognize the imminent threat a resurgent fascism poses in the U.S.

Chapter 2: Vigilantes on Parade

This chapter examines fascism as a function of the construction of alternate fantasy "realities" on the right, in which a growing base of extremists associated with the GOP believe that U.S. law and order is under threat, and that citizen fascists need to take matters into their own hands. It examines the rise of vigilante violence, focusing primarily on the Kyle Rittenhouse trial and his exoneration as a representation of intensifying street fascism in the United States. It discusses the implications of court sanctioned violence in place of professional policing.

II. Neoliberal Fascism, Cruelty, and Street Politics

Chapter 3: Neoliberal Fascism, Cruel Violence, and the Politics of Disposability

In this chapter, we argue that the United States is at a turning point in its history. As civic culture collapses, neoliberalism wages war on the public imagination, and politics is emptied of democratic values. Violence and staggering inequality in wealth and power occupy the center of power and everyday life. Violence has become the midwife of political power in U.S. politics and a valued currency of social change. In addition, cruelty has come to play a prominent role in the rise of fascist ideology and policies.

Chapter 4: Street Fascism and the Politics of Denialism

Chapter 4 further explores the rise of street fascism, examining the ways in which U.S. media culture engages in denialist discourse that erases discussions of fascism. Various mass shooter events involving fascists are dissected, including the Buffalo, New York and Highland Park, Illinois mass shootings. These events are tied to the politics of white supremacy, anti-Semitism, and white nationalism, as we examine the motives of the shooters, while analyzing the ways in which U.S. reporters have obscured this fascism in their reporting and commentary.

III. The Language of Fascism

Chapter 5: Language and Violence as Spectacle in the New Age of Fascist Politics

This chapter discusses how the spectacle of violence and its dehumanizing language have become central features of neoliberal fascism in American society and politics. It explores the argument through both the increasing toxic role of the social media and conservative online platforms as well as through popular culture and the growing extremism of the Republican Party.

Chapter 6: Language and the Politics of Lying: The Big Lie and White Supremacy

Chapter 6 includes two case studies that dissect how organized lying is central to fascism. It examines the role of *Fox News* and other right-wing media in constructing the false notion that the 2020 election was stolen from Donald Trump in favor of Joe Biden, while uncovering the practical effects of this lie on mass opinion for those who consume *Fox News*, and for Republicans and the mass public more generally. The chapter also reviews how discussions of white supremacy were systematically omitted from discussions of vigilante fascism in relation to Kyle Rittenhouse and his connections to alt-right fascists.

IV. Fascism's Fundamentalist Passions

Chapter 7: Fascist Politics and the Scourge of Anti-Semitism in the Age of Disconnected Present

This chapter argues that as social problems are treated in an isolated and disconnected way in contemporary America, it becomes difficult to see fascist politics as a new and dangerous political and social formation. It examines how various issues such as the display of anti-Semitism by Ye, the attack on public education, Ron DeSantis's shameful stunt of shipping migrants to Martha's Vineyard, and other social issues are part of a broader authoritarian attack on democracy.

Chapter 8: Fascism, White Christian Nationalism, and QAnon Rising

Chapter 8 discusses the intertwining of fascist politics and QAnon with right-wing Christianity and Christian nationalism. It examines the rising fundamentalist rhetoric of Republican officials, who seek to impose Christian identity politics on the nation. This assault on the rule of law, the First Amendment, and separation of church and state is tied directly to various right-wing campaigns, including the attempt to ban books that spotlight racism in America, and related to the demonization of liberals more broadly.

V. Fascism's Attack on Political Agency and Historical Memory

Chapter 9: The Menace of American Authoritarianism and the Crisis of Political Agency

Chapter 9 examines the notion of fascist politics as part of an ongoing crisis of political agency, historical consciousness, education, and the collapse of civic consciousness. It argues that historical memory is crucial to examine and expose the delusions of the past to understand the present. It is also crucial to use the past as a vital pedagogical resource for imagining a future that is not frozen in the methodological cleansing of history. We propose that historical memory is central to overcoming a form of moral blindness and historical amnesia that depoliticizes individuals by constraining their sense of agency and collective power of resistance.

Chapter 10: Politicizing January 6th, White Supremacy, and the Assault on Historical Memory

This chapter interrogates the lies that have been told about January 6th. These are lies of omission, first in terms of Trump seeking to erase his role in stoking the crisis. Second, we expose how discussions of white supremacy and fascism are erased from mass discourse in relation to how these impulses resonate with the public. We examine the January 6th report as an example of fascism denial within the political class, and among academics and journalists, despite available evidence that white supremacy is the primary driver of how tens of millions of Americans look at January 6th.

VI. American Society and the Turn Towards Fascism

Chapter 11: The Nazification of American Society

This chapter explores how the different registers of fascism overlap and shape language, policies, and a range of educational practices that extend from banning books and whitewashing history to forcing teachers to take loyalty oaths while enacting punishing policies aimed at Black, Brown, and transgender youth. As fascism is normalized, there is an urgent need for educators to merge a mass movement for economic and social justice with a formative culture and educational project that places matters of morality, justice, compassion, care, and civic courage above a predatory neoliberal capitalism that is destroying the planet and ushering in a new age of fascist barbarism. The chapter calls upon teachers and educators along with artists, youth, and others committed to a democratic socialist society to unite and fight for a future defined by social justice democratic values, equality, social responsibility, inclusiveness, and freedom.

Chapter 12: What Fascism is (and Isn't): The White Working Class and White Supremacy

Chapter 12 cuts to the core of what it means to talk about American fascism. It reviews the evidence that associates Trumpism, right-wing extremism, and fascism with economic insecurity. There is little to indicate that right-wing extremism, including fascist politics, is driven by insecurity. Fascism is primarily about an embrace of right-wing socio-cultural values and authoritarianism, via the normalization of fascist ideology by Trump and right-wing media. We examine Trump's speeches, looking at the ways in which he demonizes Democrats, immigrants, and people of color in favor of white nationalist-white supremacist politics, and via dehumanizing rhetoric that compares people of color to animals. This tactic of dehumanization is right out of the pages of the Third Reich's fascist propaganda.

VII. Education and the Mobilizing Passions of Fascism

Chapter 13: The Nazification of American Education

This chapter compares how education developed in Nazi Germany and details its resemblance to a variety of right-wing educational policies and practices in the U.S. The chapter focuses on a range of educational practices in the Third Reich that ranged from book burning and censorship to the gutting of the curriculum and the firing and punishing of dissident faculty. It examines these practices with references to a range of educational practices being conducted by Governor Ron DeSantis and other GOP leaders throughout America.

Chapter 14: Orwell, Totalitarian Politics, and the War on Anti-Racism in Education

Our final chapter further elaborates on Chapter 13 and the discussion of the Nazification of U.S. education. It provides an extensive analysis of the war on Critical Race Theory, charting out this rising opposition as a function of the right-wing backlash against Black Lives Matter and anti-racism. The chapter provides a framework for understanding opposition to anti-racism that draws on George Orwell's writing about the rise of totalitarianism and Big Brother monitoring regimes, which represent an eliminationist assault on critical thought.

PART ONE

Fascist Nightmares and the Cult of Violence

CHAPTER ONE

America's Fascist Problem: Rethinking Education in an Age of Conspiracy Theories and Election Deniers

In the current political landscape, fascism is on the rise and democracy is imperiled both as an ideal and promise.[1] A number of Republican politicians who ran for political office in America embrace elements of white supremacy, support white Christian nationalism, traffic in anti-Semitism, and endorse voter suppression policies, among other elements of hate politics. These officials indulge in a poisonous rhetoric that fuels a neo-fascist politics that is sanctioned by most of the Republican Party—a rhetoric of historical erasure, hate, bigotry, and disposability. At least 210 of these election-denying politicians were elected to House, Senate, and governor seats in 2022, including J. D. Vance, Marjorie Taylor Greene, and Gregg Abbott.[2] While President Biden claimed in a speech prior to the 2022 election that the election would put democracy on the block, he vastly underestimated the degree to which the resurgent right wing could usher in fascist politics in America.[3] After the election, a number of pundits, including President Biden, argued that there is some hope for democracy given that the Republican red wave did not happen as predicted, especially since a number of the "worst election deniers and kookiest candidates were sent packing."[4] Yet, as Michael Tomasky observes, while some of Trump's candidates lost, "Trumpism still won to a frightening extent [since] 176 election deniers won statewide races or seats in the House of Representatives."[5] Moreover, the GOP did take control of the House of Representatives, albeit with a small majority. Unfortunately, under the leadership of Kevin McCarthy the ultra-right wing of the

GOP is driving policy in the House of Representatives. As of this writing McCarthy has been ousted as speaker of the house and it is unclear who will succeed him. One potential candidate is far-right extremist Jim Jordan—an election denier and supporter of the January 6 attempt to overthrow the government. Fortunately, the Democrats retained control of the Senate—an arguably small reprieve for democracy. Yet, the deceptions and ideological mystifications powering the threat of fascism remain. The ghosts of fascism are still with us waiting to stamp out any vestige of democracy, however fragile it already is. Fascism in America and across the globe continues to be a spiraling probability.

What must not be forgotten is that many of the GOP politicians who were voted into office, especially Gov. Ron DeSantis, who swept to landslide victory in Florida, hold deeply anti-democratic, authoritarian positions. These are not rogue deviants; rather, they are symptoms of a much wider culture of authoritarian politics that normalizes bigotry, whitewashes history, bans books, and encourages violence. They are the new face of fascist politics haunting America. Fascist rhetoric is no longer an underground phenomenon. It has been awakened and is embraced without apology. This is a politics that basks in the language of demagogues, encourages those who trade in lies and ignorance, manipulates public opinion in the service of tyrants, embraces a ruthless display of power, demonstrates an utter disregard for the law, and fosters a passion for viciousness. Ron DeSantis's reelection in particular was troubling given the fact that many historians, opinion writers, and others, including former Secretary of Labor, Robert Reich, have made clear his links to fascism.[6]

This rebranded fascist politics exceeds and targets more than any one specific group. It extends far beyond the intensifying displays of anti-Semitism among celebrities such as rapper Kanye West (Ye) and Brooklyn Nets' superstar point guard Kyrie Irving, beyond the white Christian nationalism of religious fundamentalists such as former General and Trump advisor Michael Flynn,[7] or the overt racism of "Dilbert" creator Scott Adams who described Black Americans as "a hate group."[8] If Flynn advocates turning politics into a "spiritual war," Kanye West and Kyrie Irving want their audiences to believe that anti-Semitism is a legitimate rhetoric, that conspiracy theories are okay to peddle in public, and that "the Holocaust is an exaggeration or a falsehood."[9] The hateful rhetoric used by Republican politicians is often matched by specific acts of aggressions by a variety of far-right groups. For instance, micro-aggressions perpetuated by neo-Nazi groups are evident in the placing of anti-Semitic flyers across a number of neighborhoods in cities such as Atlanta, Georgia.[10] Neo-Nazis no longer hide in the shadows. They now appear protesting Broadway shows, declare an anti-Semitic "Day of Hate," and parade openly in protest of almost any LGTBQ+ event. Scott Adams's racism is almost expected in a climate in which individuals on the right claim they are either being victimized by liberals and the left or that "White people face discrimination and racism equal to or greater than Black or other non-White groups."[11] Adams is merely repeating another version of white replacement theory—a relatively recent label for an older version of Jim Crow and fascist ideology, which views whites as losing their political and social power due to their being replaced by immigrants and non-whites.[12]

In the age of fascist politics, extremist rhetoric is not only fueled by Trump and his followers, but also by a slew of forces including digital culture and right-wing media platforms. This anti-Semitic discourse emerges at a time "when incidents of harassment, vandalism, and violence against [Jews] have been at their highest since at least the 1970s."[13] Moreover, this rhetoric is now part of a broader language of disposability aimed at migrants, people of color, refugees, and others. As Trump's rhetoric, aimed at various prosecutors who have indicted him, becomes more reckless, including posting a photo of a judge's daughter, along with comments such as "IF YOU GO AFTER ME, I'M COMING AFTER YOU," social media outlets have exploded with violent threats. For example, a number of pro-Trump forums, messaging groups, and media platforms have posted violent threats against Fani Taifa Willis, the district attorney of Fulton County, Georgia. Similar threats have been posted against judges and others who are overseeing cases against Trump's criminal infractions. Vera Bergenruen reports in *Time* magazine that "Threats against federal judges have spiked 400% in the past six years, to more than 3,700 in 2022, according to the U.S. Marshals Service."[14]

What should be condemned here is not only such actions but also a society that allows such threats to become normalized. What should be understood and interrogated in the age of rebranded fascism is the broad-based attack by anti-democratic forces in the Republican Party and their allies on those key political, cultural, and social institutions that attempt to create informed and critically engaged citizens. Violence against civil servants is not new, what is distinct is how it has become normalized in a political culture in which truth gives way to conspiracy theories, critics are branded as enemies of America, and a major political party has become a cult willing to do almost anything to gain power. Violence at almost every level of American society has become a disturbing fixture of daily life both in wider culture and in the realm of politics.

As democratic agencies come under attack, modes of critical agency disappear in the fog of political infantilism, paving the way for the public's belief in the rhetoric of racial purity and religious fundamentalism. At the same time, we are witnessing the rise of an ecosystem of lies, a withdrawal from the language of social and moral responsibility, an obsession with crime and punishment, and the identification of adversaries as enemies of the state. We now live in a system of manipulation, staged fear, and manufactured ignorance that dissolves any vestige of disbelief, skepticism, and critical thinking. A crisis of ideas, criticism, and ideals has led to a crisis of conscience and the near collapse of democratic politics. The winds of fascism now reach deeply into the lungs of the social fabric, infecting its ability to breathe, converting it and the public it serves to the status of the walking dead.

In his 1946 essay in *Commentary*, Leo Lowenthal writes about the atomization of human beings living in a state of fear that approximates a kind of updated fascist terror.[15] Atomization for Lowenthal refers to individuals living in a social order in which they are cut off from communal spaces, reduced to disembodied agents who suffer from bouts of isolation and lack of self-worth. Trapped in a culture of harsh competition and a regressive notion of individualism, they feel powerless and are prone to bouts of cynicism and despair. For those who lack any sense of interconnection, the space of the social dissolves, leaving nothing but the emptiness of self-interest and self-survival. Central to their condition is a sense of homelessness, a kind of spiritual rootlessness. What Lowenthal understood, even in 1946, is that democracy cannot exist without the necessary educational, political, and formative cultures and institutions that provide a sense of solidarity, common good, compassion, and connectedness. And he recognized that atomized individuals—who feel divorced from their community—are not only prone to the forces of depoliticization but also to the false swindle and spirit of demagogues, discourses of hate and demonization of the other.

We live in an age of death dealing loneliness, isolation, and militarized atomization. If you believe the popular press, loneliness is reaching epidemic proportions in wired advanced industrial societies.[16] The usual suspect is social media platforms, which sequester people in the warm glow of the computer screen while reinforcing their own isolation and sense of loneliness. Notions of "friends" and "likes" have become disembodied categories as human beings disappear into the black hole of algorithms and empty signifiers. The toxic role of digital platforms cannot be overestimated when one lives in a society where feelings of dependence, compassion, mutuality, care for the other, and sociality are undermined by a neoliberal ethic in which self-interest and extreme individualism become the organizing principles of one's life.[17] Social bonds have become frayed in a capitalist society that glorifies selfishness, destroys social connections that give us a sense of agency, place, worth, and community, and traps us in ecosystem that fosters loneliness and alienation. Capitalism thrives on producing social atomization, which leaves individuals trapped in emotions infused with fear, anxiety, anger, and pervasive feelings of helplessness. Chris Hedges is right in arguing that "Social isolation is the lifeblood of totalitarian movements."[18]

Social media spaces amplify a survival-of-the-fittest ethic that breeds a culture that at best promotes indifference toward the plight of others, and at worst promotes a widespread culture of cruelty and disdain for the less fortunate. It also promotes a culture in which the self can only recognize itself in the image of the selfie, convinced as John Steppling puts it that "having an experience is identical with taking a photograph of it."[19] Power is now in the hands of the financial elite who control the means of knowledge production, culture, and all the major financial institutions.[20] Jonathan Crary, in *Scorched Earth*, captures the staggering power of transnational corporations in the following comments:

> The digital tools and services used by people everywhere are subordinated to the power of transnational corporations, intelligence agencies, criminal cartels, and a sociopathic billionaire elite. For the majority of the earth's population on whom it has been imposed, the internet complex is the implacable engine of addiction, loneliness, false hopes, cruelty, psychosis, indebtedness, squandered life, the corrosion of memory, and social

disintegration. ... The internet complex has become inseparable from the immense, incalculable scope of 24/7 capitalism and its frenzy of accumulation, extraction, circulation, production, transport, and construction, on a global scale. Behaviors that are inimical to the possibility of a livable and just world are incited in almost every feature of online operations. Fueled by artificially manufactured appetites, the speed and ubiquity of digital networks maximize the incontestable priority of getting, having, coveting, resenting, envying; all of which furthers the deterioration of the world—a world operating without pause, without the possibility of renewal or recovery, choking on its heat and waste.[21]

At the same time, violence has become normalized as part of the rhetoric of politics, sometimes with dangerous if not deadly results. Fueled by former President Trump, right-wing media, and politicians at the highest levels of government, violence is now a tool of political opportunism. It is now used in the service of power to threaten and intimidate teachers, politicians, school board members, librarians, election officials, and anyone else who defies the orchestrated lies and far-right ideologies promoted by a diverse group of white supremacists, neo-Nazis, nativists, rabid evangelicals, and other extremists.

It is no surprise that the greatest threats of violence in America, according to the FBI and a host of other government agencies, now come from far-right extremists. As Amy Goodman and Denis Moynihan note, "Political violence is on a bloody and disturbing rise in the America ... [and] Since Trump's 2020 loss, threats against election officials have intensified. The Brennan Center for Justice issued a report in 2021 that detailed reports from states across the country of numerous confrontations and threats against election workers—many laced with racism and anti-Semitism."[22]

The lust for power by corrupt politicians, major corporations, and the financial elite draws directly from the playbook of fascist politics. Umberto Eco in his 1995 *New York Review of Books* essay "Ur Fascism," was right in claiming that fascist politics takes many forms. Eco reminds us that the components of fascism often come draped in the symbols and traditions of the societies that embrace them.[23] His list of said components is worth paraphrasing and elaborating on: 1) the cult tradition and the nostalgia for those days when white powerful men ruled society; 2) the rejection of the modern world and the turn toward irrationalism; 3) a deep seated anti-intellectualism; 4) the belief that any disagreement with established power amounts to treason; 5) the fear of difference—exemplified by what Hungarian Prime Minister Viktor Orbán calls "mixed races"; 6) the appeal to fear, anxiety, and uncertainty; 7) a notion of who is worthy of citizenship based on a besieged and victimized sense of white agency and identity; 8) an ultra-nationalism that can provide the nation with a racial identity; 9) contempt for the weak; 10) an embrace of hyper-masculinity modeled after a contempt and disdain for women; 11) a selective populism in which the notion of citizenship is restricted to a privileged few—those who hold a sense of racial, religious, and political entitlement; 12) use of an impoverished vocabulary, a hatred of truth and an open embrace of lies; and 13) the destruction of historical memory and moral witnessing.

In 1944, Henry Wallace, Vice President to Franklin D. Roosevelt, published an article in *The New York Times* in which he made clear that fascism was not a foreign entity unrelated to American politics.[24] For Wallace, fascism has to be recognized and defined within a menacing American context if it was to be defeated. By expanding the definition of fascism, he pointed to what he called a "breed of super-nationalist[s] who [pursue] political power by deceiving Americans and playing to their fears … who poison the channels of public information (and put) money and power ahead of human beings."[25] Additionally, he argued that fascists need enemies and scapegoats, and that they harbor "an intensity of intolerance toward those of other races, parties, classes, religious, cultures, regions or nations."[26] There was an urgency in Wallace's argument that resonates today with the rise of authoritarianism across the globe—an urgency that speaks to a crisis of American democracy at the breaking point. Wallace saw a slow-motion nightmare in his own time. It is time to recognize a fascist nightmare that is no longer slow-moving, but galloping across the globe.

All of these attributes mentioned by Eco, Wallace, and others are at work in the updated fascist politics driving the modern Republican Party.[27] These attributes not only present an ongoing threat to social justice, democracy, equality, and freedom, but also provide an image of a fascist past—whether inspired by the genocide of Indigenous people and slavery in America or the legacy of Nazi Germany—that makes clear what the end of humanity looks like.

The spectacle of Nazi rallies holds an eerie resemblance to those Republican rallies held in the lead up to the 2022 midterm elections. Prior to these, politicians ranging from Ron DeSantis and Kari Lake to Blake Masters and J. D. Vance spewed out lies, denied election results, rejected the perils of climate change, adulated the power of the financial elite, and demonized women's rights—all to the sound of cheering crowds. Their language was laced with falsehoods, racial dog whistles, the demonization of those they disagree with, an embrace of the rhetoric of fear and often not too subtle calls to violence—all in the service of spectacularized fascism. In the runup to the 2024 presidential election, Trump escalated his violent rhetoric and threats. He "appeared to threaten Manhattan District Attorney Alvin Bragg (D) with a baseball bat and warned that any indictments brought against him could lead to 'potential death & destruction' around the country."[28] Trump has called Black prosecutors such as Bragg, New York Attorney General Letitia James, and Fani Willis racists. In doing so, he is both echoing the language used in the Jim Crow era and stoking the white supremacy movement.

Isolated individuals do not make up a healthy democratic society. In Marx's more theoretical language, alienation is a separation from the fruits of one's labor. While that is certainly truer than ever, the separation and isolation is now more extensive—governing the entirety of social life in a consumer-based society run by the demands of commerce and the financialization of everything. Isolation, privatization, and the cold logic of rationality based on a market-driven notion of efficiency, worth, and commercial exchange have created a new social formation and social order in which it becomes difficult to form communal bonds, deep connections, a sense of intimacy, and long-term commitments. The first casualty of authoritarianism is those who oppose it. In an age in which education on multiple fronts has turned toxic and repressive, thereby acquiring a depoliticizing function, for large groups of people politics has turned deadly. One consequence is that rightwing formations threaten to destroy civic culture and politics itself in America.

Neoliberalism has created a society of monsters who view the pain and suffering of others as entertainment—displaying and legitimizing a new level of cruelty. How else to explain the GOP passing an anti-abortion law in Florida that resulted in terrified physicians refusing to provide an abortion for a woman whose baby would be born with Potter syndrome, a fatal abnormality, and "would die after delivery."[29] As Maya Yang noted in *The Guardian*, "Despite the pain that the Dorberts and couples in similar situations are experiencing, the state's Republican governor, Ron DeSantis, has maintained a staunch anti-abortion stance."[30] How else to explain a comment by Alaska Republican state Representative David Eastman, who stated that "In the case where child abuse is fatal, obviously it's not good for the child, but it's actually a benefit to society because there aren't needed government services and whatnot over the whole course of that child's life."[31] Surely, this comment reveals gangster capitalism in all of its cruelty, especially when it supports the death of an abused child because it results in cost savings.

American society has degenerated into a permanent state of warfare where racism is accepted as an organizing principle of society and militarism is centered as the most powerful force shaping masculinity. Politics has taken an exit from ethics and thus the issue of social costs is divorced from any form of intervention in the world. These are the ideological metrics of political zombies. The key word here is atomization, and it is both a curse produced in neoliberal societies and the scourge of community and viable forms of solidarity. Neoliberal capitalism now preys on the fears of the alienated, fearful, isolated, and uninformed to pour gasoline on the fires of racism, hate, and bigotry.

Central to any type of politics that successfully challenges the emergence of fascist politics is the recognition of both economic structures of domination and the role played by cultural apparatuses in reproducing an authoritarian mindset and a reactionary sense of agency.[32] That is, there is a need to address those ideological and educational forces that shape particular identities, values, social relations, or more broadly, agency itself. Imperative to such a recognition is the fact that politics cannot exist without people investing something of themselves in the discourses, images, and representations that come at them daily. Rather than suffering alone, lured into the frenzy of hateful emotions, individuals need to be able to identify—see themselves and their daily lives—within progressive critiques of existing forms of domination, and see how they might address such issues not individually but collectively. This is a particularly difficult challenge today because the scourge of atomization is reinforced daily, not only by a coordinated neoliberal assault against any viable notion of the social, but also by an authoritarian and finance-based culture that couples a rigid notion of privatization with a flight from social and moral responsibility.

The cultural apparatuses controlled by the one percent are the most powerful educational forces in society, and they have become disimagination machines—institutions of misrecognition, stupidity, and cruelty. Collective agency is now atomized, devoid of any viable embrace of the social. Under such circumstances, domination does not merely oppress through its machineries of terror and violence, but also through the power of language, speech, ideology, and the mass production of lies.[33] Too many progressives and others on the left have defaulted on the enormous responsibility of recognizing the educative nature of politics and challenging this form of domination—working to change consciousness and make education central to politics itself.

Trump and his current political allies, including Elon Musk, rely on the media as disimagination machines and engines of misinformation because they understand that with an education that promotes critical analysis, thinking, and informed judgment comes the possibility of an active citizenry willing to hold power accountable while fighting to strengthen democracy itself. Critical education is the enemy of demagogues. They don't want to change consciousness, but freeze it within a flood of shocks, sensations, and simplisms that demand no thinking while erasing memory, thoughtfulness, and critical dialogue. For Trump and his current crop of political misfits running for office, miseducation is the key to getting elected.

The leaders of the modern Republican Party make a claim to mythic innocence, as James Baldwin once put it, by barricading themselves "inside their history."[34] Instead of breaking free of the smothering grip of white supremacy, too many of them and their followers have embraced a form of historical forgetting and erasure that represses and rewrites history to both suit their feral politics and mimic, without apology, the genocidal legacies of a fascist past. Innocence has now turned deadly as mythic representations of history only make space for whites who view themselves within the discourse of Christian nationalism, xenophobia, and a brutalizing nativism, all of which traps them in the grips of fascist politics.[35] Fascism in America has been expanded through a mix of white supremacy, anti-Semitism, a growing population of white evangelicals, and other right-wing Christians. As Sarah Posner, the historian of the religious right, observes, these religious fundamentalists "believe America was founded as a Christian nation and it is their duty to take it back from what they claim are anti-Christian forces who have undermined its Christian heritage."[36]

Too many progressives and leftists have failed to take the current crisis seriously by avoiding efforts to address the symbolic, structural, and pedagogical dimensions of struggle. All of this is necessary in order at the very least to help people translate private troubles into wider social issues. The latter may be the biggest political and educational challenge facing those who refuse to acknowledge that the 2022 midterm election was not only about those who believe in democracy and those who do not, but also about the possibility of America turning into an authoritarian state. The midterm elections made clear that both democracy and fascism were on the ballot. Considering the less than anticipated Republican victory, the American people will still have to bear the burden of living in a number of GOP run states that will punish anyone who is not a white Christian nationalist, white supremacist, or a supporter of a rebranded fascist politics.

While the 2022 midterms did not result in a democratic bloodbath, what cannot be overlooked is that the Republican Party has been actively putting into place a gerrymandered politics, or what can be called a form of "unconstitutional disenfranchisement."[37] In this instance, the GOP creates serious structural roadblocks that ensure their success at the polls. This is about more than the GOP's unique brand of electoral fraud, engineered by redistricting maps drawn up in GOP backrooms. It is about maligning voting preferences and undermining the fate of democratic elections. This rigging of elections is not only about unfair advantage but, more importantly, the death of democracy itself. Rigged elections coupled with the big lie fostered by election deniers when they lose elections is one of the conditions that fosters and legitimates the new, rebranded fascist politics at work in several nations, including the United States.

The sinister nightmare of a fascist takeover no longer resides in the works of dystopian fiction. It is here in the present, functioning as a lethal fairy tale defined by a contempt for democracy and heralding political doom. The threat of fascism is no longer a matter of speculation but was put to a vote in the 2022 election and will be repeated in 2024. It is conceivable that the 2024 election will transport the unthinkable from a provocative fiction to an excruciating reality. There is some hope in that a complete authoritarian rout did not happen in the midterm elections, and that the GOP did not get the power for which they had hoped. This suggests that much of the voting public is willing to fight back against the GOP's fascist political agenda. Moreover, there were hopeful signs with abortion rights advocates turning out in force, LGBTQ+ candidates running in record numbers, sending the first LGBTQ+ immigrant to Congress, and "a democratic surge among voters under age 45, but especially in the 18–29 bracket," all voting to rescue democracy.[38] And yet, we think it is crucial not to underestimate the threat of fascism in America. Moreover, the endless gloating by the liberal press over how democracy was saved because the midterms did not result in a red tsunami is as politically foolish as it is dangerous. What is crucial to acknowledge, as the historian Ruth Ben-Ghiat warns, is that "the threats to democracy remain."[39] There is a lesson to be learned here if the American public wants to keep democracy resurgent in the face of threats from an updated fascism.

CHAPTER TWO

Vigilantes on Parade

As we suggested in the last chapter, the threats to any viable notion of democracy are multiple and far exceed the workings of the electoral process. The ghosts of fascism reemerge with the normalization of vigilante violence. The specter of street brutality harkens back to the threat of classical fascism that emerged in the interwar years in Italy and Germany. While fascist aggression in those cases involved hundreds of thousands of blackshirts and brownshirts, American fascism is of a more neoliberal variety, where violence is outsourced to the base with Republican officials maintaining plausible deniability. Most notably, GOP officials and right-wing pundits stoke faux outrage over fictitious election fraud and demographic change in America as the country shifts away from a white majority. In the process, the party's base has come to believe that their country is being "stolen" from them, as they are encouraged to take matters into their own hands to save it by rhetorical fascist pundits and officials such as Donald Trump, Mark Levin, Tucker Carlson, and the late Rush Limbaugh, among others.[1]

Kyle Rittenhouse's embrace of violence in response to the rise of Black Lives Matter (BLM) is one example of vigilante street fascism from right-wing activists who believe their country is being taken away from them. This violence is overwhelmingly concentrated on the political right, with most mass shootings in America in recent years committed by reactionary activists. This is a clear warning sign—a canary in the coal mine—of a rising fascist culture that embraces extremism and authoritarian politics and is concentrated within the GOP-Trumpian base.[2]

Rittenhouse, who was in illegal possession of an assault weapon, and responsible for the death of two BLM activists, envisioned himself as a hero who was protecting private property from destruction and providing for security and stability in a time of crisis. Such vigilante acts in the name of "stability" are belied by the reality that 96 percent of BLM-related events since 2017 involved no property damage or injuries to police, and 98 percent produced no physical injuries among bystanders or participants.[3] Whether they recognize it or not, when vigilantes like Rittenhouse commit extra-legal killing in response to rising citizen activism, they send a clear and chilling message that progressive activists should fear for their lives when they take to the streets in the struggle for anti-racism, equality, and democracy. When police informally encourage individuals who commit violence and perpetuate in their ranks a culture of racist violence, no one is safe with the prospect of rising street fascism and aggression.

Rittenhouse faced numerous charges of first-degree homicide and reckless endangerment, but was acquitted in late 2021. Despite the ruling, the gravity of his actions and the fact that it was ultimately sanctioned by the legal system sets a dangerous precedent that empowers vigilantes who believe they are deputized to "enforce the law" against individuals with contrary political beliefs and ideologies. Consider the perverse nature of the events in question. Rittenhouse traveled to a city that he did not live in, in a state in which he was not a resident, in illegal possession of an assault weapon he had no legal right to wield, and killed people in the name of protecting property he did not own, in altercations that could have been avoided had Kenosha police worked to separate right-wing vigilantes from BLM activists—rather than actively encouraging them as the city's police did with Rittenhouse.[4]

The Rittenhouse case should not be understood in a vacuum, but as a trial run for fascism. It occurred within a larger political context in which other right-wing vigilantes justify their commitment to fascist violence, including murder, under the banner of "self-defense" against various perceived threats. The white men who murdered Ahmaud Arbery in Georgia claimed they had to gun him down because, although he was unarmed, committed no crime, and was of no threat to them, he *might* be a criminal. A lack of evidence to validate their suspicions did not stop them from stalking, cornering, and shooting a Black man who was jogging through a neighborhood—in the opposite direction of his killers—whom they falsely assumed with no evidence had committed burglary. One could add to this incident other acts of violence committed by right-wing extremists, including the Buffalo, New York, Highland Park, Illinois, and Jacksonville, Florida mass shootings. Beyond those acts of terror, we could include the majority of other domestic terror incidents committed in recent years by individuals on the political right. These cases reveal that citizen-led street fascism is here to stay, via spectacular acts of violence and terrorism directed against BLM activists, religious minorities, liberals, and people of color, validating a larger campaign and culture of cruelty that normalizes brute force and embraces the politics of literal disposability.

As with Rittenhouse and other vigilante killers, the defendants in the Arbery case claimed "self-defense" against a looming threat to justify their actions. This is part and parcel of the right-wing fascist program in modern times—which focuses on numerous alleged threats to white America. These include the supposed danger from people of color and lawlessness in "inner cities." Those ringing the alarm bell almost always refuse to recognize the racist aspect of the "war on crime" that is still ongoing and is directed against communities of color. It entails paranoid attacks on large cities with sizable minority populations—a target at the heart of Trump's racist claims about election fraud in Democratic strongholds. It also includes those who normalize white replacement theory—and the claim that white Americans have their backs up against the wall due to demographic change that threatens to make them a minority in "their own country." Finally, it includes the brutalist nativism and eliminationist rhetoric against the Democratic Party from officials like Trump, which frames the opposition party as the "party of crime" due to its (allegedly) overly permissive stance on immigration, which is falsely associated with rising violent crime.[5]

In the fascist mind, Trump's rhetoric about the Democrats as the "party of crime" is fuel for paranoia and fear. What does one do with a party of crime, which we are told is set on destroying America? Trump and the fascist pundits that support him leave the proper response to the imagination of their followers, thereby maintaining deniability as they stoke intensifying street fascism and vigilante violence. Despite Trump's denial of responsibility for fueling this extremism, the real-world implications of his and other pundits' rhetoric are clear at a time when right-wing insurrectionists occupy capitol buildings, seek to implement coups against the winner of a democratic election, and call for the heads of opposition party political leaders. The language of hate and racism is more than horrifically symbolic, it also creates a culture in which the normalization of violence allows unthinkable acts of aggression to be both spoken and enacted. Toni Morrison is right in arguing that cultivated rage and ignorance cut off reason and create a world of friend–enemy distinctions that "pathologize and criminalizes alleged enemies—creating an environment in which fascism can grow."[6] As the historian Federico Finchelstein notes, the central element of fascism lies in its "affirmation of the devotion of violence," and the lies that are central to a politics that historically has led to violence.[7]

In a legalistic sense, the outcome of the Rittenhouse trial raises dire concerns about a society that masks passion for vigilantism and viciousness under the guise of self-defense. Jurors in the case were instructed to issue a verdict based on how the defendant said he felt, which established a bias in favor of his actions.[8] As a result, Rittenhouse was empowered to kill, rationalizing it as "self-defense." Rittenhouse could claim that he felt endangered, even as he placed himself in a situation that produced a violent encounter. This scenario also empowers others looking to create self-fulfilling prophecies that legitimate street violence. Based on paranoid associations of progressive protest with violence, right-wing vigilantes can claim to fear societal collapse due to an epidemic of crime. They then take to the streets and take up violence themselves. In the process of seeking conflict, they put themselves in vulnerable positions, and when subject to violence, feel they must further escalate the conflict to "protect" themselves.

America is witnessing the ascendance of the reactionary right with white nationalist-neofascist hate groups such as The Proud Boys, which used the Rittenhouse decision to rally supporters to their vigilante cause.[9] The larger lesson in the Rittenhouse case, when considered alongside other right-wing acts of violence, is that state sanctions of vigilantism are a greenlight for rising extremism, with street fascists feeling empowered to "take the law" into their own hands. The Kenosha police's informal deputization of Rittenhouse represents a serious dereliction on their part, and a de facto authorization of street fascism. Protecting the public is widely recognized to be the job of police, not vigilantes looking for violent confrontations and operating with impunity.

Venerating a culture of cruelty and violence, Rittenhouse supporters depicted him as a "hero" who stood up to criminality and lawlessness.[10] The narrative overlooks Rittenhouse's history of aggression and tendency to jump into confrontations with others despite limited information. He boasted weeks prior to traveling to Kenosha that he wanted to shoot people based on undocumented suspicion of retail theft. The incident involved Rittenhouse sitting in a car across the street from a CVS, when a few individuals ran out of the store into a car, and Rittenhouse and his friends speculated that they were armed and engaged in a robbery. Despite having no immediate knowledge of what had transpired in the store, Rittenhouse remarked in real time that "I wish I had my AR. I'd start shooting rounds at them."[11] This is the individual that traveled to Kenosha, seeking violent conflict with BLM activists—a person with a history of desiring conflict and assuming it was necessary before even understanding the situations playing out before him. In cases like Rittenhouse's, the ideology of the citizen soldier—the vigilante who protects the law "because no one else will"—embraces an act first and think later mindset. With Rittenhouse, his vigilantism dovetailed with his open identification with white nationalist fascists, with whom he publicly posed for photos while flashing a white supremacist sign.[12]

The implications of the Rittenhouse ruling for social movements are dire. One possibility moving forward is that vigilante street fascists show up to progressive and leftist protests with increased frequency, feeling themselves empowered by law enforcement to "police" the events as they see fit, and act preemptively to engage in violence in the name of fighting crime and providing security and stability. Any future acts of violence they provoke will be justified in the name of self-defense, even when the violence would have been avoided had they not acted.

The potential for such actions is real, looking toward future elections and the threat of right-wing vigilantes monitoring and loitering around polling places, particularly those disproportionately populated by people of color, liberals, and Democrats. Such threats of violence could be rationalized by claims that the vigilantes are merely seeking to prevent mass voter fraud, and that they have no choice but to confront voters to verify that they are legally allowed to vote. When tens of millions of people believe that their democracy is being "stolen" from them by Democratic voters, it is impossible to say for sure how many may take to the streets to indulge in vigilantism.

Fascism's trial run also manifests itself in the prospect that Republican Secretaries of State or legislatures may engage—in the name of combating voter fraud—in voter nullification in swing states to hand an electoral "victory" in future presidential elections over to a Republican. This scenario, especially if the outcome effects the winner of a presidential election, is likely to be met by rising protest among Republican Party critics and opponents. And even if a single state's action does not affect the outcome, it will set a precedent for other states to follow in future elections. The prospect for these scenarios to spiral out of control into violence in the streets cannot be discounted at a time when one in five Republicans admit they think it is acceptable, even desirable, to engage in violence to achieve their political, social, or religious goals.[13]

For those who deny the potential of violence as a consequence of rising right-wing paranoia, a review of the evidence is instructive. With the mainstreaming of white replacement theory, a growing number of Americans and Republicans perceive racial and ethnic diversity in the United States to be a threat. The perception of a rising racial threat to white identity is linked to paranoia about elections being "stolen" from Republican Americans, and to support for taking militant action to "protect" against this alleged threat. Eight in ten Republicans agreed in a 2021 PRRI poll that "America is in danger of losing its culture and identity," while 79 percent of party members felt "the American way of life needs to be protected from foreign influence."[14] Furthermore, a majority of Republicans (51 percent) agreed that "America must protect and preserve its white European heritage," with a majority also feeling that "a culture established by the country's early European immigrants" is "important" to "the United States identity as a nation."[15] Nearly two-thirds of Republicans identified being "truly American" with being a Christian, while 53 percent viewed with alarm a changing nation before them, claiming that "things have changed so much that they feel like a stranger in their own country."[16]

These polls reveal that support for Christian nationalism, mainstreamed versions of white ethnonationalism, paranoia about foreign influences, and anxiety about one's country slipping away exist simultaneously, in overlapping ways, among the majority in the party base. Majority sentiment within the party also contends that American elections have been fundamentally perverted. Depending on the survey, between two-thirds and three-quarters of Republicans believed the 2020 election to have been stolen from Donald Trump.[17]

This sentiment was strongest among those socialized by right-wing media to accept big lie election propaganda, with concern about a stolen election being shared by 82 percent of Republicans relying on *Fox News*, and 97 percent of those relying on *Newsmax* and OAN, compared to just 44 percent of Republicans getting their information from mainstream news.[18]

Finally, the Republican Party base is increasingly home to the radical sentiment that violence is the necessary path forward to protect the nation. As polling from early 2021 revealed, nearly 40 percent of Republicans felt that "if elected leaders will not protect America, the people must do it themselves, even if it requires violent actions." This attitude was linked to partisan socialization, with consumers of right-wing media including *Fox News*, OAN, and *Newsmax* being more likely than Democrats to support violence.[19] Similarly, other polling revealed that 30 percent of Republicans agreed that "because things have gotten so far off track" as a nation, that "true American patriots may have to resort to violence in order to save our country." Republicans were nearly three times more likely to accept this rationale for violence than Democrats.[20] Reactionary fears about a country slipping away via mass voter fraud were linked to the fetishization of citizen violence, with nearly four in ten of those believing the 2020 election was stolen from Trump also agreeing that violence was needed to save the country, compared to less than one in five Americans (18 percent) overall.[21]

The polls conducted in the wake of the January 6th insurrection provide evidence of a relationship between the extremist messaging of the Republican Party and affiliated right wing media, and support for violence and authoritarianism among the party base. Rising support for a Christian, white, ethno-nationalist state that valorizes street fascism obviously cannot be sustained indefinitely without endangering anti-racist efforts, the separation of church and state, respect for the rule of law, and democracy itself. The majority of Americans—who are not Republicans—are unlikely to tolerate the toxic combination of street fascism, election subversion, and would-be dictatorial politics if Republicans succeed in the future in overturning a presidential election won by a Democrat.

It may be that the overwhelming majority of Republicans who say they support political violence are not willing to commit it themselves. Even if so, a small number of fanatics engaged in coordinated acts of violence and targeting American polling facilities or other government locations may be enough to impose chaos. Such violence could be enough to potentially cause a collapse of the American electoral system or a national implosion—if it coincides with the Republican Party's nullifying a Democratic electoral win in a future presidential election. The fusion of Republican proto-fascist coup politics with rising vigilante street fascism represents a looming threat to the country. The rule of law—and respect for the outcome of elections—cannot survive a top-down led right-wing movement that is dedicated to dismantling public trust in the electoral process and destroying electoral integrity through a combination of coup politics and violence. Short of a mass movement to roll back fascist politics, it is unclear how the country will defeat the threat of right-wing extremism.

With American democracy, however compromised, under siege, it is deeply troubling that public anxieties over the future of the nation vary so radically depending on the partisan lens through which Americans filter their political views. Polling from *The New York Times* and *Siena* provides a clue for how right-wing anxiety manifests itself in a time of rising fascist politics. The poll, conducted in late 2022, revealed that 71 percent of American voters agreed that U.S. democracy was "under threat."[22] This finding alone was difficult to interpret, since Americans have different reasons for their apprehension about the future of the republic. Still, there were plenty of reasons for Americans to worry moving into the Biden era, given the various ways that fascist politics were mainstreamed under Trumpism. These included:

- Rising white nationalism and a commitment to the idea that America is, at its core, a white country.

- An intensifying mass hysteria via the cult of patriarchal personality centered on Trump himself—with nearly two-thirds of his supporters admitting there was nothing that he could do that would ever make them reconsider their support for him.[23]

- Rising paramilitarism and the celebration of violence, via the concentration of terrorist violence on the American right and the idealization of vigilantes who militantly oppose progressive movements, people of color, and other minority groups.

- Growing indulgence in eliminationist rhetoric that undermines the very idea of democratic multi-party politics in favor of the notion that only the Republican Party can adequately represent the public.

- A continued commitment to militarism and empire—emphasizing a distinct white nationalist flavor that elevates the idea of recapturing America's lost greatness—to "Make America Great Again"—and that elevates immigration from white European countries, while discouraging it from countries with majority Black, Muslim, or LatinX populations.[24]

America is not a fully consolidated fascist republic, and opposition politics persists amidst institutional and electoral pushback against Trumpism and Republican efforts to undermine confidence in and destroy the integrity of the voting process. This much is clear when considering the numerous legal charges against Trump in relation to manipulation of election finances, theft of national security documents, electoral manipulation, and insurrection. Still, with rising attacks on election integrity and ascending street fascism, it is dangerous to pretend America had returned to a politics as usual status quo under the Biden presidency.

Despite the threats to democratic politics, the public was divided on the nature of the threat to the republic. The *Times-Siena* poll revealed that Americans—depending on who one talked to—were angry about very different things. Among those agreeing that democracy was under threat, partisanship dramatically shaped perceptions, with members of each party concentrating on the perceived dangers of the other party. Fifty-seven percent of Democrats said the Republican Party was a major threat to the country, while just 5 percent of Republicans agreed. Two-thirds of Republicans felt the Democratic Party was a threat, while just 5 percent of Democrats felt the same. Eighty-four percent of Democrats felt that Trump represented a threat to the republic, although it was just 7 percent of Republicans.

The polling data also reveals partisan patterns of disagreement on electoral democracy. Echoing the big lie propaganda popularized by Trump, most Republicans (55 percent) thought that "voting by mail" was a threat to democracy, with just 12 percent of Democrats agreeing. Sixty-two percent of Republicans believed Trump was the true winner of the 2020 election, compared to 95 percent of Democrats saying it was Biden. Regarding the conspiracy theory movement QAnon, the poll revealed that only 4 percent of independents, Republicans, and Democrats said it was "believable," although susceptibility to the movement among those who said they "don't know" if it is legitimate or not was highly partisan. Those expressing "don't know" responses about the movement included 42 percent of Democrats, 53 percent of independents, and 73 percent of Republicans. This partisan pattern was longstanding, with Republicans expressing heightened susceptibility to the movement since at least late 2020 in the run-up to the presidential election.[25]

One could attribute "don't know" responses in national surveys to mass American ignorance about political issues. But the QAnon conspiracy theory had received saturation coverage in the news from 2020 to 2022, since it was so intimately tied to Trump. A continued partisan bent to public uncertainty about the movement suggested that the problem was not simply a matter of being innocently ignorant as to what QAnon represented. The conspiracy theory should have been deemed absurd on its face, as it claims that the Democratic Party, journalists, and Hollywood are engaged in a secret Satanist cabal with the "deep state," against the Republican Party, and that they are participating in human trafficking, cannibalism, and drinking the blood of children. But in a Republican Party with numerous officials who support the conspiracy—including Trump—susceptibility to QAnon persists.

The *Times-Siena* poll is also disconcerting in that it speaks to the neoliberal myopia of American voters who overwhelmingly focus on economic metrics for assessing the state of the nation, while marginalizing concerns with the right-wing assault on democracy. While the poll found that nearly three-quarters of American voters believed serious threats to democracy existed, when asked about their national priorities, only 7 percent said the "most important problem" for America pertained to the "state of democracy." More than twice as many—19 percent—said "inflation" was the largest problem, while another 26 percent cited "the economy" more generally, including "jobs" and the "stock market." In total, the public was more than six times as likely to cite economic concerns with jobs, inflation, and the stock market than they were to cite concern with the state of democracy.

It is not surprising that Americans were concerned with inflation and unemployment—both of which are predictable developments to concentrate on in a volatile time when the nation faced global supply disruptions that greatly impacted prices throughout the COVID-19 pandemic. But to say that the public should be more concerned with the costs of goods and services than democracy itself speaks to the power of manufactured public ignorance and myopia that is endemic in neoliberal societies, where individuals are socialized to prioritize their own economic interests over the collective. This political infantilism ensured the blunting of mass awareness of the nightmare of rising fascist politics. With the withdrawal of notions of collective responsibility, fascism becomes someone else's problem to deal with—not a national priority.

Drawing on the power of Orwellian style propaganda, where basic truths are perverted and inverted, Republican Party voters embraced the message of a democracy under threat due to alleged mass voter fraud. This strategy represented an assault on the basic institutions of electoral democracy, undertaken in the name of its preservation. "Democracy" had become a rhetorical weapon used to undermine democratic governance, with 71 percent of Republicans and 37 percent of independents feeling "comfortable" voting for a candidate who thought that the 2020 election was stolen.[26]

Throughout the early 2020s, the public continued to downplay the threat of rising fascism—as personified in a potential return of Trump to political power in 2024. The *Times-Siena* poll found Trump and Biden polling neck and neck (45 to 44 percent), in a hypothetical match-up for the 2024 presidential election, as voters prepared to cast their ballots in the 2022 midterms. The enduring support for Trump matched the willingness of nearly half of the public to normalize Trump's politics, as reflected in his job approval rating throughout his presidency, which averaged 41 percent.[27]

The mainstreaming of the Trumpian assault on democracy did not disappear as America moved from a split outcome in the 2022 midterm elections, and looked toward the 2024 presidential contest. Short of Trump being successfully prosecuted for his efforts to defraud the election outcome in Georgia by demanding the state manufacture votes for him, Trumpism, and the reactionary values behind it, would persist. Despite half the country seemingly content that they had "moved on" from Trump, almost half the electorate had clearly not moved on, and were looking to future presidential contests to continue the fascist politics that emerged during Trump's presidency. This emerging politics is not only saturated with violence, it is also reproduced within a gangster neoliberal capitalism that both produces and legitimates a range of overlapping oppressions that breathe new life into it. We take this issue up in the next chapter.

PART TWO

Neoliberal Fascism, Cruelty, and Street Politics

CHAPTER THREE

Neoliberal Fascism, Cruel Violence, and the Politics of Disposability

Cruelty has always had a special place in fascist politics. Not only did it embody a discourse of hate, bigotry, and censorship, it also initiated a practice of vicious power in order to eradicate those ideas, dissidents, and human beings considered unworthy. Legacies of fascism in Hitler's Germany, Pinochet's Chile, Franco's Spain, and Mussolini's Italy, among others, mixed a language of dread, fear, and contempt with widespread practices of suppression. The repressive power of the state was utilized to eliminate any just concept of politics and the structural conditions and ideological possibilities for developing civic and democratic communities.

Under fascist regimes, however diverse, cruelty and its transformation into extreme violence occupied the very core of everyday life.[1] It was structured in relations of domination and traded in fear, insecurity, corruption, forced precarity, and the production of what Etienne Balibar calls "death zones."[2] Under such circumstances, politics and violence permeated each other, transforming all vestiges of the social state into a punishing state. Fascist politics represented a war waged not only against democracy, but against the social contract, public good, and all social bonds rooted in "movements of emancipation aimed at transforming the structures of domination."[3] The social does not disappear in this context, but is simply removed from democratic values and ruthlessly subjected to the workings of capital.[4]

Fascist regimes reduced politics to a form of barbarity,[5] creating a culture of hardness and cruelty—a politics that menaced all aspects of society, functioning as a disimagination machine that destroyed civic culture, any viable sense of inclusive citizenship, and critical thought. Delight in the misery and suffering of others was normalized as part of a wider war on social responsibility and critical institutions, creating the conditions necessary for the triumph of ignorance, irrationality, and the legitimation of what we call the politics of disposability.[6] The merging of violence and politics did more than test the limits of democracy and social justice, it also pushed at the boundaries of the unthinkable and unimaginable. As the bar for civic tolerance and social justice disappeared, a form of totalitarian terror emerged in which groups were marked out for terminal exclusion, social abandonment, and in the worst case scenario, extermination. One effect of the embrace of such a culture was what the French philosopher Etienne Balibar calls "production for elimination." He is worth quoting at length:

> In the face of the cumulative effects of different forms of extreme violence or cruelty that are displayed in what I called the "death zones" of humanity, we are led to admit that the current mode of production and reproduction has become a mode of production for elimination, a reproduction of populations that are not likely to be productively used or exploited but are always already superfluous, and therefore can be only eliminated either through "political" or "natural" means—what some Latin American sociologists provocatively call *poblacion chatarra*, "garbage humans," to be "thrown" away, out of the global city. If this is the case, the question arises once again: what is the rationality of that? Or do we face an absolute triumph of irrationality?[7]

The culture of cruelty has a long history in America. Adam Serwer, writing in *The Atlantic*, reminds us of the catalogues of subjugation on display in the Museum of African American History and Culture with its memorials of a tortured history of suffering and cruelty. He points to artifacts of inhumanity that include slave shackles worn by children, the mutilated bodies of lynched Black men, and photos of grinning whites who took enormous pleasure in the torturing of those bodies considered worthless and objects of racial contempt.[8] In the more contemporary moment, we have examples of bodies kidnapped, tortured, and imprisoned in black holes and at the Guantanamo Bay detention camp by the Bush administration.[9] Of course, it is well known that the Trump presidency made dehumanization and aggression a central element of policy in his dealings with migrants, people of color, and the separating of children at the border from their parents. The latest manifestations of brutality, worn like a badge of honor, come from a number of Republican governors, especially Florida's Ron DeSantis, who are waging an attack on trans children, using migrants as political pawns, and reviving a culture of overt white supremacy.[10] DeSantis's xenophobia does more than court with violence, he builds it into his white nationalist messaging by calling for "deadly force" against alleged drug traffickers (code for immigrants crossing the US border). DeSantis's language of violence gets more offensive as part of his bid for the presidency. For instance, he stated that "if elected to the White House, he would 'start slitting throats' in the federal bureaucracy on his first day in power."[11] Columnist Max Boot stated that DeSantis's words suggested that he was "deranged."[12] Texas Governor Greg Abbott exhibited his own callousness by sending three buses with 130 migrants, many of whom were non-English speaking and were wearing only light clothing to Vice President Kamala Harris's home in the Washington D.C. area on December 24th, 2022. That evening the temperature had plunged to 15 degrees Fahrenheit, the coldest on record. Conservative speech writer Mona Charen was right in labeling his actions as "performative malice."[13] As she notes, "Our immigration problem calls for generosity, not cruelty," a message that DeSantis, Abbott, and most of the GOP refuse to embrace.

Cruelty for the Republican Party runs deep and should be understood as part of a wider logic of disposability. For example, most GOP House of Representatives members voted against capping insulin costs, despite the fact that access to insulin is a matter of life and death for many poor people. The politics of disposability are brought in full view by the GOP's decision to prevent 2 million "dreamers" from obtaining a path to citizenship, even though the U.S. is the only home they know. Political opportunism reigns supreme for DeSantis even when it runs the risk of costing lives. Further polarizing the public debate over vaccines, DeSantis has "demanded a grand jury investigate 'criminal or wrongful activity in Florida' involving the 'development, promotion and distribution' of coronavirus vaccines."[14] This is a dangerous and absurd political stunt that endangers lives and can cause needless deaths.

Such examples are not unique. For instance, in spite of the fact that violations of child labor laws are on the rise in America, some Republican legislators are "pushing for changes at state and federal levels to roll back protections in what some see as a threat to return child labor to the country."[15] As Michael Sainato reports in *The Guardian*, this is in spite of the fact that "Young workers have much higher rates of non-fatal injuries on the job and the highest rates of injuries that require emergency department attention."[16] Even more unbelievable, 28 House Republicans voted against a bill that "would aid victims of child sex abuse and their families."[17] The culture of cruelty is especially evident in the ongoing denigration of youth through state policies. This point was brought home in a speech given by Trump as part of his roll out for the 2024 presidential election, in which he claimed that "there has been a leftist takeover of school discipline and juvenile justice." He added, "Many of these carjackers and criminals are 13, 14, and 15 years-old. I will order the Education and Justice Departments to overhaul federal standards on disciplining minors ... So when troubled youth are out of control, they're out on the streets and they're going wild, we will stop it. The consequences are swift, certain and strong and they will know that."[18] Trump's demonization of young people is reminiscent of his racist suggestion in 1989 that five Black teenagers known as the Central Park Five be executed for raping a jogger in Central Park. Though they were later proven innocent, Trump never apologized for taking out full-page ads calling for the death penalty and their execution. Welcome to the GOP's war on youth. In this view, juveniles are dehumanized, and defined as mere criminals who must be punished. If one measure of democracy is how a country treats its children, the GOP's punitive policies directed at young people suggest democracy is all but dead in America.

The Trump regime produced a range of policies that rejoiced in the anguish of others. This was evident in the cutting of safety nets and programs that included support for Habitat for Humanity, the homeless, the meals on wheels program, energy assistance to the poor, legal aid, and numerous anti-poverty initiatives. By injecting violence into politics, moving it from the margins to the center of power, Trump and his followers advanced the descent of the nation into barbarism. One consequence is that violence is now so deeply rooted in American culture that it appears to have been normalized.[19] According to data from the Gun Violence Archive, there have been over 600 mass shootings per year in the U.S. since 2020.[20] They take place daily and are barely acknowledged, and if they are noted, it is almost in purely personal terms, reduced to examining the personal lives of the perpetrators and victims. Larger systemic causes of violence are not part of the analysis. Violence has become so arbitrary and thoughtless that it no longer warrants sober reflection regarding its causes or consequences. This is especially true regarding violence, both symbolic and real, waged in the name of white supremacy by a Republican Party that is deeply racist and authoritarian. Violence, as Jonathan Schell once noted, has "steadily gained ground along with a growing faith in force as the solution to almost any problem, whether at home or abroad. Enthusiasm for killing is an unmistakable symptom of cruelty."[21]

Rarely do the corporate and mainstream media connect a rampant culture of cruelty with the legacy of fascism and its updated version of authoritarian capitalism—what we call neoliberal fascism. In the current era this connection is hard to ignore, in part because it is difficult to ignore the visibility and normalization of extreme violence and cruelty produced in social media, media coverage, and in all aspects of the entertainment industry. Violence has become part of a staged performance and mode of political theater that hearkens back to the fascist integration of aesthetics into the mesmerizing spectacle of violence and intense auras and displays of cruelty.[22] Violence has become apocalyptic and spectacularized. A theater of cruelty and violence now functions to consolidate power, shatter the bonds of solidarity, and create a culture of white supremacy and Christian extremism. The ghosts of fascism are back.

With the reappearance of fascism, democracy turns phantom-like and dark, and Americans face the plague of a hate-filled politics of disposability. In this environment, some individuals and groups are regarded as non-human, treated as excess and human waste, presented as faceless, superfluous, diseased, morally incorrigible, and as symbols of fear who are unworthy of human rights and dignity.[23] When fascism's attributes are isolated and removed from history, there is no analysis of broader systemic power relations and their overlapping layers nor comprehensive understanding of how an emerging fascist politics is part of a new totalizing formation that permeates every aspect of the social order. Following the work of Adorno and Horkheimer, there is no holistic mode of inquiry. This is to say that there is no broad-based analysis that moves beyond focusing on specialized issues, isolated problems, and individual events—such as removing the violent attack on Tyre Nichols by the police from a wider culture of violence in America and in its policing.

What remains are isolated and disconnected expressions of oppression, unrelated social movements, and narrow modes of analysis caught in paralyzing and limiting modes of inquiry. Such disconnected and fractured approaches avoid and often refuse to examine how the present historical moment bears the weight of the past, requires a broader systemic politics, and necessitates the development of theoretical and political tools essential to resist and demolish the threat of a fascist future. The catastrophes of our time are increasingly normalized by the refusal of intellectuals, academics, pundits, and various media platforms to provide any comprehensive account for developing a critical vocabulary against fascism. These actors have also failed in helping us understand how major social problems are interrelated, how they manifest in relation to other forms of oppression, how they overlap and reinforce each other, and what this totalizing form of terror means for the present and future.

America has entered into a dystopian age. It is a period marked by a new phase of economic savagery—one that since the 1970s has embraced the ideology that all social life should be shaped by market forces, and that any political, social, or economic institution that puts a curb on corporate and private interests, unregulated markets, the amassing of personal wealth, and unchecked individual and property rights, is the enemy of freedom. Under this regime of economic tyranny, social needs and social responsibility have been held in contempt along with the welfare state, the common good, and society itself. This was echoed in former Prime Minister Margaret Thatcher's infamous claim that "There is no such thing as society. There is only the individual and his [sic] family." It is precisely this regressive individual conception of self-hood with its unchecked notion of self-interest, agency, and freedom that defines neoliberalism.[24] Social problems, precarity, alienation, despair, suffering, and misery are now "individualized, and experienced as normal and inevitable."[25] Moreover, the collapse of ethics is both highly obvious and completely wedded to the neoliberal notion that any concern about social costs is the enemy of the market. With the collapse of ethics in a neoliberal social order comes a "war against all" and "us against them" ethos that not only assaults solidarity and compassion, but also the very idea of the social as a space and set of relations dedicated to the public good. As Michael Yates observes, "Capitalism is a system of stark individualism," rooted in regressive notions of self-interest and reproduces the highly destructive notion that all problems are individual issues.[26] The neoliberal ideology of self-interest is touted as the root of all social problems, ignoring the weight of systemic and structural conditions. Under such circumstances, political agency is trapped in "the normative anchor of the individual self" and becomes increasingly depoliticized.[27]

Language has been hollowed out, transformed into a consumer advertising pitch, wedded to the spectacle of game shows, made dumb by celebrity culture, weaponized as part of a war on social responsibility, and censored in schools by right-wing propagandists who idealize violence to achieve political goals. The language of politics is written in the language of capital, not ethics, justice, and compassion, making it easier to connect violence with the most lethal workings of power. Violence is now facilitated by a glut of manufactured ignorance, accelerated through the degradation of language. In the age of dwindling attention spans, language succumbs to a mediated culture of immediacy, tweets, and a degrading commercial culture that limits the imagination, politics, civic life, and democracy itself. In the age of rebranded fascism, political culture is no longer a critical culture, but undermines those civic and critical institutions and spaces in which an anti-capitalist consciousness can be developed.[28]

Under an emerging fascist politics, violence is no longer hidden behind a wall of silence. It is now worn like an honorary badge by far-right extremists in the Republican Party along with their supporters. Learned helplessness in America has morphed into learned cruelty and a retreat from the discourse of compassion, care, and truthfulness. Social bonds disappear in a neoliberal world of dwindling interconnections, atomized subjects, fractured communities, suppressed historical memory, and civic disintegration. Under such circumstances, facing life's problems is now a solitary affair reinforced by the ongoing right-wing attack on historical memory and the individualization of the social. Rachel Kaadzi Ghansah, in her lyrical and passionate commentary on "The Mystic of Mar-a-Lago," captures the shattering ideological architecture of this collapse of consciousness, integrity, and meaningful social bonds. She writes:

These days, so many of us speak the language of emergency, but where is the language of integrity, sincerity, and dedication? Gone is the ability to bear down, to think beyond ourselves, even in the most basic ways. Instead, we have been left to navigate a disabling pandemic on our own, with the most vulnerable left to their own resources. We are becoming a country anesthetized to people saying, "I am afraid for my life." The war on one another demands that we not stop to ask, "Why are you afraid?" but rather that we bear our right to be callous and to keep on. Mr. Trump gave people something to coalesce around as a communion of disdain, but it signified nothing at the end of the day.[29]

What has changed since the global economic crisis of 2007–2008 is that neoliberalism has fallen into a legitimation crisis. But American society has experienced more than a crisis. It has entered what Stuart Hall calls a new historical conjuncture.[30] That is, a period when different social, political, economic, and ideological forces come into being to give it a specific and distinctive shape. It is important to name and understand this if we are to resist it. As a rebranded form of politics, it does more than give free rein globally to finance capital, but also unleashes generic elements of a fascist past with its legacy of racial cleansing, rabid misogyny, mass violence, and the politics of disposability. This new historical moment or conjuncture represents the end of one period and the rise of another—neoliberal fascism, with its brutalizing ideological and economic baggage representing a new and relentless turning away from democracy. It signals that the old period of the social welfare state, social contract, and emphasis on constitutional rights is no longer the defining politics of American society. Liberal governing principles are now the object of a white supremacist war to eliminate this older period of American history and politics. The Trumpian slogan *Make American Great Again* [MAGA] rightly captures this new conceptual identity.

Neoliberalism no longer appeals to the old economics of private wealth creation and trickle-down benefits to either justify economic inequality or the promises of social mobility.[31] It has no solutions for mass poverty. It actively seeks to defund essential public goods such as schools, while fueling the crisis of social services, the deterioration of the public health sector, runaway drug prices, and staggering levels of inequality in wealth and power. Whatever economic growth has taken place in the last four decades benefited the financial elite at the expense of the many. All the while, economic power translates into political power, further eroding the basic foundations of the democratic state and governance.[32]

Neoliberalism fuels poverty and inequality and no longer offers a defense of its death-dealing ideology.[33] As Pankaj Mishra has noted, it cannot "improve material conditions and bring about measure of social and economic equality."[34] Incapable and unwilling to defend the misery it imposes on the American public, it now appeals to overt racism and ultra-nationalism, claiming that liberal democracy is responsible for the ongoing economic and political crises that amount to "an abyss of failed sociality."[35] Parading as a species of illiberal democracy, neoliberal fascism rejects democracy "as the incommensurable sharing of existence that makes the political possible."[36] Instead, immersed in the "pornography of power," mass-produced misery, and the bogus fantasy of unaccountability, neoliberalism updates itself, unabashedly aligning itself with anti-democratic forces across the globe that demonize, censor, and punish racial, gender, religious, and sexual minorities.[37] Dehumanization, racial cleansing, and repression are the new legitimating tools of this updated form of neoliberal fascism. Paul Mason captures this new alignment, writing:

> Neoliberalism's collapse has stripped the current model of capitalism of all meaning and justification ... the vacuum is being filled by an ideology hostile to human rights, to universalism, to gender and racial equality; an ideology that worships power, sees democracy as a sham, and wishes for a catastrophic reset of the entire global order. Worse, the number one weapon for the US right is that self-same "eighteenth-century philosophy" that [allegedly] had given Americans immunity from totalitarian rule: their individualism, which has been turned against them during thirty years of free-market rule, and their belief that economic choice constitutes freedom.

Freedom has turned ugly in America.[38] Michael Tomasky rightly observes how freedom in right-wing discourse has become detached from any sense of social responsibility. He illustrates the point by arguing that one measure of such detachment can be found at the moment when, at the heart of the pandemic, right-wing conservatives argued "that freedom included the right to cough on strangers in the grocery store."[39] Relatedly, Josh Shapiro, the Democratic-elect Governor of Pennsylvania (far from being on the left) provides a trenchant contrast of some of the ugly freedoms espoused by right-wing Republican Party politicians, such as the Christian nationalist, Douglas Mastriano, the far-right extremist he defeated in the race, and his conception of what he terms "real freedoms." Shapiro writes:

> It's not freedom to tell women what they're allowed to do with their bodies. That's not freedom. It's not freedom to tell our children what books they're allowed to read. It's not freedom when [Mastriano] gets to decide who you're allowed to marry. I say love is love! It's not freedom to say you can work a forty-hour work week, but you can't be a member of a union. That's not freedom. And it sure as hell isn't freedom to say you can go vote, but he gets to pick the winner. That's not freedom. That's not freedom. But you know what? You know what we're for? We're for real freedom. And let me tell you what, let me tell you what real freedom is. Real freedom is when you see that young child in North Philly and you see the potential in her, so you invest in her public school. That's real freedom. That's real freedom. Real freedom comes when we invest in that young child's neighborhood to make sure it's safe, so she gets to her eighteenth birthday. That's real freedom.[40]

It is worth noting some earlier ideological conceptions of neoliberalism as freedom and how they have been appropriated by the extremist elements of the Republican Party. For example, Friedrich Hayek, the highly influential Anglo-Austrian economist and neoliberal arch-theorist, argued in the early 1960s that the freedom of the individual can only be equated with the freedom of the market.[41] Freedom in this discourse reproduces the notion that social justice and ethics are irrelevant, if not dangerous to market freedoms. Freedom is removed from any notion of either social responsibility or solidarity. Collective freedom either disappears or is considered pathological or dangerous. Reduced to the radical individualism and interests of the financial elite, these earlier neoliberal notions of freedom wage war against any collective notion of political and social agency and the institutions that enable them. Related to this view is the iron-clad neoliberal position that no activity should be concerned with social and economic costs. As one of the American apostles of neoliberalism, Milton Friedman once stated, without remorse or irony, the call to social responsibility is tantamount to "preaching pure and unadulterated socialism [and that] the use of the cloak of social responsibility, and the nonsense spoken in its name by influential and prestigious businessmen, does clearly harm the foundations of a free society."[42] In this context, the crisis of social responsibility is connected to both the crisis of agency and the crisis of politics.

Under neoliberalism, the marriage of human capital and unfettered corporate interests is all that matters. As Caleb Crain has noted, relying on the insights of the émigré Hungarian intellectual Karl Polanyi, neoliberalism has morphed into a form of fascism that "strips democratic politics away from human society so that 'only economic life remains,' a skeleton without flesh."[43] With the crisis of capitalism and the rise of fascist politics in America, especially among the leaders of the Republican Party, moral, social, and ethical considerations have become objects of intense disdain, elevating a culture of cruelty and violence to unthinkable heights as a political tool and organizing principle of society.

At the heart of the violence sweeping across America is a contempt for human rights, equality, and justice. In this logic, compassion for the other disappears, the connections that tie human beings together are scorned, and the institutions that offer the possibility of a just society are eliminated. Identities and desires are defined through a market logic that favors self-interest, a survival-of-the-fittest ethos, and unchecked individualism. Violence toward the poor in the United States cuts across party lines. The neoliberal chokehold on both parties is on full display in their lack of compassion and policies for the poor. Over 40 million Americans lived below the poverty line in 2022, and as Liz Theoharis notes, "at least 53 million Americans still relied on food banks or community programs to keep themselves half-decently fed, a shocking number in a country as wealthy as ours."[44] She adds that "right above the 40 million Americans who officially live in poverty, there are at least 95–100 million who live in a state of chronic economic precarity, just one pay cut, health crisis, extreme storm, or eviction notice from falling below that poverty line."[45] Yet, there are few attempts among those in power to address staggering levels of inequality and poverty in America.

Little is said about raising the minimum wage; Senator Joe Manchin killed the Child Tax Credit, resulting in 3.7 million children falling below the poverty line. Senate Minority Leader Mitch McConnell celebrated a staggering $858 billion military budget that excluded any help for those caught in the vice of staggering debt, living from one pay check to the next. The hardships and debt produced by a privatized health care system, stagnant wages, and rising interest rates boggle the mind, and yet, there is almost no talk about creating universal health care, free childcare, and free education. The military budget expands to grotesque levels along with the concentration of wealth in fewer and fewer hands. Gangster capitalism is now on steroids.[46] Even worse, the GOP now talks about eliminating Social Security and Medicare—a shocking indictment of neoliberalism and its disastrous effects in the richest country in the world.

Under neoliberalism, life-draining and unending competition is a central concept for defining human relations, if not freedom itself. In a society of winners and losers, the movement from hatred to violence against the other is easily normalized. Not only is this type of neoliberalism deeply rooted in a fascist form of irrationality, it also embraces totalitarian impulses that legitimate and produce relentless acts of both mass violence and the daily violence and misery waged under the rule of gangster capitalism.

In the age of a coarsening neoliberal fascism, violence appears without limits and intrudes on every imaginable aspect of everyday life, not just in relentless mass shootings. Not only has it produced a massive degree of fear, insecurity, and aggression, it has also, because of its pervasive and often spectacularized presence, diverted attention from the conditions that produce it. Aligned with a permanent war culture, neoliberal fascism now merges entertainment with political theater. In doing so, it widens the traditional sphere of politics to expand the boundaries of its white supremacist and ultra-nationalist ideology and hatred of democracy. Selfishness and greed now coalesce with a mode of militaristic violence in which the suffering and death of those considered excess and disposable becomes a source of entertainment and pleasure—a rancid source of amusement, which obscures policies of raw contempt. Under neoliberal fascism, the aestheticization of politics has become complete.

This ecology and mass production of an image-based hate-politics provides the conditions for accelerating the turn to militarized violence by right-wing extremists. One distinctive feature of neoliberal fascist violence is its use of the old and new media as a form of theater that manipulates people's feelings and emotions along with their personal fears and anxieties. Right-wing media have become echo chambers that serve as a staging ground for normalizing and enabling the increasing political violence, mass shootings, and militarization of American society. As the social sphere is shredded, any meaningful notion of politics experiences its own destruction, accompanied by the rise of extremist groups and a public drawn to racist and xenophobic rhetoric and actions. In this instance, brutality is increasingly aligned with a politics of cultural and racial purification. As violence disconnects from critical thought, ethical sensibilities are neutralized making it easier for right-wing extremists to appeal to the alleged exhilaration and experience of pleasure and gratification provided by the abyss of moral nihilism, lawlessness, and the operation of power in the service of mass aggression.

The militarization of American society is almost complete, representing what William J. Astore "calls a peculiar form of collective madness."[47] Rather than a source of alarm, it is a source of pride as force replaces not only democratic idealism as the main source of U.S. influence abroad, but is normalized as an organizing principle of society.[48] There is no longer much difference between the militarization applied abroad and the militarization now applied at home. War culture now connects both foreign and domestic policies as the punishing state at home increasingly mirrors a foreign policy that prioritizes systemic violence. A weapons culture has replaced a culture of shared democratic values. Safety is regressively associated with personal security, surveillance industries, and unconstrained gun rights. The prison and its lockdown rituals now provide the model for public schools, social services, airports, and increasingly malls, churches, supermarkets, and synagogues. Right-wing Republicans view the Social Security administration and its programs with contempt, while celebrating nativistic-inspired borders and Homeland Security.

There are no protective spaces left in America. The foreign terrorists that the U.S. has fought abroad have now come home. As the Anti-Defamation League documents, "over the past decade ... about 450 U.S. murders [have been] committed by political extremists. Of these 450 killings, right-wing extremists committed about 75 percent. Islamic extremists were responsible for about 20 percent ... Nearly half of the murders were specifically tied to white supremacists."[49] Homegrown extremists now pose the greatest threat of violence to Americans. A militarized and violent America presents itself as a pure distillation of white supremacy, radical Christian nationalism, and bigotry.

A permanent war culture has collapsed the line between domestic terrorism and the violence produced in the name of a war on terror abroad. Military weapons are now in the hands of the police. Domestic terrorists rather than foreign terrorists represent the greatest threats of violence in America. The ecological war against the planet and the threat of nuclear war cannot be separated from a permanent war mentality that shapes both domestic and foreign policies. War fever dominates the public imagination and has become heroic. It is embodied not only in the language of right-wing ultra-nationalism but also in the authoritarian nationalism embraced by far-right neo-Nazis, the leadership of the Republican Party, white supremacists, and white Christian fundamentalists.[50]

Neoliberalism expands the war machine along with the mentality that supports it. In its upgraded form of fascist politics, it produces nuclear stealth bombers, such as the B-21 Raider, which threaten humanity and cost close to $750 million apiece. The December 15th, 2022, military budget amounts to $858 billion, making the United States the "world's largest military spender ... which [is] 39 percent of total global military spending."[51] and is a symbol of both political insanity and a psychological addiction to apparatuses of death. The latter is one element of a war machine that ignores problems such as staggering levels of poverty, homelessness, a crumbling health care system, a punishing carceral state, and a collapsing ecosystem. But it does more. It also poisons everyday life by banning abortions and books, gutting social security and social services, expanding an overly militarized police force, and increasing the growth of jails while cutting funding for public schools. Also at risk under the banner of neoliberal policies are women's rights, environmental protections, trade-union rights, and civil rights.[52]

Cruelty now parades as theater in the media matched only by policies that steal people's time, dignity, and lives. The time has come to take fascism down, not simply through the ballot box, but through a massive collective struggle and uprising that can bring this deadly politics and the gangster capitalism that supports it to a halt. This call for a full-fledged attack on fascist politics is especially relevant at a time in which socialist ideals are being revised. Calls for a universal income, defunding the police, health care for all, a renewed recognition of the structural nature of racism, state violence, and staggering levels of inequality point to a growing socialist consciousness in America. Capitalism is a laboratory for fascism, and any viable mode of resistance must begin by calling for eliminating rather than reforming it. But to do so, as Barbara Epstein notes, it is crucial for a viable resistance movement to move beyond a "fragmented Left held together by a vague commitment to a more just, egalitarian, and sustainable world ... lacking a common focus or basis for coordinated action."[53] The starting point for fighting rising right-wing extremism lies in rebuilding a critical mass consciousness and a progressive multi-racial movement that is capable of dismantling the oppressive ideological and structural regimes of neoliberal fascism.

As David Harvey has stressed, the fundamental problems of capitalism "are actually so deep right now that there is no way that we are going to go anywhere without a very strong anti-capitalist movement."[54] Now is the time for abolishing neoliberal fascism rather than attempting to soften its policies. The notion of a compassionate capitalism as preached by President Clinton's former Secretary of the Treasury, Robert B. Reich is an oxymoron.[55] The time has come for a strong anti-capitalist movement that reimagines and acts on how society should be organized along socialist democratic principle. America requires a united, multi-racial, multi-gendered movement of working people dedicated to a strategy of direct action for fundamental social transformation. It necessitates a radical vision along with what C. Wright Mills once called "big ideas," to give shape to a unified revolutionary movement.[56] It needs a new militancy that draws from struggles of the past to forge the appropriate weapons to fight this scourge of fascism.

Fascism is on the rise across the globe along with the atrophy of civic culture and the political imagination. Without a politically radical educational and political movement to fight it, the deadly virus of fascism will reach its endpoint and democracy, even in its most tepid forms, will cease to exist. One source of hope comes from the words of James Baldwin, which were written in another time of crisis. He writes: "Not everything that is faced can be changed; but nothing can be changed until it is faced."[57] The urgency of the times demands that we remove the blinders before it is too late and face the impending fascist threat. The urgent question of what kind of world we want to live in is no longer rhetorical, it is a vital call to action. Collective resistance is no longer an option waiting to unfold, it is a necessity with no time to spare.

CHAPTER FOUR

Street Fascism and the Politics of Denialism

The militarization of American society entails not only street fascist vigilante violence, but also includes the erasure of the white supremacist motives of those who engage in such activities. In a culture that embraces militarism and normalizes a gun culture committed to routine acts of mass violence, it makes sense to speak of America as the world's leading warfare state.[1] When such militarism is associated with rising white supremacy, and with the facade of "democracy" that America celebrates, individuals are deprived of a basic understanding of the fascist political ideology driving white nationalists to commit street violence. Hence the systematic efforts from public intellectual-pundits, scholars, journalists, and officials to erase serious discussions of fascism, and to avoid discussions linking fascism to rising right-wing violence. The enduring, if not shameful, silence of the corporate and liberal media on the issue in America is hard to miss and inexcusable given the ongoing assault on all levels of society. Will Bunch, writing in *The Philadelphia Inquirer* is right in stating, "It's been already way past time for the American media to start using the f-word—fascism—to describe this ideology that continues to transfix the core voting bloc in one of America's two major political parties."[2]

Examining recent cases of street fascism, we see how denialism pervades American media discourse, particularly concerning the 2022 mass shootings in Buffalo, New York and Highland Park, Illinois. Payton Gendron was responsible for murdering ten Black people in Buffalo, with motivations that traced back explicitly to fascist ideology. In Highland Park, Robert Crimo murdered seven people at the Jewish synagogue he targeted, and had a history of indulging in racist and anti-Semitic rhetoric online.[3] These terror incidents involved individuals who explicitly identified with fascism or with fascist principles and symbols. U.S. reporters—operating in a culture of denialism that envisions fascism as something that "can't happen here," consistently omitted this word from public discourse when discussing these shootings and their perpetrators.

As numerous scholars have documented, fascism denial is endemic to American political culture.[4] Media references to fascism and Trumpism were almost non-existent throughout Trump's presidency, although reporters did at times refer to him as "authoritarian," while regularly reporting on his administration within the context of "populist" politics and "populism" as an ideology.[5] "Liberal" media outlets, including *The New York Times* and MSNBC were 2.5 to 4 times more likely to discuss Trump within the context of "authoritarian" politics and "authoritarianism" than they were to discuss him as "fascist," "fascistic," or to refer to "fascism" more generally. And references to Trump as "populist" or to "populism" more broadly were four to five times more common than discussions of fascist politics or fascism.[6] These trends are revealing of American political culture and the denialist impulse as pertaining to fascism. Populism is widely recognized as a generic term that refers to the wisdom of "the people" and to corruption on the part of a political class and "elites." The term can be used in positive or negative ways—and applied to progressive or right-wing movements. The same is not true of fascism. By avoiding the "F" word in U.S. media discourse, journalists avoid condemnation from Republican officials in the midst of the reactionary surge within the party. These journalists soften their discussions of rising right-wing extremism, indulging in euphemisms that prevent the public from recognizing the gravity of the threat from fascist politics. They may also refrain from using the word fascism because it provides room for analyses that could call into question a savage capitalism that has morphed into fascist politics.

A dominant trend in America is for academics—including fascism experts themselves—to ritualistically avoid discussions of fascism as applied to the Trump administration and Republican politics. The historian Paul Street documents this pattern in painstaking detail in *This Happened Here*, reflecting on the fact that most academic historians tend to treat fascism as a political, economic, and social development that emerged and thrived in Europe during the interwar years. Their discussions of fascism today simply do not apply to American politics.[7] Fascism in this instance is frozen in a historical straitjacket. By defining fascism in such a myopic way—and by academics defining it out of existence—one conveniently avoids discussion about its development in contemporary politics. One also refuses to learn from history.

As Street documents, American political officials routinely avoid conversations of fascism. In the Democratic Party, numerous officials, including Barack Obama, Hillary Clinton, Tim Kaine, and Joe Biden, begrudgingly recognize the fascist threat to American politics. These concessions in the case of Obama, Clinton, and Kaine came in private conversations; they were not made in public. With Biden, the recognition of fascism rising is begrudging, and made at various episodic junctures during crisis movements such as following the January 6th insurrection at the U.S. Capitol.[8] Clearly, the Republican Party is also dead set on avoiding discussions that describe its politics as fascist, meaning that the two major parties of the American political system are at the forefront of official denialism of the fascist threat. Finally, Congressional Democrats and Republicans avoid references to the specter of rising fascism in their official commentaries on the floors of the House and Senate. A review of the statements made by these officials during Trump's four years in office finds not a single reference to "fascist" or "fascistic" politics or to "fascism" in relation to the Trump administration.[9]

The consequences of intellectual, journalistic, and official fascism denial arise alongside an intensifying assault on American democracy. Working to reinforce a state of manufactured ignorance in American political culture, various political actors—including officials, journalists, and academics—fuel a war on truth via the destruction of historical memory. To them, fascism is something that happened a long time ago—a vague or ambiguous label that may be loosely tossed around, or ignored entirely, without a substantive understanding of what it entailed and the dire threat to democracy that it represented. From this perspective, it is not worth talking about in any substantive or extended way in relation to contemporary politics. As these discussions are driven from public discourse, Americans fail to learn about the classical era of fascism. And if they do not know what fascism is, how can they consider whether the components of classical fascism are relevant to American politics in the twenty-first century? Of course, as Primo Levi, Hannah Arendt, Frantz Fanon, Paul Gilroy, and many others have made clear, fascism is never entirely interred in the past, defined by precise characteristics. On the contrary, specific historical conditions produce fascism in different forms, and these forms have emerged once again. Fascism is far more indeterminate and part of the rhythms of everyday society than most critics are willing to acknowledge. Primo Levi was right in stating that "Every age has its own fascism and we see the warning signs wherever the concentration of power denies citizens the possibility and the means of expressing and acting on their own free will."[10]

America's history of fascism denial set the foundation for media reporting and commentary on the Buffalo and Highland Park mass shootings. These events were almost entirely disassociated from any discussion of fascism. With the Buffalo shooting, Payton Gendron was a self-identified fascist, who posted a manifesto on white replacement theory, warning that a Jewish global elite was seeking to replace white Americans with immigrants, people of color, and "inferior" races.[11] Gendron referred to himself as an "ethnonationalist" who "wish[ed] all the Jews to hell." He wrote:

> What I'm advocating for is the gentiles vs the Jews. We outnumber them 100×, and they are not as strong by themselves. But by their Jewish ways, they turn us against each other. When you realize this you will know that the Jews are the biggest problem the Western world has ever had. They must be called out and killed, if they are lucky they will be exiled. We cannot show any sympathy towards them again.[12]

Gendron sought to livestream his murders from the Buffalo grocery store, through a zip code he selected because of its concentrated Black population. He was inspired by Dylann Roof, the white supremacist neo-Nazi who murdered nine Black people in a church in Charleston, South Carolina in 2015, and Patrick Crusius, who murdered 23 people in an El Paso, Texas Walmart in 2019. Crusius, like Roof, was a white supremacist who targeted that particular Walmart due to the concentration of LatinX people in the area. Finally, Gendron drew inspiration from the New Zealand mass killer Brenton Tarrant, who targeted more than 50 Muslims in two mosques in 2019 based on xenophobic concerns about a Muslim invasion. Much of Gendron's manifesto was plagiarized from Tarrant's white supremacist writings, which explicitly embraced white replacement theory.[13]

Scholars studying these mass shootings refer to a "contagion and copycat effect," with these acts of right-wing terrorism being global in nature and constituting a transnational extremist movement.[14] In an age of instant communication across borders, the culture of cruelty embodied in rising fascism provides fertile ground for efforts to criminalize religious minorities, women, and people of color and to treat them as disposable. Spectacular acts of terror are pursued under the banner of fascism. Which is to say that American officials and pundits, and leaders across the world stoke outrage and anger over immigration and against minority groups, providing legitimacy to the hatred that underlies these mass shootings. Right-wing terrorism is outsourced to the most militant wing of the GOP base—the street fascist vigilantes. Republican officials wipe their hands of responsibility via "plausible deniability," since they never explicitly encourage the mass shootings. Still, the fact that most mass shootings arise from the political right, with many of these shooters drawing explicitly on right-wing officials for inspiration, is unmistakable evidence of a cross-pollination between official messages and grassroots action that complement each other to form a fascist right menace.

Indirectly speaking to the cross-pollination of fascist messages and action, news reports following Gendron's attack documented how various Republican officials and right-wing pundits had done their part to mainstream white replacement theory. *The Anti-Defamation League* reported that *Fox News* primetime host Tucker Carlson "elevated the conspiracy theory that Democrats are plotting to replace 'legacy American' voters with immigrants in more than 400 episodes of his show and discussed the falling white birth rate and shifting gender roles, another key component of the conspiracy, in over 200 episodes."[15] Carlson's reach was expansive, as he was the highest rated cable primetime news host prior to his firing in 2023, attracting an audience of over 4 million viewers.[16]

Contributing to the normalization of white replacement theory, Republican leaders explicitly advocated it or openly associated with known supporters in the run-up to the Buffalo terror attack. Republican House Representative Elise Stefanik charged Democrats with attempting to "overthrow our current electorate" via amnesty efforts for unauthorized immigrants that would empower non-citizens to vote. Republican Senator Ron Johnson claimed white replacement theory was "the Democrat grant plan" for America, claiming that "I've got to believe they want to change the makeup of the electorate."[17] Republican Representative Matt Gaetz tweeted that "Tucker Carlson is CORRECT about Replacement Theory as he explains what is happening to America."[18] Republican Representatives Paul Gosar and Majorie Taylor Green are also affiliated with the theory, participating in a conference organized by anti-Semite and Holocaust denier and leader of the fascist Groyper army group, Nick Fuentes.[19] Neofascist replacement theory benefited from mass support within the Republican base as well, with polling at the time of the Buffalo attack showing that 61 percent of Republicans agreed "a group of people in this country are trying to replace native-born Americans with immigrants and people of color who share their political views."[20]

As for the Democrats, Joe Biden lamented the Buffalo attack, while avoiding language that would present the threat within the larger context of rising fascism in America and across the globe. He warned of "a hate that through the media and politics, the internet, has radicalized angry, alienated, lost and isolated individuals into falsely believing that they will be replaced—that's the word, 'replaced'—by the 'other'—by people who don't look like them and who are therefore, in a perverse ideology that they possess and [are] being fed, lesser beings."[21] Biden's response was deeply problematic, in that he essentially recognized the white supremacist and fascist underpinnings emanating from the Buffalo shooter and others like him, while watering down his message regarding the severity of the threat. "Hate" and "radical" are hollow substitutes for recognizing a fascist assault on multi-racial democracy, equality, the rule of law, and the basic right to life for people of color and religious minorities. This softened Democratic response is a classic example of enabling fascism, purveyed by a party that knows full well the dangers the nation faces, but seeks to avoid partisan blowback from Republican officials and right-wing pundits who are empowered to traffic in the rhetoric of fascism with impunity.

Echoing the Democrats' "hands-off" approach, and obscuring Republicans' embrace of white replacement theory, the news media have suppressed a sustained discussion of rising fascism in America. A review of the *Nexis-Uni* database in the two weeks following the Gendron massacre found virtually no references to "fascism" or "fascist" politics in relation to his terrorist attack.[22] *The New York Times* devoted not a single news article, column, or editorial to the topic. Of *Fox News*'s nine reports, only one referenced Gendron as a self-described fascist. At *MSNBC*, none of the four programs mentioning Gendron discussed his fascist politics. And of *CNN*'s 26 transcripts mentioning Gendron, about a third (nine) referenced the attack within the context of fascist politics or fascism. In total across the four venues, this represents ten references out of 91 news segments and articles—or just 11 percent that referenced fascism. Put another way, the vast majority of reporting on Gendron's massacre—89 percent—were stripped of any larger contextual discussion of Gendron's motives, thereby suppressing recognition of the contemporary far right's embrace of fascism. These findings run contrary to cliched notions that fascism is such an overused term in American discourse that it is stripped of all meaning.[23] Just the opposite appears to be the case—the concept is so infrequently discussed in cases where reporting clearly merits such a discussion that Americans are unlikely to have much of an understanding of how contemporary right-wing politics is now inextricably linked with the politics of fascism.

As with Gendron, American media continued to downplay a sober assessment of the fascism threat following Robert Crimo's terror attack in Highland Park just a few months later. It was not difficult to identify a basic profile of Crimo as an individual who participates in fascist politics based on a review of his online and other activities. The profile for mass shooters had become almost standard by the time of his July 4th shooting—a young, white male known to be an awkward recluse engaging in hate-filled social media networking and posts, who had few friends outside the people he engaged with online, and who indulged in right-wing political content and posts that were compatible with fascist politics, used an assault rifle to commit a horrific act of terrorist violence, with a disproportionate number of the victims being religious minorities and people of color who were targeted in a disproportionately minority-populated community.[24]

Biden's response to Crimo's crimes was to condemn the "senseless violence"—echoing a common response to terrorist mass shootings that obscures the cruelty, barbarity, and political ideology driving them, and favors the dubious notion that these attacks result from mental illness. Trump explicitly adopted this response following the

El Paso terrorist attack, announcing that "mental illness and hatred pulls the trigger, not the gun," after 23 people were murdered by Patrick Crusius.[25] The reality of the matter is that psychologists conclude that mental illness has little to do with these sorts of crimes. The vast majority of individuals suffering from mental health challenges are not violent, and they certainly do not commit mass shootings.[26] Rather than illuminating discussions of mass shootings in America, the emphases on "senseless" violence and mental health serve to obscure a thoughtful discussion of these attacks as rooted in the ascendance of a deadly culture of cruelty that indulges in acts of mass violence as a manifestation of fascist ideology. This violence is directed against "undesirable" groups that are increasingly seen as a threat to the nation. This is the politics of disposability, applied in service of white supremacy.

In Crimo's case, the signs were clearly present that fascist ideology motivated his actions. His association with Trumpism was documented, as he was previously observed attending a Trump rally prior to the 2020 election, as well as other Trump-related events.[27] He fused his support for Trump with an indulgence in "alt-right" politics, demonstrated by a photo of him wearing a shirt with "Pepe the Frog," the mascot of choice for alt-right fascists.[28] These facts were all known within days of Crimo's July 4th attack, meaning that reporters had adequate context to draw from when reporting on his motivations.

Unlike Gendron, Crimo did not explicitly refer to himself as a fascist. But no such reference was necessary considering his blatant indulgence in extremist politics. This included his identification with the "alt-right"—a movement that valorizes white supremacist politics, white replacement theory, violence, and fascist principles. His online social media posts and behavior included anti-Semitic iconography and indulgence in Christian "alt-right" media messaging. He used his YouTube channel to flash the three-fingered white supremacist "OK" sign, and had a lightning bolt tattoo on his right hand—a "cracker bolt"—which is a neo-Nazi symbol derived from the SS that calls back to the days of the Third Reich, and which is now adopted by Proud Boys fascists.[29] Crimo had reportedly visited a local synagogue in Highland Park weeks before the July 4th terrorist attack, seemingly to "scope" out the location as a potential target, and five of the seven victims of his assault were reportedly Jewish themselves, with his attack occurring within blocks of the synagogue.[30]

Our review of Nexis Uni reveals a similar pattern for reporting in Crimo's case, documenting how America's embrace of the politics of cruelty and fascism was suppressed. A search of various major media reporting mentioning "Crimo" and the "Highland Park" terror attack in the two weeks following the massacre shows there were no references to "fascism," "fascist" politics, or to Crimo himself as a fascist in 18 *New York Times* articles. The pattern was the same in other venues. Fascism was omitted from all of *CNN*'s 72 segments covering Crimo's violence, while discussions of fascism were also absent from all of *Fox News*'s 16 segments, and from *MSNBC*'s 17 programs. References to Crimo as a terrorist or as having engaged in an act of terror in the week following his crimes were also almost entirely missing from reporting. References to terrorism appeared once in *The New York Times*, three times on *Fox News*, not once on *MSNBC*, and nine times on *CNN*. In total, references to terrorism appeared in 12 of 104 news articles or segments for all the outlets examined—or in just 11.5 percent of all reporting—meaning the overwhelming majority of news stories—nearly 90 percent—omitted discussions of Crimo's mass shooting as an act of terrorism or as intended to terrorize residents of a heavily Jewish community.[31]

In place of a discussion of fascism, reporters preferred generic and less controversial classifications of Crimo's attack, with stories overwhelmingly referring to him as a "shooter" and to his "shooting." In the week following the Highland Park shooting, these terms appeared in 14 of the 15 articles run by *The New York Times*, in all of *MSNBC*'s ten programs, in 66 of 67 *CNN* programs, and in all 12 *Fox News* segments. This by itself should be unsurprising to those who study the news, given the well-known episodic bias to U.S. news reports, which focus heavily on specific events without providing much historical context. But we are aware of no media critics who expected a sustained—or even cursory—history lesson about historic fascism in most of the news reports on Crimo's crimes. Rather, even as a simple descriptor, stories could have included references to his politics as fascist. This classification would have fit well with an episodic bias, in that various facts about Crimo himself that appeared to motivate his actions—including his anti-Semitism, Trumpian inclinations, and support for "alt-right" white supremacy—were all available for reporters to emphasize as part of the larger story of the Highland Park shooting. These were clearly newsworthy subjects in terms of helping Americans make sense of what happened and making the connection to fascism.

When reporters did attempt to provide context for Crimo's motivations, the information provided was incredibly superficial and at times wrong. For example, *The New York Times* ran a story on July 7th, three days after the terror attack reporting that "the motive for the shooting is unknown," and failed to provide readers with any substantive information about Crimo's background as explored in this chapter, or about his extremist ties.[32] CNN ran its own report, also three days after the shooting, quoting Highland Park's mayor, who reflected that "It's one of those things where you step back and you say, 'what happened?' How did somebody become this angry and hateful?" while Crimo's uncle contended that there "were no signs that I saw that would make him do this. Everything was normal."[33] Most egregious was *Rolling Stone*'s reporting, which framed Crimo as "politically completely indifferent" and as "more apolitical troll than extreme ideologue"—a characterization that was plainly inaccurate and that erased from the discussion Crimo's history of embracing Trump and "alt-right" neofascist ideology.[34] Reporting from these venues speaks to the denialist impulse that mystifies fascist politics, erasing the extremist motivations that drive vigilante violence.

The "lone wolf" narrative has come to dominate U.S. political discourse and commentary on mass shootings. These are individuals, Americans are told, who are deeply disconnected and alienated from the world around them. The reality of rising street fascism in America is quite the contrary. Right-wing terrorism is committed by individuals who are piped into larger networks of extremism that stoke outrage over demographic change, and with supporters of fascist politics coming to believe they are under assault—their backs up against the wall in "their own country." The only choice, they believe, is to "fight back" against the "white replacement" that is looming in front of their eyes, and that amounts to a "White Genocide." It takes serious, willful ignorance to consistently fail to connect the dots in terms of understanding the politics that drive modern mass shootings, the majority of which—two-thirds by 2020—were committed by right-wing ideologues.[35] This ignorance, however, is not surprising in an exceptionalist country that prides itself as the world's greatest democracy, and that is defined by a mass culture that sees fascism as something that "can't happen here."

Substantive concerns with the assault on democracy should be on the minds of Americans as they ponder the havoc wreaked by the politics of disposability. Right-wing ideologues and their supporters treat tens of millions of Americans—religious minorities and people of color—as a threat to be neutralized in favor of the maintenance of white supremacist privilege and power structures. Compounding the problem, Americans idealize freedom through a myopic neoliberal prism that privileges the market economy and the freedom of individuals to pursue profit and prestige without constraint. A culture of immediacy idealizes the consumption of widgets—in pursuit of enhanced personal prestige and status—and as the ultimate symbol of human progress and achievement. In the process, the nation refuses to ask: what about collective freedom from fascism? What about the right of people of color, women, and religious minorities *not* to be criminalized in their own country? What about basic principles of justice and democracy—which require that powerful racial groups not reign supreme over others? In a society that is too busy fixating on narrow forms of identity that center on fetishized commodity consumption, larger questions about rising fascism and the threat to democracy are omitted from public discourse.

The consequences of neoliberal myopia and the erasure of fascism from our memory are dire. When people are afraid to leave their homes for fear of being murdered by a mass shooter, it is a sign of a broken society. When these terrorists tie their political program to suppressing the results of democratic elections, and to reimposing white supremacy, something is deeply wrong. When society is characterized by tens of millions of people who condone the use of violence for political and other ends—that is a society that cannot and will not engage in the critical self-reflection necessary to neutralize the rising fascist threat to the republic.

PART THREE

The Language of Fascism

CHAPTER FIVE

Language and Violence as Spectacle in the New Age of Fascist Politics

Violence has seen an almost unthinkable upsurge in America. Violent language and imagery are now a defining characteristic of American culture and acts of violence erupt in even the most protected spaces, engulfing almost every facet of U.S. life. The horror of COVID-19 and the iniquitous treatment of its sufferers have revealed a healthcare system driven by profits and staggering inequalities in wealth and privilege. Suffering in America during the pandemic was needlessly intensified by a neoliberal culture that stigmatizes basic safety precautions such as mask wearing and mass vaccination requirements.[1]

Gun violence and mass shootings have become so routine that most of them escape any public attention, even though this is the leading cause of death among children. In fact, according to the Gun Violence Archive, "the US has suffered more than 160 mass shootings in the first 15 weeks of 2023 ... That's an average of more than 1.5 mass shootings every day so far this year."[2] Racist police brutality persists despite the massive protests after the murder of George Floyd. Mass shootings in Monterey Park and Half Moon Bay in California along with the murder of Tyre Nichols point to a culture of violence deeply rooted in American history, culture, and its most basic institutions, compounded by the emergence of right-wing extremist violence. All these threaten everyday American life.

Every aspect of society is increasingly militarized, producing a culture in which violence becomes a defining discourse of politics. Once on the fringe of American society, political violence is now at the center of power and political life. David French, writing in *The Atlantic*, states that in the aftermath of the January 6th attack on the Capitol, "Death threats have surged across the country. As terrorists realize death threats work, they are using them more often."[3] Such threats are waged against election officials, public health workers, teachers, librarians, and even "Republicans who voted for President Joe Biden's infrastructure package" or who supported Donald Trump's impeachment, such as Liz Cheney and Adam Kinzinger.[4] Death threats to the Capitol Police and lawmakers are the highest they have been in decades.[5] It appears that for right-wing Republicans, everyone who defies Trump's and the GOP's anti-democratic ethos is an enemy. In the Trump era, intimidation has become a defining feature of governance, politics, communication, and everyday life.

It gets worse. In the aftermath of the FBI raid on Trump's Mar-a-Lago Palm Beach home, threats of violence accelerated to an alarming degree against judges, politicians, media pundits, and almost anyone else who might have played a role in initiating or justifying the necessity of the raid. NBC reporters Ben Collins and Ryan J. Reilly stated on "pro-Trump internet forums," threats emerging from anonymous sources told their followers to "'lock and load'" and "agitated for civil war."[6] Kenny Stancil reported in *Common Dreams* that "It wasn't just anonymous posters threatening to mow down their perceived political enemies. For instance, highly influential reactionary Steven Crowder tweeted, 'Tomorrow is war,' followed less than 12 hours later by, 'Today is war.'"[7]

Additionally, numerous Republican politicians and those running for office also engaged in threatening rhetoric. For example, right-winger Kari Lake, the failed GOP nominee for governor of Arizona, stated after the FBI search at Trump's residence, "Our government is rotten to the core. These tyrants will stop at nothing to silence the patriots who are working hard to save America." "If we accept it," she added, "America is dead."[8] Alan Feuer, writing in *The New York Times*, noted that a number of Republican figures reacted to the search at Mar-a-Lago with not only calls to dismantle the FBI, but also with the claim that such actions "had triggered 'war.'"[9] A number of Republican politicians, such as Rep. Marjorie Taylor Greene, made references to "civil war" on social media. This ramping up of threats with the implied recourse to civil war and violence was also echoed by Joe Kent, a Trump-backed candidate in Washington's 3rd Congressional District who stated on a podcast run by Steve Bannon, "We're at war."[10]

The threat of violence has become a standard GOP response to almost any issue, including its use against women fighting for reproductive rights, against those who oppose gun restrictions, and against educators and librarians who oppose banning books. Senator Lindsay Graham stated on *Fox News* that "If there is a prosecution of Donald Trump for mishandling classified information ... there will be riots in the streets."[11] It is hard not to interpret Graham's remarks as a both a retaliatory threat in the service of political opportunism and a veiled claim that Trump, regardless of his lawlessness, is above the law. This menacing climate was reinforced by former President Donald Trump, who in a radio interview warned that if he were charged for mishandling classified documents, there would be "[big] problems in this country the likes of which perhaps we've never seen before," adding, "I don't think people of the United States would stand for it." Soon afterwards, Trump went as far as to use the inflammatory language against Senate majority leader, Mitch McConnell, who against Trump's wishes voted favorably for a bill to fund the federal government through mid-December. Combined with a racist reference to McConnell's wife, Trump stated that McConnell must have voted for the legislation "because he has a DEATH WISH."[12] No subtlety here. While running for the 2024 presidency, Trump has promised to "pardon any of his allies if they face charges from Biden's Justice Department."[13] Trump's embrace of violence, disregard for the law, and appropriation of fascist models of leadership is quite clear in his promise to avenge his followers and seek retribution against his enemies if elected for a second term. Robert Reich, the former Secretary of Labor in the Clinton administration, noted that "Trump's rhetoric is dangerous. We have already seen the consequences of what happens when Trump invites a mob to the streets."[14]

Laura Italiano, writing on *Insider*, noted that immediately following the FBI raid on Trump's Florida residence, references to violence and "civil war" in online spaces increased by 106 percent. She also quoted Alex Friedfeld, a researcher with the Anti-Defamation League's Center on Extremism, who stated that "Extremist anger has not been that high since the lead-up to January 6."[15] She noted that the rise in violent rhetoric, including death threats, occurred on "unmoderated websites such as 4Chan, Stormfront, Patriots.win and MyMilitia.com, and on extremist chat channels on Gettr, Gab and Telegram, and even in the form of certain hashtags on mainstream sites like Twitter and YouTube."[16] In light of this accelerated surge in right-wing violent rhetoric, numerous menacing threats against federal agents and their families appeared on multiple online and social media platforms. Additionally, the federal judge who issued the Mar-a-Lago search warrant was threatened. Unsurprisingly, U.S. Attorney General Merrick Garland, who stated that he "personally approved the decision to seek a search warrant in this matter," has been the subject of numerous death threats by online users, with some writing that he "needs to be assassinated" along with the call "to kill all feds."[17]

A variety of analyses attempting to explain the increase of violence in U.S. society have appeared in the mainstream press. These explanations range from what David French calls a "miserable political culture ... that tolerates no dissent" to the increasing predominance of bellicose, dehumanizing, and apocalyptic language used by right-wing politicians (including Trump himself), prominent right-wing pundits such as *Fox News*'s Tucker Carlson (who was fired in 2023), and far-right cable TV outlets such as such as *OAN* and *Newsmax*. All these sources contribute to a formative culture of lies, hate, misinformation, and white supremacy.

The pervasiveness of violence goes beyond right-wing media. Violence passing as news, entertainment, and sports dominates—and it becomes normalized as increasing numbers of Americans believe that it is an acceptable tactic to drive politics, culture, government, and even school policies. The pervasiveness of such views is in part confirmed by Professor Robert Pape, a political scientist from the University of Chicago, whose studies of political violence find that violent populism is on the rise in America. According to Pape, "The equivalent of 21 million U.S. adults believe two radical beliefs. One, that Joe Biden is an illegitimate president because he stole the 2020 election, and two, that the use of force to restore Donald Trump to the presidency is justified."[18] Even though 62 percent of Americans support a ban on semi-automatic rifles, "most Republicans, supported by the gun lobby, remain opposed to gun reform."[19]

Right-wing figures also embraced violence as a means of bonding, offering their followers the muscular allure of a spectacularized fascism mediated through and enlivened by the false claim that white masculinity is in crisis, aggrieved, and under assault by people of color. Violence is no longer hidden behind a wall of silence; it is now encouraged, sensationalized, and placed on display by most of the Republican Party as a badge of honorable political discourse. Furthermore, such violence is now inscribed in a language that attempts to normalize itself through its appeal to common sense, where it escapes rational analysis and is taken-for-granted. The language of the Republican Party and its supporters not only displays a visceral hatred for truth, democracy, and justice, it also makes a corpse out of everyone who does not believe in its right-wing ideology. It does so in a language that is spectacularized, emotive, and bereft of reason and any sense of justice. In this case, language is weaponized as an expression of apocalyptic rage.

The spectacle of violence and its dehumanizing language have become central features of an upgraded form of neoliberal fascism, revealing itself as "a capitalistic principle."[20] Yet, in spite of a massive increase in bellicose rhetoric, the deeper racial, political, class, and gender registers producing violence within American society are largely ignored by the mainstream media. One consequence is that language has simultaneously succumbed to the spectacle and become a central part of the microphysics of power. How else to explain the drama surrounding the cult-like admiration of Trump, irrespective of his lawlessness, corruption, racism, and petty narcissism? Drained of any democratic substance, language has become a complicitous force in the acceleration of violence and white supremacy. One example can be found in the militant imagery embraced by far-right extremists that maximizes the pleasure of racist violence—endowing their position with a fascist edge. This is a language immersed in a kind of violence that celebrates white nationalism, along with a regenerating cult of aggression, as a legitimate tool of political power. We have seen this celebration of politics as theater before in Nazi Germany. Reich Minister for Propaganda, Joseph Goebbels, stated this view clearly in 1933 with the comment that politics is "the highest and most comprehensive art there is, and we who shape modern German policy feel ourselves to be artists ... the task of art and the artist [being] to form, to give shape, to remove the diseased and create freedom for the healthy."[21]

The philosopher Byung-Chul Han rightly argues that "society today is gripped by a general process of decline of the social, the common and the communal."[22] As language is shaped by a neoliberal logic in which it is privatized, individualized, commodified, and stripped of any social responsibility, public spheres collapse under the attack of a fascist politics that both atomizes and depoliticizes people. Both mainstream and right-wing language turn violence into a spectacle, though for different political reasons. In both cases, the decoupling of violence from larger political, economic, and social issues removes critical thought and political action from normative debates. This failure to provide a broader comprehensive political analysis is purposeful on the part of right-wing extremists. The reduction of violence to a spectacle encourages its use in the service of reproducing a high pleasure quotient among its followers, neutralizing individual ethical sensibilities while shattering any meaningful bonds of solidarity. Under such circumstances, language is aligned with capitalism's death drive and forces of brutality, annihilation, the mass production of human misery, and the destruction of the planet itself. Culture is now defined largely as a site of war, as violence is aligned with forms of political opportunism and pragmatism that appear to have no limits. In the current geographies of culture, language, and violence, there is little room for the privileged space of agency, except as the location of rage, revenge, and macho ebullience.

Culture and politics now resemble a war zone of ambient fear and denial that functions to erase people's awareness of the real social, economic, and political conditions that are destroying people's lives. Instead of embodying shared values, much of cultural politics has turned deadly and functions as an educational force in the service of fascist ideals and white supremacy. Saturated with the language of violence and degrading images, this manifestation of culture numbs people to the plight of others, lessening the care, attention, and moral sensibility that are necessary ingredients for a democratic society. The language of violence promotes voyeuristic identifications and a debilitating consumerism that undermine the critical faculties, making us insensitive to cruelty and the loss of our political agency. Fascism has boldly extended its fight into the realms of culture, education, and aesthetics—and in doing so, feeds off isolation, loneliness, anger, and outrage at work within the social fabric of America. At the same time, it creates fertile ground through disinformation machines for the colonization of mass consciousness, the undoing of civic morality, and the production of forms of learned helplessness that undermine any critical form of resistance. There is more at work here than the spectacularizing and normalization of violence and its destruction of civic life; the spread of fascist politics occurs through self-normalizing processes that render this discourse a commonplace part of the everyday.

This new brand of fascism in the U.S. poisons language by weaponizing it as a political apparatus that mobilizes a culture of fear, denigrates those human beings considered disposable by a language of dehumanization, and legitimates violence as an act of war. In the current post-Trump era, words are emptied of substantive meaning and reason is overtaken by lies and the forces of irrationality. The modern conscience collapses as it is overcome by doctrines of hate, white supremacy, revenge, and the death of ethical standards. New and oppressive pedagogical relations and modes of persuasion extend from social media to numerous online platforms. These new regimes of indoctrination and propaganda take on an unparalleled significance in the production of knowledge, identities, agency, values, and social relations. Under such circumstances, language no longer functions as simply a repository of meaning and facts; it has turned toxic and takes on a new significance in its ability to shape values, social relations, and actions.

In this new era, it is crucial to recognize not only the political, institutional, and cultural conditions at work in turning politics into a form of civil war, but also to identify the sites, policies, and regimes of power that exploit the fears, anxieties, loneliness, and rage that have been produced by a capitalist society that is synonymous with a culture of cruelty, war, aggression, and death. Under neoliberalism, domination has become internalized, politics has collapsed into the personal, and meaningful registers of the social and public sphere have largely disappeared. As we mention through out this book, social problems are defined through the regressive neoliberal language of individualism—in which all troubles are reduced to pejorative categories such as a lack of ambition and resilience, personal failings, individual deficits, and laziness.

Critical education—and critical thinking itself—both as a form of schooling and in the larger cultural realm, are under attack by white supremacists, religious fundamentalists, and right-wing anti-intellectual reactionaries. Those who oppose Trump and his politics are viewed as enemies to be humiliated, attacked, doxed, subjected to death threats, and in some cases assassinated.[23] At work is a form of depoliticization that prevents individuals from translating private troubles into systemic considerations and eliminates any meaningful notion of community as a crucial form of collective resistance. The policies now embraced by the modern Republican Party have accelerated communal violence and threats of political violence while lessening the public's resistance to the impending rise of fascism.

Violence in the age of the spectacle breaks down the threshold between the living and the dead, and offers those who view irrationality, anti-intellectualism, and whiteness as forms of redemption the power to express themselves through a sense of community forged in the apotheosis of war. The scent of death is everywhere in America produced by extremists who have blood in their mouths. Many Republicans are now united by an ideology that aligns with Walter Benjamin's notion that war and violence become the central tools used to destroy democracy, justice, equality, and hope. Yet there is more at stake here than the undermining of democracy. There is also a "frenetic hatred of the life of the mind," coupled with menacing threats of violence against those considered racially impure and politically dangerous.[24]

The death march of neoliberal capitalism has alienated people by locking them into a privatizing and commodifying worldview that makes them insensitive to the suffering of others. It also creates a language, a set of legitimating institutions, and cultural apparatuses that turn the revolutionary potential of overcoming a capitalism in crisis into a catastrophe for which the only solution is the drum beat of fascist politics.

Aided and abetted by conservative echo chambers and multiple media platforms, mass anger, hatred, and despair are channeled into the spectacle of violence. Violence as a legitimate political discourse is coupled with fascist iconography consisting of Twitter storms, torchlit rallies, military pageantry (loved by Trump), and endless replays of right-wing thugs storming the Capitol. While the Republican Party celebrates vigilantes such as Kyle Rittenhouse as heroes, the mainstream press denounces his action while decontextualizing his appalling violence, showering him with media attention without connecting him to a long legacy of racist violence in America. Representations of violence both celebrated and portrayed without context expand the logic of the fascist "spectacle into the field of politics," while misdirecting possibilities for real social change. [25]

It is crucial to understand how these elemental machineries of death function at global, national, and state levels if they are to be challenged and resisted. Neoliberal capitalism, even as it is going through a major crisis, has morphed into a fascist politics that is embraced and proclaimed openly through a language and set of policies that are rooted in U.S. history and culture. Domination has always merged the economic and pedagogical. New forms of criminalization arise, punishing more aggressively those teachers, journalists, critical intellectuals, and others who use language, education, and new digital and media technologies to advance matters of freedom, equity, and justice.

Under such circumstances, the reach of oppression is accentuated, colonizing the body and the mind. Material forms of domination are legitimated through a language that flattens culture, degrades critical thought, and produces pedagogical and symbolic forms of repression. This is a language that both criminalizes dissent and a range of social problems and increases the reach of the punishing state. Neoliberal capitalism works through a predatory economic system which increasingly poisons and undermines language, beliefs, and the social imagination through cultural apparatuses such as public and higher education, the media, and other cultural institutions. This suggests a crisis of not only economics and politics, but also of education and agency.

Once again, it is important to stress that fascism appropriates the call to violence as theater, a form of entertainment in which the masses can express intense emotions while forfeiting critical thought. Under the Republican Party's upgraded version of fascist politics, pageantry and theater are not used to educate people or empower them with the tools of self-determination. On the contrary, it simply offers them a chance to express themselves—part of what Ernst Bloch once called the swindle of fulfillment. The logic of violence has expanded into the crisis of consciousness and identity. Violence in this instance is not simply normalized, but habitualized via cultural apparatuses and pedagogical practices used by the Republican Party and the corporate elite. This type of fascist politics must be analyzed and challenged through a new understanding of the marriage of politics, culture, power, language, and agency.

In the new age of violence and fascist politics, culture has become a central domain for producing the ideas, identities, and values conducive to drawing people into authoritarian social relations. Under gangster capitalism, powerful pedagogical and cultural apparatuses constantly work to mobilize anger in the interests of a reactionary politics that convert diverse spaces into war zones. Nowhere is the centrality of culture as an educational force more evident than in its elevation of violence as a viable political strategy, along with its ability to convince large segments of the American public that civic institutions and public spheres nurturing a critical sensibility are no longer crucial to preventing democracies from sliding into authoritarianism. Thin conceptions of democracy under neoliberalism have given way to a global rejection of liberal democracy. The modern Republican Party is translating anti-democratic rhetoric into policy. This is evident in voter suppression laws, the banning of books, attacks on teachers and LGBTQ students, and policies criminalizing librarians who refuse to censor and remove material from schools and public libraries.

It is crucial for those who believe in a radical democracy to analyze the role that educational, ideological, and cultural domains play as both forces for domination and as sites of resistance and contestation. Power is not simply about domination, and domination is not simply about economics and other institutional structures. Moreover, resistance is not limited to economic issues or to a singular instance of repression. Pierre Bourdieu was right in stating that "the most important forms of domination are not only economic but also intellectual and pedagogical and lie on the side of belief and persuasion."[26] For theorists such as Pierre Bourdieu, Antonio Gramsci, Stuart Hall, Angela Davis, and Jürgen Habermas, it was crucial to understand how totalitarian ideas generated loyalties, what legitimation strategies they used, and what role culture and education played as forms of legitimation. Furthermore, the politics of legitimation raise important questions about how culture, technology, and power now merge into new pedagogical and cultural institutions that produce powerful hegemonic strategies to get people to support authoritarian regimes and surrender their political agency to a dystopian vision. Central to any critical notion of resistance is an analysis of the tools authoritarian regimes use to maintain their authority. In addition, there is the fundamental question of how these tools can be analyzed in terms of their methods of production, circulation, and reception. These issues are important to address if these new cultural formations are to be resisted, and at the same time redirected to enable a critical understanding of the ideological and material relations that support gangster capitalism and its slide into fascist politics.

As civic culture is wiped out, literacy becomes an object of scorn, and politics is reduced to theater, it is all the more crucial to reclaim a language of public life, the social contract, and community. At the very least, such a language would enable the critical analysis of the historical and socially constructed categories of truth, politics, and ethics. It would offer a comprehensive notion of politics, one that illuminates the diverse connections that join institutions, power relations, and the habits of everyday life. In addition, this language would make legible matters of class, inequality, iniquitous power relations, systemic racism, and a politics of common sense. It should also offer a vocabulary for deepening the connections among diverse groups, social movements, and competing solidarities. Following Stanley Aronowitz, Angela Davis, and Barbara Epstein, a viable notion of resistance needs a new language for rethinking theory, politics, and power. It would also include a discourse for relating education to social change, a theory of institutional structures, a developed notion of public intellectuals in the age of digital media and tyranny, and a theory of critique and possibility.[27]

The Republican-backed and corporate-controlled cultural sphere weakens civic life and confirms fears of a vanished future while keeping existing class, racial, and gendered hierarchies in place. Therefore, central to the fight against fascism and the existing culture of violence is the need for a new language and understanding of politics, and the development of a revitalized strategy to unite people across class and racial lines against an oppressive language, set of policies, and ideas that are part of the Republican legislators' fascist playbook. The latter embodies a culture of organized irresponsibility that is fundamental to erasing historical memory, encouraging a loathing for the truth, resuscitating the politics of whiteness wedded to racial cleansing and violence, and legitimating the use of the state as an agent of force and conquest. Trump has inaugurated a political era in which violence is licensed and incited. He has encouraged violence at his rallies, sanctioned violence to achieve political goals, and created a climate in which threats of violence as a form of political opportunism are normalized. Under Trumpism, violence is "a way of moving history forward and bringing about change in society."[28] One consequence is the emergence of extremist groups such as the Proud Boys and Oath Keepers who believe that with Trump's imprimatur, they have a license to engage in violence against those who oppose Trump's ideas and policies, especially the notion that he legally won the 2020 presidential election.

Any viable form of resistance must address how language, mediated through an image culture and a pedagogy of gangster neoliberal capitalism, works to legitimate repression, dehumanize human beings, manufacture ignorance, disseminate lies and disinformation, and deny people their crucial needs while pushing them into a desperate attempt to merely survive. In this context, the language of right-wing violence does not simply legitimate white nationalism and white supremacist ideology, but also guides and expropriates experience, thus making it even more necessary for the left to make education central to its struggles over matters of agency, desire, and the longing for community.

What the left needs to make clear is that the political, medical, and economic crises many Americans are experiencing are not matched by a crisis of ideas—that is, by a critical understanding of the conditions that produced the crises in the first place. Fascist politics no longer hides behind the call for market freedoms, small government, and individual expressions of rights. For example, Trump's hatred of dissent not only reveals itself in his view of the free press as an "enemy of the people," but also in his disdain for any institution that does not promote the willful narrative of white nationalism. How else to explain his call for a commission to establish what he embarrassingly labeled "patriotic education," a term one associates with dictatorial and fascist regimes? By ignoring these issues, any form of potential resistance engages in a form of self-sabotage.

Those embracing the language of fascist politics expect those who still believe in the promises of a socialist democracy to live in silence, to look away, to exercise history as a curse, and as James Baldwin once stated, collaborate "with the authors of one's degradation."[29] Its pedagogical purpose is to make dominance seem natural for the oppressed while securing the levers of domination for the financial elite and those who adhere to white supremacy. Against this updated and accelerated culture of spectacularized violence, theater of cruelty, and criminalization of social problems and dissent is the need to develop a vision that weds the core values of justice, equality and solidarity to a working-class mass movement that is anti-capitalist and offers a vision of what democratic socialism looks like. Such a movement must begin by introducing immediate reforms, such as expanding the child tax credit and forgiving student loans. It should also address long-term systemic changes such as universal health care, eliminating poverty, redistributing wealth and power, instituting a living wage, dismantling the carceral state, free quality education, environmental justice, protection of unions, and the ensuring of long-fought rights of minorities of class, religion, ethnicity, and race.

The call to address the material conditions that promote social and economic oppression must be matched by a call for a new set of values, which offer new forms of agency, solidarity, dignity, and freedom. The precondition for creating a mass movement in defense of a socialist democracy demands a project in which matters of consciousness, agency, and identity are connected not only to enlarged political and personal rights but also economic rights. The latter suggests a new embrace of a cultural politics capable of overcoming the crisis of depoliticization, historical memory, and agency that have become the precondition for gangster capitalism and its rebranded version of fascist politics. Against this anti-democratic neoliberal ethos, with its relentless cycles of violence, war, misery, despair, and emotional plagues, the left needs to further accentuate and embrace a language that is capable of developing a cultural politics that is both forward-looking and offers the possibility for fundamental change. This includes "a program that gives people something to fight for, not just something to fight against."[30] We see indications of such a project among the Black Lives Matter movement, youth struggling against gun violence, the ongoing push for unionization, diverse movements fighting systemic racism, the battle for reproductive rights, and the mass youth-led movement for climate justice. But this is just the beginning.

President Biden is only partly right in stating that the GOP has become a "semi-fascist" party that "embraces political violence." We fear he is being too diplomatic in his rhetoric. America has a full-fledged fascist problem that must be addressed if it is to think its way to a different politics and future. But America is not alone. Across the globe, the struggle over politics faces the threat of becoming less a rivalry between political parties than a struggle between rebranded fascism and democracy itself. We live in dangerous times that demand a revitalized vision, language, strategies, social formations, sacrifices, and even more unified and powerful modes of collective resistance.

CHAPTER SIX

Language and the Politics of Lying: The Big Lie and White Supremacy

Organized lying is central to the politics of contemporary fascism. It not only collapses the boundaries between good and evil, informed judgment and manufactured ignorance; it also serves as a powerful cultural force for normalizing violence. It draws on the cult of personality—in which what *The Leader* says goes—and is systematically tied to white supremacist messaging that treats people of color and religious minorities as disposable. The language of racism and the U.S. culture of lying are also tied to violence in the cases of "Big Lie" election propaganda and vigilante street fascism. In the latter case, men like Kyle Rittenhouse are valorized as providing stability and security in response to the rise of Black Lives Matter (BLM), which is framed in right-wing commentary as a menace to society.[1] Big lie propaganda serves as fuel for racist attacks on disproportionately minority populated cities, which are characterized as the center of the Democratic assault on democracy. Lies about mass voter fraud also drove faux public outrage that led to the January 6th insurrection.

Despite Republican denialism that the party has embraced white supremacy, election propaganda about voter fraud was implicitly framed to direct public outrage at communities of color. Cities like Philadelphia and Detroit were the primary focus of Trump's ire, as he claimed that more than a million people fraudulently voted in these cities, throwing the election to Joe Biden.[2] Never mind that Trump and his legal team never presented concrete, tangible evidence of mass voter fraud. Or that the largest influx of new votes for Biden in 2020 (compared to Hillary Clinton in 2016) came from suburban and exurban voters, not from cities.[3] With the cult of personality that undergirds fascism, what *The Leader* says is gospel, regardless of whether there is substance to his claims.

Modern white supremacists view people of color and the Democratic Party as an existential threat to the republic. Cities like Philadelphia and Detroit, among others in the rustbelt and northeast, lean heavily towards the Democrats, so they are predicably a focus of attack by a conspiracy theory-indulging, white nationalist-embracing figure like Trump. Philadelphia's population is 58 percent Black and LatinX, while Detroit's is an overwhelming 86 percent.[4] These cities were caught up in Republican attacks on electoral democracy in a country that has seen the rapid mainstreaming of white replacement theory—which posits that the Democrats and people of color represent an invading force that threatens the nation's virtuous white majority.

Looking at the rise of white replacement theory, Southern Poverty Law Center (SPLC) polling from 2022 revealed that most Republicans—53 percent—agreed "somewhat" or "strongly" that "the changing demographics of America pose a threat to white Americans and their culture and values." In conspiratorial flare, this sentiment overlapped with the accusation that the demographic shift was part of a premeditated Democratic plan to overturn America's white majority. Reinforcing this point, the SPLC poll found that 68 percent of Republicans, 42 percent of independents, and 35 percent of Democrats agreed "somewhat" or "strongly" that "The recent change in our national demographic makeup is not a natural change but has been motivated by progressive and liberal leaders actively trying to leverage political power by replacing more conservative white voters." Finally, paranoia about conspiracies to replace white voters were associated with perceptions of mass voter fraud in the 2020 presidential election. As the SPLC poll found, 76 percent of those who agreed that the 2020 election was fraudulent also agreed "somewhat" or "strongly" that the "recent change" in U.S. demographics was "not a natural change" but part of the attempt by liberal officials to "replace" white conservative voters.[5]

There is ample evidence that Trump and *Fox News* operated as disinformation machines to popularize big lie election propaganda. Trump was told by his advisors that there was no evidence of voter fraud, and pushed the narrative anyway.[6] Echoing Trump's propaganda, *Fox News* was also aware that there was no tangible evidence of mass fraud.[7] The consistent lying about fraud resulted in serious damage to the voting company, Dominion Voting Systems, which filed a lawsuit against *Fox News* alleging financial damage to their reputation due to their and other right-wing media outlets' "barrage of lies" against them, which the company felt falsely implicated them in conspiracy theories about voter fraud.[8]

Despite *Fox*'s denial of wrongdoing, it should have been clear to critical observers during and following the 2020 election that the channel was committed to disseminating the big lie. *Fox News* anchor Mark Levin hosted Kenneth Starr, the former special prosecutor in the case of Bill Clinton's sexual infidelity investigation, who claimed without evidence that Democratic state officials in Pennsylvania committed "illegal" and "unconstitutional" acts by recognizing fraudulent votes.[9] *Fox* host Lou Dobbs insisted Trump take "drastic action" to combat voter fraud, including pressuring the Supreme Court to reverse Electoral College votes in swing states that favored Biden.[10] Tucker Carlson speculated that voter fraud was committed by "dead people" who voted "in large numbers."[11] Other *Fox* hosts, including Sean Hannity, Jeanine Pirro, and Maria Bartiromo, explicitly linked Dominion to claims of voter fraud.[12]

Various actors involved in the case recognized, in one way or another, that *Fox* had trafficked in voter fraud propaganda claims. Judge Eric Davis reflected that "Fox News and its news personnel continued to report Dominion's purported connection to the election fraud claims without also reporting on Dominion's emails" to the network that presented evidence undermining said claims.[13] Davis wrote, "Given that Fox apparently refused to report contrary evidence, including evidence from the Department of Justice, the [legal] Complaint's allegations [from Dominion] support the reasonable inference that Fox intended to keep Dominion's side of the story out of the narrative."[14]

In the aftermath of various filings regarding Dominion Voting System's lawsuit against the *Fox News* network, it was revealed that Rupert Murdoch, and *Fox News* channel hosts knew that Biden had won the election and that there was no evidence of fraud on the part of Dominion Voting System. Privately Tucker Carlson, Sean Hannity, and Laura Ingraham knew that Trump had lost the election and derided him, along with Sidney Powell and Rudy Giuliani. Hannity allegedly wrote that Trump "was acting like an insane person in the weeks following the election." Carlson thought Powell was "dangerous" and wrote to a producer that "Powell was lying." Ingraham told Carlson that Powell was "a complete nut. No one will work with her. Ditto with Rudy [Giuliani]." Murdoch and his most prominent hosts all lied to the *Fox News* audience in order to pander to their right-wing audience, keep their ratings high, and protect their stock prices.[15]

Rather than accepting responsibility for its trafficking in baseless voter fraud claims, *Fox* reiterated its commitment to those claims. The outlet continued to repeat claims from the Trump administration about illegal voting in Detroit and Maricopa County, Arizona, with *Fox*'s legal team responding to the Dominion case by claiming that their reporting involved "accurately" covering "questions" that were being explored "on newsworthy subjects" and "pending allegations" about the election.[16] Considering the baseless nature of the fraud allegations, this defense amounted to claiming that *Fox* was validated in disseminating Trump and his supporters' lies. This argument was only possible if *Fox* was operating from the assumption that Trump's claims were not outlandish, but deserved to be seriously considered despite a total lack of evidence.

Dominion's lawsuit sought to repair the damage done to the company's reputation and its ability to remain in business, providing voting tabulation systems in more than two dozen states for in-person and mail-in voting. And there was considerable evidence that Trump and *Fox News*'s big lie propaganda had a significant effect on the way people look at elections—and by association, how they look at companies like Dominion, revealed by our statistical examination of national survey data from the Pew Research Center, and of polling on Americans' media consumption habits and attitudes about voter fraud in the 2020 presidential election season.[17] Americans were asked about what outlets they relied on as "a source of political and election news." They were also asked "As far as you know, how big of a problem has voter fraud been when it comes to voting by mail in U.S. presidential elections?"

Utilizing statistical regression analysis, we analyzed the Pew survey to see whether there was a significant relationship between *Fox News* consumption and attitudes about mail-in voter fraud, while accounting for other factors, including respondents' partisan affiliation, ideology, education, gender, income, race, age, and consumption of various other information sources, including Trump's campaign itself, social media platforms such as Facebook and Twitter, print newspapers and news magazines, broadcast news outlets, National Public Radio, and *The New York Times*.

Our findings validate Dominion's position that *Fox News* played a *significant* role in cultivating public support for the big lie among the outlet's consumers. Compared to those relying on print newspaper and print magazines, individuals relying on *Fox News*, Trump's campaign messaging, and social media for information were significantly more likely to agree that voter fraud was a serious concern in relation to mail-in voting. These findings persist after controlling for all the other demographic variables included in this analysis like partisanship and ideology, undermining the claim that *Fox News* viewers (due to these factors) were already predisposed to accept voter fraud claims. Contrary to *Fox* consumption, attention to *The New York Times*, National Public Radio, and *CNN* were significantly associated with being less likely to accept claims about mail-in fraud.[18]

A deeper dive into the data reveals that nearly six in ten Americans (59 percent) consuming *Fox News* as their "major" source of news believed that mail-in voter fraud was a "major" problem in the United States. This is in comparison to 35 percent of those relying on *Fox* as a "minor" source for information, and just 11 percent of people who did not rely on it at all. In total, an incredible 93 percent of heavy *Fox* viewers thought mail-in fraud was a major or minor problem for the country, compared to 74 percent of those using *Fox* as a minor source of information, and just 37 percent for those not relying on it at all. These are not only significant, but large differences in beliefs between the three groups.

A critical analysis of Pew's survey data suggests that Dominion had a serious case against *Fox News*. The outlet's attacks, coordinated with the Trump administration against the integrity of democratic electoralism, are not something to take lightly. They represent the weaponization of language, in pursuit of a rolling-coup effort against the government itself, which culminated in the January 6th insurrection at the Capitol. This attack would not have occurred had it not been for Trump and his media allies stoking a culture of fear and paranoia in which right-wing Americans came to believe that they were losing their democracy—that it was being actively stolen from them—by Democrats, liberals, illegal immigrants, and people of color. *Fox*'s settlement of the suit with Dominion—a $787 million payout—speaks to the serious grievances that Dominion brought forward, and to the dubious journalism that *Fox* pursued by normalizing big lie election propaganda.

Local institutions of vote counting in the United States have for decades successfully tabulated election results without systematic evidence of voter fraud.[19] With Trump and his allies empowered to promote their propaganda, dire concerns remained in the wake of the 2020 election. Republican state legislatures may nullify state majorities that favor a Democratic presidential candidate in the future, citing baseless claims of voter fraud. A future election involving Trump or another big lie Republican raises the potential for disastrous effects as the party endlessly beats the drums of paranoia and fear over dubious claims of fraud. Without Republicans facing a penalty for trafficking in this propaganda, it is unlikely that the assault on U.S. elections will recede in the future. Moreover, it is dubious to believe that *Fox* and other right-wing disimagination machines, however exposed for promoting contempt for both their viewers and journalism as a whole, will refrain from disseminating bigoted and conspiratorial modes of thinking that promote the political and economic interests of those forces in American society at war with democracy. As Federico Finchelstein notes, under regimes of fascism, truth and violence had little to do with reason and were viewed as "authentic expressions of ideology, and especially the ideas of the leaders."[20] As such, reality is shaped according to "ideological imperatives [and was] rewritten in the logic of absolute truth"—expressed as the affirmation of a culture of lying and a politics of fear.[21]

One case in point is the media construction of the Kyle Rittenhouse trial. The language of violence manifested itself even more explicitly in a culture of lying when considering how the news media covered the trial. As discussed in Chapter 2, at the heart of the Rittenhouse case is a fight for national identity. Will the U.S. deteriorate into a full-on embrace of a culture of vigilante street violence and white supremacy, and the cruelty that they embody? Or will progressive and democratic forces fight back against these reactionary forces? In an age of spectacle, terrorism, and disposability, people of color are on the front lines of a battle in which the stakes are nothing less than the country's commitment to equal rights, the rule of law, and democracy. The Rittenhouse case suggested that the news media were not up to this struggle in terms of their capacity to provide basic information to the public about the specter of white supremacist politics and street fascism.

Much of the right-wing discourse on the Rittenhouse trial admonished the "liberal" media for pushing a false narrative that Rittenhouse himself is a white supremacist. Some prominent examples included Glenn Greenwald lamenting on *Fox News* that the media were impugning Rittenhouse:

> If you relied on the media, you should feel betrayed. You know, I'm somebody, before I was a journalist, who worked as a lawyer inside courtrooms for more than a decade. So I knew it's very difficult to cast a judgment about an event this complex without seeing the evidence at trial. So I waited before forming a judgment, and when I did sit down to watch the trial, I was infuriated that everything I had been taught to believe by the media was radically different than the facts of the case as they developed … multiple media outlets around the world, like the biggest ones in Brazil, in Holland, in the UK, have all repeatedly reported that the people that Kyle Rittenhouse killed were black, because they were misled by the American media who kept saying this was a white supremacist on a terrorist hunt. And therefore they naturally presumed, because they were again deceived by the American media, that his victims were black.[22]

Greenwald also insisted on Tucker Carlson's *Fox* program that U.S. media "deliberately cultivated this false narrative from the start that he was a white supremacist," implicating journalists in a premeditated fraud perpetrated against the American public.[23] Other commentators made similar claims, for example at The Hill, where Robby Soave commended Rittenhouse in his interview with *Fox News* for being "restrained" despite allegations "from figures in the [Biden] administration and mainstream media" that he was a white supremacist.[24] Former *Rolling Stone* commentator Matt Taibbi similarly chastised journalists for having "made a lot of assumptions" about Rittenhouse "that maybe didn't turn out correct," and repeated the lament about white supremacy: "As a reporter I would be afraid to use that word about someone that I didn't have a pretty serious collection of evidence, [that he] had beliefs like that. Because I would be afraid of libel suits, frankly."[25]

Generally speaking, the claim that U.S. journalists are guilty of purveying a liberal bias is incredibly problematic. Decades of academic studies conclude that U.S. media are primarily characterized by an official source bias that encompasses deference to both major political parties, with the privileging of one party over the other depending on which party is in control of Congress and the White House.[26] U.S. journalists have themselves conceded that an official source bias privileging the party in power is how they report on politics, undermining the notion that they systematically favor Democrats and liberal perspectives.[27]

More specifically, efforts to avoid a public discussion of the white supremacy problem in relation to Rittenhouse's behavior and politics reveal a larger reactionary political culture that seeks to suppress serious and sustained discussions of racism and rising fascism in America. In Greenwald's case, the effort was self-serving, directing attention away from his own tacit support for white supremacy, via his routine association with Tucker Carlson's "white power hour," which consistently mainlined white supremacist values and white replacement theory into America's veins.[28] To review the facts explored in Chapter 2, Rittenhouse attended a BLM-related event in Kenosha, Wisconsin, in opposition to a movement that explicitly identifies itself as anti-racist and as opposing police brutality. He embraced the idea of preemptive violence, with little to no understanding of the situation in which he found himself, and assumed that violence was the preferred path forward. Rittenhouse was also a known affiliate of white supremacist Proud Boys, posing with them in a picture in which he and they flashed white power signs. Given this situation, it was hardly inappropriate for journalists to raise questions about his associations with white supremacy and fascism.

Contrary to reasonable expectations, and contradicting the baseless laments from right-wing pundits, U.S. reporters went out of their way to consistently *avoid* discussions of white supremacy and fascism in relation to the Rittenhouse trial and his actions in Kenosha. Utilizing the Nexis Uni database, we examined all the transcripts and articles in major "liberal" U.S. media—including *The New York Times*, *CNN*, and *MSNBC*—between November 1st and 23rd, 2021, in the weeks before the Rittenhouse ruling, and in the days after it—to understand how salient the white supremacy narrative was in these venues. In that time, we found 150 articles in

The New York Times referencing Kyle Rittenhouse, 328 transcripts on *CNN*, and 72 transcripts on *MSNBC*. Of those 550 transcripts and articles, not one referred to Rittenhouse as a "fascist," or discussed his case within the context of rising "fascism" in America. Although Rittenhouse's trial was highly salient in the news, discussions of white supremacy were not. Of the 550 transcripts and articles we examined, Rittenhouse's name appeared within 50 words of a reference to "white supremacy" or "white supremacist" politics in a minuscule number of instances. Just four articles in *The New York Times*, eight on *MSNBC*, and ten on *CNN* included discussions of white supremacy or white supremacist politics—translating into 4 percent of all their reporting and commentary content devoted to Rittenhouse.

A closer examination of media content finds that explicit references to Rittenhouse as a white supremacist were virtually non-existent in the "liberal" media outlets in question. Only one story in *The New York Times* contained an explicit link between Rittenhouse and white supremacy, with reporters quoting Derrick Johnson of the NAACP asserting that the verdict in his case "is a reminder of the treacherous role that white supremacy and privilege play within our justice system."[29] Examining *CNN*'s ten segments that mentioned white supremacy, three of them did not discuss the term in relation to Rittenhouse, but were instead discussions of the (at the time) ongoing trial involving white supremacists participating in the Charlottesville violence in 2017. Another five segments included discussions in which program guests actively denied that Rittenhouse was a white supremacist.[30] Finally, three segments associated Rittenhouse and his trial with white supremacy.[31] One segment quoted Democratic Congresswoman Rashida Tlaib who warned in the wake of the Rittenhouse verdict that "our justice system is broken. It protects white supremacy."[32] The second segment referenced a civil rights activist who concluded that Rittenhouse's acquittal was "a win, for white supremacy."[33] The final segment discussed Rittenhouse "posing for photos in a t-shirt" that read "Free as F," while making a hand gesture that "prosecutors say has been co-opted as the white supremacist okay sign."[34]

Most of *MSNBC*'s eight segments also failed to associate Rittenhouse with white supremacy. Two of them included guests who denied he was a white supremacist. Another two referred to white supremacist groups celebrating Rittenhouse's acquittal.

Four segments directly acknowledged the white supremacy issue in relation to Rittenhouse himself. One referred to his public association with the white supremacist and fascist Proud Boys.[35] Another discussed his acquittal related to "the rampant voter suppression targeting communities of color," and "the extreme gerrymandering targeting communities of color," which are "all about trying to preserve white supremacy in the face of major [national] demographic shifts."[36] A third segment discussed "traveling across state lines" with an AR-15 to intimidate people as "absolutely white supremacy."[37] A final segment referred to the judge in the Rittenhouse case as excluding evidence from the trial that he had flashed a white power sign in meeting with the Proud Boys.[38]

In total, out of 550 articles and television segments examined, eight of them explicitly discussed white supremacist politics in relation to Rittenhouse, his actions, and his politics. This represents less than 1.5 percent of all reporting. These results demonstrate that U.S. media have overwhelmingly downplayed discourse on Rittenhouse and white supremacy, while completely ignoring his case in relation to the threat of rising street fascism and its embrace of a culture of cruelty and spectacle.

It is difficult to argue that Rittenhouse's politics were divorced from white supremacy. Although he claimed in his post-trial interview with Tucker Carlson that he is not a racist and even supports BLM, he also openly identified with white supremacist Proud Boys members after he was released from prison on bail. And in that interaction, he flashed a hand sign widely associated with the white power movement. No one made him do these things. He actively associated with this group of his own volition. Considering the circumstances, a critical reader who is open to recognizing the threats of rising white supremacy and street fascism would be validated in asking: why would news reports systematically exclude discussion of Rittenhouse's racist political affiliations, particularly in a trial that relates to him killing BLM activists? The omission of such a discussion, however, is entirely predictable in a political culture where U.S. officials, journalists, and Americans en masse avoid discussing or recognizing white supremacist and fascist politics. In a country where fascism "can't happen here" and Americans believe they long ago transcended the plague of racism, emphasizing these two issues would endanger the dominant public notion that the U.S. is a color-blind, exceptional democracy that rises above all other nations.

For broadcasters like *Fox News*, the obsession with framing the "liberal" media as fixated on white supremacy has real propaganda value. It allows right-wing political figures, reactionary media, and their supporters to project their own extremist values onto others. If reporters are extreme, paranoid, and deranged in their fixation on fictitious white supremacy, right-wing political actors are free to continue normalizing these values, with little to no risk of public blowback. This means the further mainstreaming of the politics of cruelty, the intensifying militarization of society, and a legitimation of the assault on people of color who seek to spotlight white supremacy and fascism.

Clearly, *Fox News* prefers the strategy of projecting its extremist politics onto the "other." Our review of Nexis Uni finds that of the venue's 105 segments during the period examined that referenced Rittenhouse, *Fox* included a discussion of "white supremacy" or "white supremacist" politics in 55 of them, or 52 percent of the total. By acting as a disinformation machine that manufactures ignorance and outrage against the "liberal" other, *Fox News* provides the vital function for the fascist right of mobilizing its increasingly reactionary base, while lending credibility to their political ideology. In doing so, *Fox* acts to roll back the gains made by anti-racist and anti-white supremacy activists in the BLM movement. As readers will see in subsequent chapters, this white supremacist program has other planks outside of erasing discussions of street fascism. One is the attack on Critical Race Theory and efforts to discuss ongoing racism and racial inequality via American elementary, secondary, and collegiate education settings.

PART FOUR

Fascism's Fundamentalist Passions

CHAPTER SEVEN

Fascist Politics and the Scourge of Anti-Semitism in the Age of Disconnected Present

Hard truths are often hidden in grim realities. Repeatedly, far-reaching events appear, suggesting a profound political and moral reordering of the social fabric. Yet while these events are often warning signs—flashes of impending danger—they are largely ignored by political and financial elites as well as by the corporate media, all of whom are inclined to isolate such events and engage with them as if they were unconnected from each other. Treated in isolation, they are quickly devoured and disappear into a neoliberal, image-driven society that is dominated by a culture of short attention spans and exchange values. In a capitalist order that has turned dark and increasingly unable to deliver on its promises, social and systemic problems appear disconnected, individualized, or reduced to personal narratives, and quickly vanish in a neoliberal disimagination machine that relentlessly tries to normalize a misery-soaked state of affairs.

Notable events, warnings, and crises are now rendered digestible, insulated, and politically insignificant, eliminating the necessity for in-depth analyses. This politicized and ideologically and pedagogically regressive approach to understanding the world offers no threat to the systemic capitalist relations of power and its darker mechanisms and effects, which are often hidden from view. Lost here, for instance, are the connections between the pending crisis of environmental collapse, rampant inequality, the threat of a nuclear war, rising authoritarianism, collapse of civic society, rising anti-Semitism, and the war on women's reproductive rights. When disconnected, such events do not raise cause for serious alarm. Under such circumstances, the problems that emerge out of and lead to a broader crisis are not merely overlooked but covered up. At the same time, engaged and informed critiques and the critical institutions that support a strong democracy are viewed with contempt. One consequence is that such warnings quickly disappear from public attention despite speaking to profound changes percolating in society that necessitate a critical understanding of the emergence of new political formations—impending forms of domination, and potential modes of resistance.

The discourses of liberal, mainstream, and dominant politics are too often disconnected from a fascist past and from the overlapping connections of the social problems they attempt to address. In this instance, they are marked by an analytic approach that treats issues in isolation. Such analytic approaches are incapable of making visible how various moments of violence and oppression inform and relate to each other. Removing issues from an historical and relational context makes it difficult to understand how they fit into a broader pattern of domination and reinforce each other. For example, there is no connection being made between Elon Musk's attack on journalists who disagree with him and the ongoing right-wing attack on teachers, librarians, and school board members who reject censoring books, curricula, and critical thought in general, all of which are part of a wider attack on democracy and its institutions. There is little understanding of how attacks on public schools, which usually take the form of defunding, relate to increasing inequality and the staggering concentration of wealth in the hands of the financial elite. Nor is the attack being understood as part of a broader assault on public goods and institutions. At the same time, the rise of mass shootings is seen as unrelated to a culture of violence that has been central to fascist politics—a culture that includes sports, the militarization of everything, mass entertainment, and video game culture. Book banning in America cannot be removed from right-wing attempts to flood the schools with white Christian fundamentalist and white supremacist ideologies. Violence against people of color is too often removed from the rise of the carceral and punishing state. Attacks on the welfare state and public goods are rarely analyzed as part of the unchecked drive for profit under neoliberal capitalism. Attacks on LGBTQ communities, trans people, people of color, and Indigenous groups are not examined as part of the politics of disposability that once led to the rise of totalitarian regimes of terror, concentration camps, and mass murder. The demonization of those considered unworthy of citizenship, along with the rise of anti-Semitism, racism, xenophobia, nativism, and the war against transgender youth, are habitually removed from the legacy of fascism and its drive for racial purity and cultural genocide.

When the media fail to connect Governor Ron DeSantis's racist treatment of migrants with Kanye West's promotion of a virulent brand of anti-Semitism and former President Trump's dining with an incorrigible neo-Nazi and white supremacist, it is more than a serious political mistake. It is a form of complicity that contributes to the emergence of fascist politics in America. While some pundits have connected these specific events to an emerging authoritarianism, they still fail to both name the ongoing development of fascism in America and recognize that it takes different forms in various societies and historical formations. They dismiss any talk of fascism. We repeat this point throughout this book because we refuse to view fascism as an historically fixed past event.

Primo Levi was right in stating that every age harbors the elements waiting to emerge in a re-branded form of fascism. Fascism is not some abstract idea that is permanently located in the past; it is a definable set of attributes that people such as former President Trump, Hungary's leader Viktor Orbán, Italy's Prime Minister Giorgia Meloni, and India's Prime Minister Narendra Modi exploit and magnify. As renowned historians such as Timothy Snyder, Sarah Churchill, Ruth Ben-Ghiat, and Jason Stanley make clear, fascism is never entirely interred in the past; it is a dangerous ideology that may go into remission but never disappears. This position has also been argued by the Black Panthers and a range of Black historians who view the emergence of the KKK as the first organized expression of fascism. We believe that fascism is far more dangerous than authoritarianism; the latter is too general a category and does not signal the specificity of such a dangerous movement that includes the current brand of fascist politics.

Fascism is a recurrent and infinitely flexible phenomenon and points to atrocities, the outlawing of books and bodies, withdrawal of citizens' rights, and the unimaginable horrors of the camps. As a present danger, it must be confronted. The refusal to acknowledge that fascism can appear in multiple forms—often lying dormant in a society until certain forces unleash it—reinforces the willingness of individuals to retreat into silence or ignore the seriousness of the emerging threat. There is no room for silence or complicity. In the face of a culture with limited political horizons, it is crucial to learn from history and cultivate a critical consciousness in order to overcome the moral vacuity, manufactured ignorance, and incitement to stupidity that gives rise to the fascist subject. Kelly Hayes, speaking in a Movement Memos podcast published by *Truthout*, is right to say:

> We must also understand that there can be no ethical silence in the face of fascism. Silence is complicity and cooperation, which helps facilitate atrocity. That might likewise be hard to hear. But how many liberals and leftists have fallen silent on trans issues as the Republicans make the elimination of trans people from public life the new centerpiece of their politics?[1]

Fascist politics saturate American society. Authoritarian signals are everywhere. These include calls for racial purity, voter suppression, hyper-militarism, anti-Semitism, white supremacy, white Christian nationalism, a culture of cruelty, raging inequality, and an expanded politics of exclusion and disposability—all of which are burning democracy to the ground. Yet, in too many cases, the larger significance of these incendiary calamities is missed because they are treated as separate from each other. Examples are not difficult to find. The three seemingly disparate events we mentioned above, Florida Governor Ron DeSantis's demonization of migrants, Kanye West's public displays of anti-Semitism, and former president Donald Trump's hosting of Nick Fuentes, a well-known white supremacist, anti-Semite, and Holocaust denier at his Mar-a-Lago resort in Palm Beach, Florida received a great deal of attention but were easily forgotten. All these events were largely decontextualized in the mainstream and corporate controlled media, treated as isolated issues, and as such, illustrate the hegemonic power of a politics of disconnection.

On September 13th, 2022, Ron DeSantis shipped two planeloads of Venezuelan migrants from Texas to Martha's Vineyard, allegedly to draw attention to what he claimed to be the Biden administration's failed border policies. The lawful asylum seekers were told by DeSantis's staff that they would be provided with jobs and "up to eight months of cash assistance for income-eligible refugees in Massachusetts, apparently mimicking benefits offered to refugees who arrive in the United States through the country's official resettlement program, which the Venezuelans were not part of."[2] They were also provided with a fake brochure titled "Refugee Migrant Benefits," though they did not qualify for such benefits.

Judd Legum reports in *Popular Information*:

> Several migrants told NPR they were told the flight was going to Boston, not Martha's Vineyard. According to the migrants, a woman who identified herself as Perla also said that, if they traveled to Boston, they could receive "expedited work papers." The allegation that the migrants were misled is legally significant. It would mean that the flights were not just heartless, but potentially criminal.[3]

DeSantis was criticized in the liberal media on a number of counts, including lying, committing a criminal offence, engaging in illegal trafficking, misusing state funds, kidnapping, and using this stunt as a publicity device to showcase his reactionary ideology regarding immigration.[4]

Very few analyses gave much attention to how DeSantis's act was connected to a white supremacist ideology and white nationalist agenda. Nor did they give much attention to the way the stunt resembled a segregationist past in which White Citizens' Councils in the South protested against attempts by activists in the early 1960s who traveled to the South as Freedom Riders to integrate the interstate bus system.[5] Not only did the segregationists and armed mobs confront the freedom riders when they pulled into Southern cities "with bats and firebombs,"[6] they also "passed out leaflets and placed wanted ads in Southern newspapers to recruit Black families with the promise of jobs up north" as part of an inhumane plan to send busloads of Blacks up North. "The deceptive and inhumane plan was a response to the heroic Freedom Rides."[7] Like DeSantis, Southern segregationists wanted to retaliate against Northern liberals. Unfortunately, the story of how this segregationist past was reproduced by DeSantis and echoed the Jim Crow era of racist policies and violence was underplayed in the mainstream and liberal media. Not only did DeSantis build on the legacy of American white supremacists such as former Governor George Wallace, he also took a lesson from the history books of fascism in trying to ride white supremacy and nationalism to further his political career.

The mainstream and liberal media also failed to pick up on the connection between DeSantis's publicity stunt of using migrants as political pawns and his attempt to erase the history of the Jim Crow era, and how both are part of his larger project of a politics of racial disposability. For instance, few have made the connection between this racist legacy and DeSantis's passing of laws that banned books about Black history and racial narratives from schools and libraries, along with limiting what teachers can teach about racism—a policy that clearly indicates how DeSantis is following in the footsteps of the Nazification of education in Hitler's Germany.

Almost nothing was said about the connection between these incidents and DeSantis's claim that it was the "American revolution that caused people to question slavery [and that] nobody had questioned it before we decided as Americans that we are endowed by our creator with inalienable rights and that we are all created equal. Then that birthed abolition movements."[8] As Professor Sarah Pearsall noted: "The claim by DeSantis is completely incorrect. Numerous individuals had questioned slavery before the American Revolution. Of course enslaved people had resisted the system since its inception, but there were also tracts by colonists [and] early abolitionists on both sides of the Atlantic [including] Quakers; their efforts in some cases predated the outbreak of the American Revolution."[9] DeSantis's lies, policies, and embrace of historical revisionism cannot be separated from the current attempts by the GOP to erase migrants and Black and Brown people from history in order to prop up a white nationalist agenda. Meaghan Ellis, relying on the work of historian Seth Rockman, a professor at Brown University, rightly argues that DeSantis's reading of slavery is especially "pernicious because it places black people outside the category of 'we' and 'Americans' [while pretending] that enslaved African and African-descended people aren't worth taking seriously as people whose opinions about slavery might matter, then or now."[10]

James Baldwin was right in arguing that this whitewashing of history makes it clear that whites do not want to know the sordid racist past of American history and, as a result, lock themselves in a history that is frozen and shaped by lies, whitewashing, and malicious propaganda.[11] DeSantis's historical ignorance is about more than refusing a future free of racism and the enactment of a more just world. It echoes a legacy in which Trump and his right-wing extremist supporters refuse to tell the truth about America's history while fashioning the present in the image of a Jim Crow past. The historian Robert S. McElvaine captures this GOP return to a racist past. He writes:

> Today's right-wing extremists seek to "Take Back America" in two senses: back from those who are not white or not male and back to the time when straight white males were in charge. An essential part of their overall quest to effect a second "Restoration" of white man's rule is an attempt to restore the ignorance of American history that had prevailed before 1964.[12]

Ron DeSantis has made clear in both his statements and policies that fascist politics is alive and well in the United States. Following in the footsteps of Viktor Orbán, the authoritarian leader who has turned Hungary into a fascist country, DeSantis has waged a war on immigrants, targeted gay and transgender youth, purged voters, banned books in Florida schools, limited what teachers can say about racism and other critical elements of American history, and used state power to punish businesses, evident in his ruthless and vindictive attack on Disney. *New York Times* writer Frank Bruni notes that DeSantis released a campaign ad prior to his re-election race for governor in which he portrayed himself "as a divine instrument, a holy messenger, fashioned precisely into his current form and set specifically on his present mission by God ... The 'God' ad signals that any presidential bid by DeSantis, who is clearly plotting one, will aggressively court Christian nationalists and, in the process, empower them."[13] He has also used the police to punish Black voters who disagree with his policies, used politics to punish his opponents, appointed anti-abortion judges to the courts, attacked first amendment rights to free speech, "signed a law to bar transgender athletes from girls' and women's sports," and waged a war on higher education. A federal judge in Florida called DeSantis's attack on higher education "positively dystopian."[14] There is little doubt that DeSantis has turned Florida into a laboratory of fascist politics. Politicians and scholars alike, including Robert Reich (former Secretary of the Treasury from the

Clinton administration) and the historian Ruth Ben-Ghiat, have labeled DeSantis a fascist, and they are right.

The stark elements of a fascist past, reproduced in the pathologies of the current historical moment, took place in 2022 in another series of events, which stemmed from the same display of racism and embrace of the politics of disposability. From October to December 2022, the rapper Ye (formally known as Kanye West) spent a considerable amount of time performing as the celebrity poster child, spewing out a barrage of dangerous anti-Semitic comments. Joining numerous celebrities who have massive followings, such as Brooklyn Nets guard Kyrie Irving, public figures such as Alex Jones, and politicians such as GOP representative Marjorie Taylor Green, Ye found himself squarely in the company of neo-Nazis, proto-fascists, and a gaggle of diverse demagogues who shared his views. Ye appeared to delight in flooding the media, along with his nearly 32 million followers, with hateful rhetoric that stoked fear, normalized white supremacy, and "ramp[ed] up the risk of violence in a country already experiencing a sharp increase in antisemitism."[15] Indifferent to how his anti-Semitic rhetoric is aligned with both a Nazi history of genocide and current acts of violence against the Jewish community, particularly the 2018 massacre at the Tree of Life synagogue in Pittsburgh, Ye acted out his hatred of Jews and support for white supremacy with impunity while endorsing ideas, concepts, and actions that not only incite violence, but are potentially murderous.

Ye has a disturbing history of anti-Semitism that has become more menacing over time. During the past decade, his quest for media attention, cultural power, and political influence has become more vitriolic and alarming as he moved from uttering offensive anti-Jewish and self-hating anti-Black racist remarks to playing with a fascist aesthetic, and more recently, providing a full-fledged apology for Nazi ideology.[16] Early on in the last decade, he began to integrate white supremacist symbols into his fashion aesthetic. For instance, he turned a confederate flag into a shirt in 2013. A decade later, he donned a sweater at the Yeezy Paris Fashion Week Show emblazoned with the phrase "White Lives Matter" on its back. The phase has been adopted by white supremacist groups in response to the rise of Black Lives Matter (BLM). In October 2022, Ye's anti-Semitic outburst took a dangerous turn when he tweeted that he "would be going 'death con 3 on Jewish people,' a dark and possibly confused reference to the defense readiness condition (DEFCON), an American military term for heightened readiness in the face of a threat."[17]

While appearing on *InfoWars* with far-right, Sandy Hook conspiracy theorist Alex Jones, Ye praised Hitler with his comment "I see good things about Hitler," claimed he loved Nazis, denied that the Holocaust took place, "accused Jews of being pedophiles," and chastised the "Jewish media" for claiming that the "Nazis and Hitler never offered us anything of value to the world."[18] Soon after airing these views, he stooped to another low, reinforcing his image as "a vile repellent bigot" by posting an image of a swastika inside the Star of David. He then added, "Let's always remember this as my final tweet."[19]

Ye has emerged more recently as a public menace, a symbol of vindictive chaos, and a warning sign of a rising fascism in the United States. His contempt for racial justice, equality, and civic integrity correlates perfectly with his personal embrace of fascism and is symptomatic of the plague of authoritarianism that now bears down on every aspect of cultural, political, and economic life in the United States. Fascism begins with hateful and dehumanizing language, opening the space for unimaginable violence. Ye's language fundamentally *structures* as much as it expresses white supremacist and anti-Semitic thought, and in doing so, functions in the service of violence, deception, and cruelty while collapsing the distinction between truth and lies, good and evil.

Ye's lies, comments, and actions merge the hateful and the delusional, and in doing so, help to mainstream and normalize fascist politics and its discourses of terminal exclusion, social abandonment, and dehumanization. His bigoted ideas and comments offer support for a range of white supremacists and anti-Semitic extremists who brazenly occupy public spaces with their fascist symbols and ideas. Celebrity wealth and power can bring about serious consequences in the real world. For instance, on Saturday, October 22, 2022, Ye's followers in Los Angeles rallied on a freeway overpass, displaying a banner declaring "Kanye is right about the Jews."[20] Ye's anti-Semitic rhetoric fuels and legitimates the hateful messages and videos produced in a range of media platforms used by white supremacists to wage violence against trans and queer people and other marginalized groups who "are at disproportionate risk of experiencing violence and mental trauma."[21] As a public figure, he has a massive following, especially among the young, and his influence does more than legitimize conspiracy theories and fascist ideology; it also shapes consciousness, normalizes bigotry, lowers the tolerance for violence, inspires racially motivated death threats, and creates a culture of fear and rage. Ye's language and actions are just one indication that we live at a time in which totalitarian forms are with us again.

Ye's influence and racist ideology expands far beyond his public persona. Prior to his interview with Alex Jones, he dined with former President Trump at his home in Florida. The dinner came as no surprise, since Ye has long supported Trump. What caught the mainstream media's attention was that Ye was accompanied by Nick Fuentes, an architect of the so-called "Groyper" movement of internet trolls whose project is to protect and preserve white, European-American identity and culture. Matthew Chapman describes Fuentes as a high-profile extremist who seeks "to push white supremacist ideology into the political mainstream, has previously compared himself to Adolf Hitler, and advocates for the creation of a white, Christian theocratic ethnostate in which Jews and nonwhite people are barred from political power."[22] Jacob Crosse adds that "Fuentes is not just another 'far-right' operative. He is an unapologetic racist, Christian reactionary, admirer of Adolf Hitler, and Holocaust denier. In addition to glorifying Hitler, Fuentes has called for violence against Black people, Jews, women, immigrants, and LGBTQ persons. Fuentes' words have led to real-life violence and death."[23] Stanley Cohen provides a scathing commentary on Fuentes that speaks as much to his profound stupidity and hatred as it does to the culture of manufactured ignorance that nourished him. He writes:

> Nick Fuentes is the consummate petty political grifter—an enduring pre-pubescent cerebral wreck who, with accomplished ease, went from triumphant 16-year-old student council president to freshman college dropout ... Along the way, as a 20 something scholarly virgin, his diverse and extensive travel and personal experience has taken him from the leadership podiums of figurative trailer parks from coast to coast ... shouting out burn the libraries ... burn the libraries to the cheer of those whose archive experience is largely limited to scanning headlines

of thought-provoking treatises shelved at Super 8 check-out counters.[24]

In the face of adverse publicity, Trump denied knowing Fuentes the ultimate grifter, but at the same time, "the former president has refused to condemn Fuentes's white supremacist views"—a pattern that links back to his first presidential campaign.[25] Some prominent Republicans criticized the dinner event but declined to condemn Trump for hosting racist anti-Semites—a further example of the degree to which the GOP and Trump have embraced and welcomed white supremacists, anti-Semites, neo-Nazis, and a fringe group of ideological fanatics into the highest levels of political power.[26] Of course, the GOP has a long history of hypocrisy around this issue. For instance, most of the GOP remained silent in the face of Trump's association with neo-Nazis, such a former KKK leader, David Duke. They failed to condemn his claim that "there were very fine people" among the Charlottesville neo-Nazis, not to mention his endorsement of the Proud Boys in a debate with Joe Biden.

Given the mainstreaming of American fascism, it is understandable, as Jonathan Greenblatt, CEO of the Anti-Defamation League said in an interview, that the majority of American Jews live in fear of being objects of violence. And rightly so, given that "not only are incidents of violence against Jews at their highest levels since the 1970s, but the level of public animosity toward Jews is higher than it's been in recent memory."[27] Of course, this widespread fear of violence is not limited to the Jewish community, as exemplified by the violence being waged by the right wing against gay people, Black and Brown people, women, and the LGBTQ community. When analyzed as isolated events, Ye's comments and actions cover up a wider and long-standing history of racial cleansing and violence rooted in the same principles of anti-Semitism and racism that led to past policies of extermination, unimaginable horrors, and intolerable acts of mass violence.[28]

While these events deal with different issues, they are connected to each other as part of what Clarence Lusane characterizes as "a neoliberal, race-based version of all-American authoritarianism [that is] targeting every facet of public life."[29] He adds, "Don't think of this phenomenon as right-wing conservativism either, but as a more dangerous, even violent movement whose ultimate aim is to overthrow liberal democracy."[30] He is only partly right since he is too cautious to name America's current slide into racist demagoguery and bigotry for what amounts to a rebranded crisis of fascism. Fascism is not on the horizon; it is present at the highest level of politics. It saturates everyday life, culture, and politics with its ominous and dangerous racial threats, lies, conspiracy theories, ever present barrage of rage, revenge, and macho ebullience, echoed in the whining discourse of white replacement theory and its false appeal to the loss of white privilege.

This updated fascism, as Geoff Mann notes, does not draw its energy from calls for a "rebirth of classical fascism's New Man."[31] He adds:

> This is a world in which [an] emergent fascism draws much of its energy from the dark and bitter nostalgia that fuels the contemporary right … today's emergent fascism is a political programme that indicts the present as a crime against the past. For much of its white base, the point is that the life they have "always lived" was not a disaster, that they are being "replaced" on the stage of history, that progressive politics turns what was a source of pride into an object of shame.

To his credit, Lusane states that "a true authoritarianism could indeed come to power in this country. And as history has shown, that could just be a prelude to a full-blown fascism."[32] We may not have a full-blown fascism yet, but we do have a Republican Party supported by a range of financial institutions, media pundits, politicians, and Supreme Court justices who support the GOP's deeply authoritarian politics. We also have the ghosts of fascism re-emerging in the hard-wiring of the public imagination regarding white, racist notions of citizenship, support for racial hierarchies, anti-Jewish hatred, and a frozen conception of cultural differences and histories. In this context, as David Graeber has observed, fascism travels easily in a society "with extremely limited political horizons, indifferent to the habits of oligarchy, as though no other politics are possible."[33]

Neoliberal capitalism's emphasis on economic and moral individualism has paved the way for fascist politics. It prospers on separating individuals from society and furthers the collapse of the critical institutions crucial to a substantive democracy. In this discourse, there is no self-determining collective subject in politics, only disembodied individuals held together by the allure of cults, demagogues, and the strong odor of hate. This type of social atomization denies that individuals are interconnected, and, as Albert Einstein once argued, reproduces the greatest crisis of the time, which leads people to believe that meaningful social relations have no value and that the notion that we are bound together as human beings via the workings of the democratic social state is a liability.[34] This call to reclaim, strengthen, and expand the social state, the collective tissue of mutual care, and the common good must be matched by theoretical discourses and a politics that can deal with social issues within a broader comprehensive politics. It must reclaim those spaces in which books, blogs, journals, social media, and the like provide a formative culture in which people become critical thinkers and are politicized rather than depoliticized. It means learning from history in order to claim a sense of collective agency, love, and care.[35]

The project of creating a socialist democracy begins with these questions: "Who are we? What kind of society do we want to live in? How do we articulate ideas to actions to make it possible?" One might add that an emancipatory politics means that freedom cannot be either individualized or removed from the quest for economic and social justice. The late cultural critic, Audre Lorde, furthered this argument by insisting that any viable leftist politics must refashion struggle in collective and intersectional terms. In her words, "There is no such thing as a single-issue struggle because we do not live single-issue lives."[36]

Khalid Lyamlahy adds to Lorde's call for a united front, arguing for a return to a politics that focused on "silent questions and neglected connections," "played with the limits of the obvious," developed a language that generated a "more active affinity between people," and engaged in pedagogical practices and cultural work that highlighted a politics that refused to "divorce itself from social institutions and material relations of power and domination."[37] Such language would make clear, for instance, that DeSantis's migration policies share with Ye's and Trump's anti-Jewish hatred the rewriting of citizenship as the exclusive domain of white Christians and "is not only restrictive but has let loose the hounds of social violence."[38] In this discourse, citizenship is no longer equated with human dignity; this abuse is reinforced, if not normalized within a larger discussion of dehumanization, racial capitalism, and white supremacy and must be addressed within a broader conversation about rights. Within a politics of connections and totality, the importance of historical consciousness, memory, moral witnessing, inclusive citizenship, and equal rights provide a more capacious analytic scaffolding that makes visible overlapping themes, often hidden connections, and relations of power that fuel fascist politics.

America is once again in the presence of a modern form of barbarity that thrives in a broad-based socio-economic context that disappears when its varied features—ranging from racial cleansing and the censoring of history to ultra-nationalism—are separated from each other. Under such circumstances, the violent histories of the past disappear along with the notion that the future does not have to replicate the present. Under neoliberal fascism, historical memory, cultural memory, social solidarity, and the living world of human interconnections fade into oblivion under the force of annihilating nihilism.

Fascism blossoms in a society that fails to address its overlapping forms of oppression, ignores broader symbolic and material constraints, and limits its analyses to narrow, distinct issues. Fascism is a language of erasure and suppression and uses words as theater to provide spectacles that offer audiences the thrill of cathartic violence. Fascism thrives on the language of dehumanization, bolstered by the politics of disconnection. As a discourse of erasure, fascism embraces ignorance and thoughtlessness. It eliminates those protecting spaces that enable individuals to question, think, analyze, and hold power accountable. Wedded to the politics of disconnection, it refuses to align the struggle over immediate needs with a call for broader structural changes. Disguised in new forms, fascism is the enemy of historical consciousness because it does not want its dark history revealed. Not only is fascism a discourse of terror and displacement, it is a project that assaults those ideas and institutions that enable individuals to understand the potential of education, language, and theory to reveal how power and resistance are interconnected and can be woven into the landscapes of politics.

Progressives and the left need a language and politics that address root causes in their interconnections. Rather than focus on individual solutions, there is a dire need to expose and confront the historical, structural, cultural, educational, and institutional underpinnings of authoritarianism in all its forms. There is a lesson to be learned here from C. Wright Mills who in his work on the sociological imagination calls upon left to connect personal troubles and issues such as personal debt and unemployment with larger public issues such as racism, staggering levels of economic inequality, and right-wing attacks on democracy. He also stressed the importance of situating social institutions, modes of resistance, and power structures in the arc of unfolding histories. What is crucial for educators to learn here is that reframing the "history of the present" in order to challenge the abyss of fascism demands a new language, politics, ethical grammar, sense of political agency, and a renewed effort to make matters of consciousness and education central to politics. The fracturing of politics has become a form of complicity with neoliberal fascism, and it must be challenged in order to imagine a society free from the scourge of hatred, bigotry, inequality, racism, and a crippling individualism. Progressives and the broad left need a robust language, energized politics, and an international social movement that captures the enormity of the danger fascism poses in the current historical moment. This is a language that rebuilds and reimagines, believes in the possibility of another world, and insists on radical change. Given the existence and danger of rising fascism, the urgency of the times demands the resurgence of a mass movement—"more attentive to the intersections of race, gender, disability, and climate catastrophe"—willing to act, resist, and give democracy room to breathe again.[39] In an age of capitalist corruption, mass suffering, and social atomization, it is crucial to develop new forms of solidarity along with a new understanding of what we share in terms of values, visions, and the kind of society in which we want to live. Socialist democracy is no longer an ideal waiting to be born; it must be grasped with urgency, essential to a future in which we can realize life beyond the nightmares of neoliberal fascism.

CHAPTER EIGHT

Fascism, White Christian Nationalism, and QAnon Rising

Chapter 7 situated the rise of fascist politics in America within the context of the growth of white supremacy, anti-Semitism, and Christian fundamentalism. In this chapter, we look closer at the intertwining of these trends via the growing popularity of white Christian nationalism and QAnon fascism. We document the disturbing process through which reactionary interpretations of American identity increasingly define GOP politics, with the predictable consequence of adopting the politics of disposability as applied to non-whites, women, and non-Christians. Ascending fundamentalist rhetoric on behalf of the Christian right and QAnon is part of a larger effort to impose Christian identity politics illegally and officially on the nation. This assault on the rule of law, the First Amendment, and separation of church and state is tied directly to right-wing campaigns, including the attempt to ban books that spotlight racism in America, and the larger effort to demonize Democrats and liberals.

The whitewashing of history is a vital part of America's racist politics, particularly the effort to erase discussions of how American institutions are structured to perpetuate discrimination and racial inequality. The public memory of the nation's racist past erodes with efforts to deprive younger generations of an understanding of the U.S. history of embracing white supremacy. This campaign is linked to the devaluing of the history of fascism, with nearly two-thirds of young Americans unaware that six million Jews were killed in the Holocaust, and with a majority underestimating the total by more than four million.[1]

The campaign to erase history includes book bans across the nation that are coordinated by various right-wing groups with ties to reactionary Christian politics, and that implicitly endorse white supremacy. They seek to remove from the classroom any references to Critical Race Theory and racism, gender studies and misogyny, and any references to LGBTQ+ identity and struggles. Book banning has increased significantly across America in recent years. According to the American Library Association, there were 681 attempts to ban books in the first eight months of 2022 alone, with an "unprecedented" 1,651 books being banned from schools and libraries. This is more than double the number in 2021 and quadruple the bans in 2019.[2] Most of the bans are in battleground and Republican states, including Florida, Pennsylvania, Tennessee, and Texas. They are focused on books that address race and racism, sexism, and LGBTQ+ identity.[3]

Moms for Liberty and *No Left Turn in Education* both rely on eliminationist rhetoric that seeks to dehumanize by writing people of color, and LGBTQ+ individuals out of existence, and to remove them from the way Americans think about national identity. *Moms for Liberty* announces on its webpage that it is "empowering parents" and "fighting for the survival of America" by "teaching the principles of liberty in our homes and community."[4] The group represents a prominent example of how right-wing women are coopted into larger efforts to impose extremist, religiously inspired, and dehumanizing political ideas. In this case, *Moms for Liberty* seeks to coerce schools and libraries into erasing the struggles of disadvantaged groups from national discourse. By framing the conflict as a fight for the nation's "survival," they indulge in an eliminationist all-or-nothing rhetorical framing that implicitly envisions their struggle as one in which white heteronormative Christians win or lose in their battle with people of color, religious minorities, and those from disadvantaged groups.

The misogyny in far-right politics is more complex than simplistic conceptions of sexism would recognize. This is not simply about men telling women how to think and what to do. *Moms for Liberty*'s leadership is comprised entirely of white women, a point that helps in revealing who they are "empowering."[5] These activists incorporate Christian fundamentalism into their politics, offering a model of religious theocracy in which being "American" and a "patriot" is conflated with right-wing Christian identity. *Moms for*

Liberty's national chapter coordinator explicitly acknowledges that "God has called on me, and equipped me, to do my part in service to Him and our country."[6] This comment speaks not only to the racist politics of banning anti-racist books, but to the misogynistic overtones of the movement, which associates religious authority with paternalism via references to a higher power as "him."

No Left Turn for Education relies on similar messaging that idealizes white Christian nationalist principles. The organization's website explicitly engages in whitewashing propaganda, declaring that "there is one race, the human race," featuring a video of a white and Black child walking hand-in-hand. The message is clear: to focus on issues such as racism and racial inequality is unacceptable, as these aspects to critical pedagogy and learning must be marginalized and omitted from the "education" experience. The group's founder, Elena Fishbein, condemns the "infiltration" of public education with "progressive ideology" and "indoctrination," describing schooling in America as "tainted" and "biased," with leftists engaging in the "subversion" of learning. Included in her list of laments is that educational lessons emphasize "diversity," "racism," "justice," "equity," and "privilege."[7] Inherent in this message is that education would be better if it did not discuss these issues, or stress them as part of the learning experience. This, again, is the politics of disposability, with people of color and religious minorities and their struggles safely placed out of sight, out of mind.

The right-wing attack on public education is notorious for gaslighting teachers and those committed to critical thinking and learning. The rhetorical strategy is to frame "bias" as the problem, leaving the impression that there is some unbiased and neutral education that can be achieved. This is a red herring. A closer look at *No Left Turn for Education* reveals that the group's founder envisions proper education to be about inculcating the young with an ideology that celebrates and seeks to "restore American patriotism in the classroom," eliminating any "curriculum that promotes guilt, defeatism and victimhood, while exacerbating pessimism and lack of responsibility."[8] Through these efforts to silence critical pedagogy, groups struggling for equality are dehumanized by the shift to a right-wing nationalist "education" that masquerades as academically neutral and objective.

No Left Turn celebrates the "1776" curriculum from Hillsdale College as an ideal template for learning. Hillsdale College is a well-known right-wing Christian institution that attracts students who are explicitly looking for perspectives that privilege right-wing Christianity.[9] The lesson one is left with after engaging with the messages from *No Left Turn* and *Moms for Liberty* is clear—acceptable education in America necessitates omitting any curriculum that emphasizes racism, sexism, classism, justice, and other forms of prejudice that perpetuate inequities in society. To focus on these issues is to be "biased." Alternatively, elevating right-wing principles and values such as nationalism, "family values," and worship of the Founders constitutes an objective education experience.[10] Social psychologists refer to this practice as "naïve realism"—the act of assuming that there is one knowable reality that can be observed and recognized.[11] Embracing naïve realism as a rhetorical strategy, right-wing education activists pretend that their own values and beliefs are, by definition, objective, factual, and represent the truth, while portraying bias as something that others practice—in this case, leftist educators. This projects outrage over bias onto others, while concealing the blatant nationalistic, racist, and Christian nationalist biases driving the right-wing education reform movement.[12]

Moms for Liberty and *No Left Turn* are not alone in idealizing white Christian nationalism. White Republican officials now repeatedly call on the United States to declare Christian nationalism a central part of the country's identity. Republican House Representative Marjorie Taylor Greene refers to the GOP as "the party of Christian nationalism."[13] Former Pennsylvania Republican gubernatorial candidate and big lie election propagandist Doug Mastriano referred in his campaign to the separation of church and state as a "myth," and called on his party to "take our state back" from secular Democrats, promising that "my God will make it so."[14] January 6th insurrection supporter and Republican Representative Josh Hawley pronounced that "we are a revolutionary nation because we are the heirs of the revolution of the Bible—without the Bible, there is no America."[15] Such rhetoric channels an eliminationist message, assaulting identities that do not fit the Christian nationalist ideal that is romanticized by the GOP. This is most apparent in Hawley's claim that "no America" exists outside of one placing a Christian nationalist and fundamentalist identity at its core.

Republican leaders' rhetoric extends beyond claims that the U.S. is a Christian nation into announcements that God selects these officials to save the nation. Republican Governor Ron DeSantis compared himself to Jesus, endorsing an ad claiming that God sent him on the "eighth day" of creation to "take the arrows" and "stand firm" against "unrelenting attacks," seemingly in opposition to leftist indoctrination in schools.[16] Similarly, former President of the United States, Donald Trump referred to himself as "the chosen one" and as the "the savior of western civilization."[17] Such blatant invocations of Christian savior politics by a governor and president represent the ultimate manifestation of Christian nationalism, with the country's most prominent leaders explicitly claiming they are hand selected by God for the sake of humanity.

The Republican Party's celebration of the U.S. as a Christian nation does not occur in a vacuum. It is part of a larger campaign by the Republican right to adopt a Christian nationalist program that defines how the country talks about its social, political, and spiritual identity. A 2022 University of Maryland poll reveals pervasive support for Christian fundamentalist principles that venture into authoritarian territory. Although 57 percent of Republicans agree the U.S. Constitution does not allow "the government to declare the U.S. a Christian nation," more than six-in-ten (61 percent) think it should do so anyway.[18] This sentiment runs blatantly contrary to Constitutional law. The First Amendment explicitly states that Congress "shall make no law respecting an establishment of religion" and that individuals retain the right of "free exercise" of religion independent of government interference. Furthermore, Article 7 states that "no religious test shall ever be required as a qualification to any office or public trust under the United States." These legal provisions were clearly put in place to avoid the imposition of government dominated by religious theocracy.

The fusion of right-wing Christianity with fascism relies heavily on the convergence of white supremacy, authoritarianism, contempt for the rule of law, and eliminationist messaging that seeks to delete and dehumanize non-Christian identities from the national consciousness and from what it means to be American. The roots of this extremism are longstanding. The United States is an outlier in comparison to other wealthy countries in its commitment to religiosity—measured by the percent of Americans who claim that religion "plays a very important role in their lives."[19] America's outlier status helps to explain how far-right Christians like Greene, Hawley, and DeSantis indulge in white Christian nationalist messaging without fear of electoral backlash.

Christian fundamentalist ideology is written into the nation's history. Fifty-five percent of Americans said in 2022 that the U.S. Constitution is "inspired by God," while 36 percent of Americans and 49 percent of Republicans thought the U.S. "is and has always been a Christian nation."[20] Speaking to notions of American exceptionalism, 64 percent of Republicans and 71 percent of white Evangelicals believe "God has granted the U.S. a special role in human history," compared to 35 percent of independents and 32 percent of Democrats.[21] Beyond these sentiments, many Americans want major political changes to further entrench Christian nationalism into the national psyche. In 2020, 49 percent of Americans, 89 percent of white Evangelicals, and 67 percent of Republicans said the Bible "should influence the laws of the United States."[22] Only a few years earlier, 57 percent of Republicans agreed that Christianity "should be established as the United States' national religion." The same poll found that 28 percent of Americans, 41 percent of Republicans, and 68 percent of white Evangelical Protestants believed the Bible "should have more influence on laws than the will of the people."[23] To circumvent the separation of church and state, a large minority of Americans want the supreme law of the land rewritten. Forty-two percent want religious leaders "to have a direct role in writing" a new U.S. Constitution, while 46 percent think that the Bible should be "a source of legislation."[24] These sentiments are a blatant endorsement of Christian theological rule, overriding the rule of law and basic democratic principles.

Fascist politics are historically linked to patriarchal personalities who seek to lead their nations to greatness and intensify misogynistic hierarchies. We see the same with Christian-fascist white nationalism, via efforts to venerate masculinity and that abhor the challenges feminism presents to patriarchy. In 2020, 53 percent of white Evangelical Protestants and 60 percent of Republicans agreed that the U.S. "punishes men for acting like men," while 56 percent of white Evangelicals and 63 percent of Republicans agreed that the nation had "become too feminine." Toxic masculinity as a socio-political trait was reflected in the sentiment, held by 57 percent of Republicans and 55 percent of white Evangelical Republicans, that the U.S. needs "a leader willing to break some rules if that's what it takes to set things right." For years, that leader was clearly Trump, with nearly two-thirds of his supporters conceding that there was nothing he could ever do as president that would make them lose support for him, even as he sought to circumvent the law in various ways related to violent suppression of progressive dissent and protests of racial injustice, and by encouraging insurrectionist violence on January 6th.[25]

The effort to erase the history of white supremacy coincides with rising Christian nationalism. Seventy percent of white Evangelicals and 79 percent of Republicans claim that the "killings of black men by police are isolated incidents," compared to 43 percent of Americans overall.[26] As religious scholar Robert Jones documents, the refusal to acknowledge racial profiling and police brutality as social phenomena is rooted in the greater susceptibility of white Christians to accept racist and white supremacist beliefs, including support for celebrating Confederate monuments, refusal to recognize the legacy and effects of generations of slavery on black Americans today, openness to stereotypes about black people as lazy and undeserving of public aid, and a general negativity toward "people of other races."[27]

The cross-pollination between religious extremism, cultism, and white supremacy on the American right is virulently manifested in the example of QAnon. The movement is fascist in its politics, between its identification with anti-Semitism, its indulgence in conspiratorial cult politics and a slavish devotion to Trumpian strongman politics, and its eliminationist orientation toward multiparty politics and the Democratic Party.

QAnon's ties to Trumpism are undeniable. In the run-up to the 2020 election, the former president retweeted QAnon accounts routinely. On July 4th, 2020 alone, he retweeted from QAnon accounts 14 times. In the months prior, he retweeted from such accounts another 90 times. He was eventually suspended from Twitter and Facebook for stoking the January 6th insurrection, which itself included a significant QAnon contingent.[28]

Trump's ties to QAnon deepened after he left office. As *The New York Times* reported in late 2022, Trump continued to repost from their accounts on his social media platform, Truth Social, and reportedly "amplified content" from 30 different QAnon accounts to his millions of followers, "reposting their messages 65 times since he became active on the platform."[29] In total, Trump disseminated QAnon posts more than 150 times from 2020 through 2022.

While Trump was actively flirting with QAnon prior to the 2020 election, he still claimed to be ignorant to what the movement represented. In the wake of the election, the evidence of his support for the movement became increasingly difficult, and then nearly impossible to deny. He met in the White House as president and collaborated with numerous QAnon activists, including "My Pillow" CEO Mike Lindell, ex-felon and retired general Michael Flynn, and his lawyer Sydney Powell. The meeting with Lindell and Powell involved the three strategizing about how to overturn the election results.[30] When asked about QAnon, Trump recognized its supporters "like me very much," and described them as people who "love America."[31] When NBC reporter Savannah Guthrie asked him about retweeting QAnon accounts, he told her the movement was "very much against pedophilia. They fight it very hard," but also gaslit Guthrie by claiming that "I know nothing about it"—presumably allowing him plausible deniability for his attempts to mainstream QAnon's politics.[32]

By 2022, Trump had transitioned into a full-blown romance with QAnon. As *Vice* reported, by the fall of that year, he had "shared a picture of himself wearing a Q lapel pin, overlaid with the QAnon phrases, 'The Storm is Coming' and 'WWG1WGA' ('Where we go one, we go all')."[33] He also featured a QAnon-linked song entitled "WWG1WGA" at one of his rallies in Pennsylvania. The same song appeared in one of his campaign videos.[34]

QAnon represents a complicated amalgamation of various phenomena and beliefs. It can be accurately classified as a neofascist movement that implicitly draws on a right-wing interpretation of Christianity in terms of its quasi-religious undertones. These include the veneration of Trump as a demagogue and semi-religious figure, who is seen as a savior working to defeat Satanic forces in the Democratic Party, media, and Hollywood. Complimenting the movement's extreme paranoia, QAnon draws heavily on a white Evangelical demographic base that is notorious for embracing a Manichean ideology rooted in religion and distinguishing between the forces of light and darkness—good and evil. This trend is most apparent in news reports that document how QAnon is most prominent in right-wing Christian communities, and polling revealing that white Evangelicals are more likely than other

Christian denominations and non-Christians to fall into QAnon-style thinking, agreeing that "Donald Trump has been secretly fighting a group of child sex traffickers led by prominent Democrats and Hollywood elites."[35]

QAnon also draws on fascist and anti-Semitic values. Their claim that Democratic leaders are vampiric pedophile Satanists is recycled from Nazi-era propaganda and echoes the "blood libel" claims offered by the Third Reich, which maintained that Jews must be persecuted because of their efforts to drink the blood of children.[36] This propaganda is based in the notoriously anti-Semitic Russian propaganda pamphlet, "The Protocols of the Elders of Zion," which was popularized in the early twentieth century, and warned of a secret Jewish plot to conquer the world.

The anti-Semitic underpinnings of QAnon are endemic to the movement. *Morning Consult* polling from mid-2022 reveals that half of the movement supporters believe that "liberalism" as a social and political force has "equipped Jews to destroy institutions, and in turn gain control of the world."[37] A deeper examination of QAnon's politics reveals its indulgence in other aspects of fascist ideology. Its members worship the cult of personality, blindly believing that Donald Trump will defeat the "deep state" pedophiles by publicly executing Democratic officials, including Barack Obama, Hillary Clinton, and Joe Biden, imposing himself as the de facto dictator of America. When various predictions from Q-influencers about when this revolution will happen fail to materialize, Q's rank-and-file re-interpret the trajectory of the movement, predicting new ways in which Trump's assumption of power will materialize. Similarly, cults are notorious for re-reading failed prophecies about the end of the world after they fail to occur, a point that has not been lost on journalists assessing QAnon.[38] As fascism goes, the cultist attachment to Trump overlaps well with the blind worship of demagogues like Mussolini and Hitler in the classic era of fascism.

QAnon is also fascist in its support for authoritarianism and dictatorship. Its adherents see Trump as a would-be dictator who should and will rule over America and defeat the devious, omnipresent "deep state" pedophilic threat. Such a view necessarily means contempt for democracy, as Americans saw on January 6th, with numerous QAnon adherents participating in the failed insurrection and attempt to reimpose Trump as commander in chief. Finally, QAnon's fascist politics are revealed in its endorsement of eliminationist politics. The movement sees Trump's political adversaries in the Democratic Party as demonic and beyond the pale; as an existential threat to society and to children. It explicitly calls for the public executions of Democratic leaders. Trump echoes this rhetoric in his attacks on Biden, who he refers to as "an enemy of the state," and in his calls to imprison Obama, Clinton, and Biden.[39] Eliminationist ideology and politics were also at the core of Third Reich fascism, specifically with the demonization of Jews as a threat to Aryan "pure blood." Jews were depicted as a fifth column threat working on behalf of communist revolution, and referred to broadly as fueling the threat of "Jewish Bolshevism"—a threat to be eradicated to preserve the integrity of the German republic.[40]

Despite the undeniable link between Trump and QAnon, U.S. political discourse has shied away from referring to the movement as fascist in orientation. Our review of the Nexis Uni database examines news coverage for 2022 revealing 478 articles that mentioned QAnon in *The New York Times*. Of those articles, only three referenced QAnon as a fascist movement, and those references were all in book review articles, without a single news story, op-ed, or editorial making the connection.[41] Similarly, other "liberal" media venues, including *CNN* and *MSNBC*, ran hundreds of segments in 2022, with only 5 percent of reports discussing "fascism" or "fascist" politics alongside QAnon.[42]

U.S. political and media culture consistently downplay the risks of rising fascism in relation to Trump, the far right, and contemporary American politics. For years, commentators, scholars, reporters, and government officials assumed it "can't happen here" in a country priding itself in democratic exceptionalism. The toxic blend of reactionary Christian fascism and conspiratorial eliminationist QAnon politics represents an existential threat to the republic—not so much because of a thousand fundamentalists who failed to occupy the Capitol building, but because the leader of one of the two major parties explicitly associates with right-wing extremist politics. This threat is a ticking time bomb that could unravel the republic and its commitment to the rule of law, mass consent, secularism, and liberal democratic principles.

PART FIVE

Fascism's Attack on Political Agency and Historical Memory

CHAPTER NINE

The Menace of American Authoritarianism and the Crisis of Political Agency

The specter haunting the U.S. consists not only of an impending right-wing fascism, but also the inability of conscience, morality, and justice to catch up with reality. America is closer than ever to tipping into the abyss of an upgraded fascist politics. The latest indications of this include how the GOP is seeking to deputize vigilantes to prevent abortion seekers from even leaving their own states to seek abortions in other states, the mass production of conspiracy theories, attacks on LGBTQ+ youth, and the normalization of white replacement theory.[1] The list also includes the enactment of voter suppression laws, the ongoing attempts by the Republican Party to engage in election denialism, right-wing brainwashing in K-12 education,[2] the banning of books, and threats against librarians for refusing to remove censored books from their library shelves.[3] As we have noted in Chapter 5, the rise of fascist politics is also present in the increasing use by Trump, his political allies, and various right-wing pundits, of a relentless rhetoric of fear, threats, and violence in the service of consolidating authoritarian political power. This anti-democratic discourse of violence also functions as a defense of "so called Christian nationalist identity ... and the fierce growth of white racism that" comes with it.[4] This is a language of blood, soil, and extermination. We have seen this before in much darker times.

    What is even more disturbing is the simultaneous crisis of political agency, historical consciousness, and the collapse of civic responsibility that has made it possible for the threat against democracy to flourish. Politics in America is no longer grounded in a mutually informing regard for both its residents and the institutions that provide for their well-being, freedoms, and civic rights. With the collapse of conscience has come the breakdown of politics as the foundation for democracy.

As Freedom House and the Economist Intelligence Unit have reported, democracy is losing ground around the world as more people reveal a liking for authoritarian leaders.[5] The most recent examples of this global trend can be found in the rise of Donald Trump in America, Viktor Orbán in Hungary, Ferdinand Marcos Jr. in the Philippines, and Narendra Modi in India, among others. According to Freedom House, in 2020 "nearly 75 percent of the world's population lived in a place that saw a decline in rights and freedoms."[6] Moreover, the report found that America saw "an 11-point decline in freedom since 2020, making it one of the twenty-five countries to suffer the steepest drops over the 10-year period."[7] It is worth noting that "the group ... ranked 151 countries and 45 territories ... based on criteria that included electoral processes, political pluralism, etc."[8]

The turn towards fascist politics in the U.S. has a long history rooted deeply in acts of genocide. This includes acts against Native Americans, slavery, Jim Crow violence, the erasure of historical memory, and updated forms of systemic racism buttressed by white supremacy. It also includes the rise of the punishing state, staggering inequality, unchecked political corruption, and a pervasive culture of fear and insecurity. As history is blindsided by the new Republican Party, an intentional erasure of political and social memory in America proves that fascism lives in every culture and that it only takes a spark to ignite it. We mentioned earlier, the Republican Party elite now views historical memory as too threatening a resource to learn from in order to address a range of existing political, economic, and racial problems.[9]

The GOP's goal is to disable memory in order to incapacitate forms of critical agency and the connection between what we know and how we act. The far right's attempts to erase history presents itself as a form of patriotism whose actual purpose is to control historical knowledge in order to normalize white supremacy and legitimate authoritarianism.[10] History in this instance can only function to facilitate learned helplessness and manufactured ignorance. As historical consciousness is repressed and disappears, the institutions and conditions that give rise to critical forms of individual and collective agency wither, undoing the promise of language, dissent, politics, and democracy itself. Consequently, politics becomes more ruthless and dangerous at a time when the forces of normalization and depoliticization work to unmoor political agency from any sense of social responsibility. Angela Davis rightly asserts that this attack on historical consciousness represents first and foremost an attack on education, an attack that must be taken seriously. She writes:

> What we are witnessing are efforts on the part of the forces of white supremacy to regain a control which they more or less had in the past. So, I think that it is absolutely essential to engage in the kinds of efforts to prevent them from consolidating a victory in the realm of education. And, of course, those of us who are active in the abolitionist movement see education as central to the process of dismantling the prison, as central to the process of imagining new forms of safety and security that can supplant the violence of the police.[11]

In an age of demagogues and aspiring autocrats, not only do democratic norms, values, and institutions fade, but in their absence the pathological language of nativism and unchecked lawlessness are reinforced through "Vivid images of invasion and demographic warfare [that enhance] the allure of the rebranded fascism," as Paul Gilroy notes.[12] While Trump has become a flashing signpost for white supremacy and Christian nationalism, he is only symptomatic of the party's deep-seated racism. Indeed, the racism that drives the Republican Party has never been far beneath the surface. Recall, as Thom Hartman notes, "the #2 guy in the Republican House Caucus, Steve Scalise of Louisiana, [once stated] that he was 'David Duke without the baggage,' and ... Reagan's Education Secretary, Bill Bennett, [stated] that 'If it were your sole purpose to reduce crime, you could abort every Black baby in this country, and your crime rate would go down'."[13]

How do we explain the Republican Party's current "love of white supremacist militias and their embrace of both Nazi and Confederate iconography," or their aggressive systemic policies of voter suppression, their racialized language of law and order, and their relentless attack on transgender youth and their guardians.[14]

What excuse can be given for a Party that supported Blake Masters, the former Arizona Republican Senate Candidate who, as Jonathan Chait reports, "has suggested January 6 was a false flag directed secretly by the FBI ... blamed gun violence on Black people. ('It's people in Chicago, St. Louis, shooting each other. Very often, you know, Black people, frankly.'), [and] has endorsed the 'great replacement' theory."[15] Chait goes on to claim that "Neo-Nazi blogger Andrew Anglin gave Masters a fulsome endorsement on the white-supremacist site the *Daily Stormer*."[16] Equally despicable was the Party's endorsement of Carl Paladino for a House seat in New York, who stated that Adolf Hitler was "the kind of leader we need."[17] Then there is Doug Mastriano, the failed Republican candidate for governor of Pennsylvania who according to Eliza Griswold writing in *The New Yorker* embodies "a set of beliefs characterized as Christian nationalism, which center on the idea that God intended America to be a Christian nation, and which, when mingled with conspiracy theory and white nationalism, helped to fuel the [Jan. 6] insurrection."[18] Finally, but not least, the flames of white supremacy are glaringly evident in the relentless defense or dismissal by Trump and his political allies of the violence that took place on January 6th at the American Capitol.

Alarming echoes of the past have long been evident in a Republican Party that supports Trump's description of undocumented Hispanic/LatinX immigrants crossing the southern border as "animals," "rapists," and "vermin."[19] They were silent, if not overtly supportive, when he disparaged Black athletes, claimed that all Haitians have AIDS, and repeatedly used the language of white nationalism and white supremacy as a badge of identity and as a tool to mobilize his supporters.[20] It is worth remembering that in a different historical context, Adolf Hitler spoke of Jews, LGBTQ+ people, and political opponents in the same terms. In both historical and contemporary cases, demagogues created a cultural politics and discourse that allowed people to think the unthinkable. Paul Gilroy gets it right in stating that there is a need to understand "Fascism as a recurrent and infinitely translatable phenomenon."[21]

America has become more closely aligned with the nightmare of fascism. Examples include the Republican Party's attack on electoral integrity, judicial independence, critical education, and voter rights, coupled with its unabashed defense of corruption, white nationalism, and support for oligarchs such as Viktor Orbán in Hungary. As language is stripped of any substantive meaning and reason is undermined by conspiracy theories, falsehoods, and misinformation produced by the right's disimagination machines, the ideological and institutional guardrails designed to protect democracy begin to collapse. Wajahat Ali, writing in *The Daily Beast*, rightly states that not only has the Republican Party lost its moral center, it is also waging war on those institutions vital to a democracy. He writes: "But how can a democracy survive when the GOP has been devoured by a right-wing extremist movement whose members are advancing Christian nationalism, promoting anti-Semitic and anti-LGBTQ+ conspiracy theories, and are willing to purge and dismantle these very same institutions to achieve their goal of minority rule? It can't."[22]

There is more at work here than what many liberals call a constitutional crisis. More specifically, the ideals and promises of a democracy are not simply being weakened by the GOP and their followers. Rather, the threat is far more serious because democracy itself is being replaced shamelessly with the plague of fascist politics. The rule of gangster capital and economic sovereignty is now coupled with ruthless attacks on gender, sexuality, reproductive rights, and a re-energized umbrella of white supremacist ideology and white terrorist policies.[23] As Michael Gillespie notes, neoliberal capitalism has "a death grip on power," and is led by a financial elite and group of "corrupt war mongers bent on popularizing their particular brand of studied indifference to human suffering, war profiteering, and militant imperialism."[24] The poisonous roots of racial capitalism and its egregious system of inequality can no longer be criticized simply for its casual nihilism, numbing lack of compassion, or its detachment from the social contract. Instead, it has far exceeded these social disorders and tipped over into the barbaric abyss of an upgraded fascism.

As neoliberalism severs itself from democratic values and resorts to blaming the victim, it easily bonds with the poison of white supremacy to divert attention from its own economic and political failures. The free-market "utopia" has lost its legitimacy due to its ruthless policies of austerity, deregulation, destruction of the welfare state, galloping immiseration, and scorn for any vestige of government responsibility. Neoliberalism now joins hands with a fascism wrapped in the American flag. In this discourse, neoliberal fascism blames all social problems, including the absurd claim that white people are victims of racism,[25] on people of color, anti-racist rhetoric and ideas, progressive social movements, and almost any source capable of holding power accountable. Central to neoliberal ideology is the normalizing tactic of claiming there is no alternative to gangster capitalism. This has proven to be a powerful pedagogical tool buttressed by the reduction of political problems to personal issues, which serves to infantilize people by limiting opportunities to translate private issues into systemic consideration. While neoliberal ideology in the economic sphere has been weakened, this depoliticizing pedagogical tactic still carries enormous power in dismantling the capacities for self-reflection and forms of critical analysis crucial to a vibrant and engaged democratic polity. As Viktor Frankl argued in a different historical context, such reductionism is "the mask of nihilism."[26] Gilroy advances this argument and states that under such circumstances, democracy has reached a dangerous point. He writes:

> As ailing capitalism emancipates itself from democratic regulation, ultra-nationalism, populism, xenophobia and varieties of neo-fascism have become more visible, more assertive, and more corrosive of political culture. The widespread appeal of racialized group identity and racism, often conveyed obliquely with a knowing wink, has been instrumental in delivering us to a situation in which our conceptions of truth, law and government have been placed in jeopardy. In many places, pathological hunger for national rebirth and the restoration of an earlier political time, have combined with resentful, authoritarian and belligerent responses to alterity and the expectation of hospitality.[27]

Such warnings by Paul Gilroy, Timothy Snyder, Jason Stanley, Ruth Ben-Ghiat, Sarah Churchill, Robin D. G. Kelley, and others raise the crucial question: In what kind of society do Americans want to live?

Additionally, there is the question of what kind of future we envision for upcoming generations, especially at a time when such questions are either ignored or relegated to the dustbin of indifference by politicians, pundits, and propaganda machines that harbor a contempt for democracy. As culture is weaponized, the horrors of the past are forgotten. Books that speak to struggles for freedom and address issues of social injustice are banned by Republican legislatures in various states.

As Robin D. G. Kelley observes, the lesson here is that such practices have no interest in exposing children to historical narratives in which "courageous people risked their lives to ensure freedom for themselves and others ... The implication of this right-wing logic is that America is great, slavery was a good idea, and anti-racism sullied our noble tradition."[28]

Such policies are about more than suppressing dissent, critical thinking, and academic freedom. The more radical aim here is to destroy the formative culture necessary to create modes of education, thought, dialogue, critique, values, and modes of agency necessary for individuals to fight civic ignorance and struggle collectively to deepen and expand a sustainable and radical democracy. Under such circumstances, the warning signs of fascism are overlooked, ignored, and run the risk of being normalized.

In the current historical moment, ethical horizons are shrinking, and politics has taken on a deeply threatening stance. This is made clear by the growing popular support for Trump and his political allies who exhibit contempt for both democracy and a sustainable future while embracing the most profoundly disturbing anti-democratic tendencies, particularly the mix of ultra-nationalism and white supremacy. Crucial here is Rob Nixon's notion of "slow violence" because it highlights theoretically those forms of power and violence "that occur gradually and out of sight, a violence of delayed destruction that is dispersed over time and space, an attritional violence that is typically not viewed as violence at all."[29] The slow violence of authoritarianism is evident in voter suppression laws, the subversion of election machinery, the embrace of white supremacist policies that define who counts as a citizen, and the use of Republican legislatures to purge critical thinking from public schools and undermine the courts. Trumpian calls to "restore greatness" are code for restoring America to a time when only white people had access to spaces of power, politics, and citizenship.

Weaponized disposability and its language of unbridgeable identities are integral to American political culture. They fuel the misery that goes unmentioned in an era of staggering inequality produced by neoliberal capitalism. Such violence, while destructive to democracy, is not of the eye-catching type that immediately grabs our attention because of its catastrophic visibility. As Nixon points out, such violence is rarely newsworthy regardless of how toxic it may be.[30] Yet, it demands a rethinking of power and its workings as part of the hidden curriculum of violence, one that can only be made visible through a serious and concerted historical and relational understanding of politics and the forces that shape it. Slow violence is often something that is only visible in a totality of events, visible only through a politics that is comprehensive and functions to connect divergent and isolated forms of oppression. For instance, the right-wing attack on schools that demand students not wear masks in the classroom—if viewed as an isolated event—misses the larger issue at stake in this form of attack, which is the goal of privatizing (if not eliminating) public education and privatizing responsibility for protecting oneself from a killer pandemic.

Authoritarianism embraces violence as a legitimate tool of political power, opportunism, and a vehicle to quash dissent and terrorize those labeled as "enemies." These alleged enemies are either people of color or those considered insufficiently loyal to Trumpism—or those who oppose the white-Christian reactionary view of women, sexual orientation, and religious extremism. Fast violence, in this instance, is not hidden; it is displayed by the Republican Party and the financial elite as both a threat to induce fear, and as a spectacle to mobilize public emotions. In this context, theater as spectacularized violence is more important than reason, truth, justice, and measured arguments. Violence and lies inform each other shattering facts, evidence, democratic values, and shared visions. As James Baldwin once observed in "A Talk to Teachers," Americans "are menaced—intolerably menaced—by a lack of vision [and] where there is no vision the people perish."[31]

This twenty-first-century model of right-wing fascism legitimizes the ideological and political framework for a cowardly defense of an insurrection intended to overthrow the 2020 presidential election, and the claim that Joe Biden did not fairly win the presidency. Lethal violence is embraced as a strategy and then denied and covered over with lies in order to disavow its consequences, however deadly. The GOP's support for unchecked gun rights is inseparable from both its own propensity for violence and the mass shootings which have become normalized in America. Grocery stores, parades, synagogues, schools, churches, and the streets themselves have become arenas used by the far right to induce fear and further connect personal safety to the purchase of military-style weapons. The culture of violence is now inextricably connected to the culture of fear, lies, cruelty, and the emergence of hyper-militarized groups that support Trump's fascist politics, such as the Oath Keepers and Proud Boys.[32]

As the House Select Committee investigation of the January 6th attack on the Capitol clearly demonstrated, there is overwhelming evidence that the former president's claim of a stolen election was the animating cause of the attempted coup, and that he and other high-ranking members of his party were criminally responsible for the violence that took place.[33] As the report noted, "The central cause of January 6th was one man, former President Donald Trump, who many others followed … None of the events of January 6th would have happened without him."[34] The nine-member House committee made clear that the insurrection gravely threatened democracy and "put the lives of American lawmakers at risk."

The House report methodically laid out the argument that Trump and his allies plotted before the attack to engage in a larger coup aimed at both undermining the 2020 presidential election and whatever remained of American democracy. Trump and his sycophantic associates such as White House Chief of Staff Mark Meadows and Rudy Giuliani made a mockery of the law by trying to pressure the Justice Department, state officials, Vice President Pence, election officials, and others into aiding his goal of reversing Biden's election.[35] Trump and his followers did more than engage in seditious conspiracy—they normalized crime, corruption, state terrorism, fraud, lies, and violence.

As Cassidy Hutchinson, a former aide to Mark Meadows made clear during her deposition before the January 6th hearing, Trump both incited and encouraged the violence on January 6th. She told the committee that "Trump knew a mob of his supporters had armed itself with rifles, yet he asked for metal detectors to be removed. She also recounted how his desire to lead them to the Capitol caused a physical altercation with the Secret Service." The security set up by the Secret Service was implemented to prevent Trump's armed supporters from attending the rally space outside the Ellipse where he was scheduled to speak. Drawing on Hutchinson's testimony, David Graham points out, "Trump didn't care. 'They're not here to hurt me,' he said. He demanded that the Secret Service 'take the fucking mags away' [magnetometers used to detect metal weapons], and added, 'They can march to the Capitol after this is over.'"[36] Once again, Trump promoted mass violence and revenge as a form of political opportunism, regardless of the consequences. It is unfortunate that

Trump's call for the public to arm themselves in order to overturn a stolen election acquired legal legitimacy through a recent Supreme Court ruling supporting the carrying of guns in public.[37] This is not to suggest that the Supreme Court legitimized the coup. Instead, it legitimated the conditions that both make and encourage the conditions for mass violence by ruling that people can carry concealed weapons without applying for a proper permit or due cause.

Less we forget, the January 6th insurrection, now revealed as an organized coup, resulted in the deaths of at least five people and injuries to 140 police officers. More than 840 rioters were charged with a crime. Trump's response to the assault on the Capitol and the ensuing violence was to claim that the mob was engaging in a form of legitimate political discourse and that the attack "was not simply a protest, it represented the greatest movement in the history of our country to Make America Great Again."[38] Peter Wehner writing in *The Atlantic* rightly notes that such comments and actions suggest that Trump was not simply "a criminal president, but … a seditious madman."[39] Bennie Thompson, the House Select Committee chair, stated that Trump was a traitor to his country who engaged in "an attempted coup. A brazen attempt … to overthrow the government. Violence was no accident. It represented Trump's last stand, most desperate chance to halt the transfer of power."[40]

As of November 2023, Donald Trump is the first current former president to be charged with four indictments and 91 felony counts in four criminal cases in Washington, New York, Florida and Georgia. Yet, despite the growing revelations about Trump's penchant for corruption, sedition, lies, violence, willingness to overthrow democracy, and the almost irrefutable image of him as a would-be dictator willing to do anything to secure power, his "polling position with Americans overall is one of his best, and he remains the front-runner for the 2024 Republican nomination." Incredulously, a recent *NBC News* poll found that "a majority of Americans (55%) now believe that Trump was either not or only partially responsible for the rioters who overtook the Capitol … That's up from 47% in January 2021."[41]

What appears missing from much of the coverage of January 6th is that it cannot be solely attributed to Trump and Trumpism—his revised brand of fascism. The roots of such violence and the politics that inform it lie deep in American history and its machinery of elimination and terminal exclusion. But the deep affinity for violence in America can also be found in the neoliberal capitalist system that has produced massive inequality, misery, violence, and suffering, while threatening the future for an entire generation of people. The roots of the current age of counter-revolution are also present in the falsification of history, degradation of language, attack on the ethical imagination, a massive abuse of power, the emergence of disimagination machines, the cult of the strong leader, the rise of the spectacle, and the perpetuation of mass violence similar to what took place under fascist regimes in Italy and Germany in the 1930s.[42]

The signposts of fascism and its threat to democracy become even more obvious and dangerous when individuals surrender their agency, capacity for critique, morality, and humanity for the plague of totalitarianism. Such dangers make it even more necessary to understand the pedagogical forces at work that undermine political agency, reinforce lawlessness, and pave the way for what Adorno once called the authoritarian personality. What is being promoted in the current counter-revolutionary moment is an attack on historical consciousness, memory, and remembrance, which are elements of history that keep alive traditions that speak to human suffering, moral courage, and the struggle for democratic rights, public goods, and social responsibilities.

If the current move towards an upgraded fascism in both America and across the globe is to be resisted and overcome, it is crucial to develop a new language and understanding regarding how concerns of agency, identity, and consciousness are shaped in terms that are both repressive and emancipatory. This suggests that the struggle over agency cannot be separated from the struggle over consciousness, power, identity, and politics. Politics is defined as much by the educational force of culture as it is by traditional markers of society such as economics, laws, political institutions, and the criminal legal system. The poisons of bigotry, anger, hatred, and racism are learned and cannot be removed from matters of culture, education, and the institutions that trade in shaping identities and consciousness. As a long tradition of theoreticians and politicians—ranging from Antonio Gramsci, Louis Althusser, and Raymond Williams to Stuart Hall and Vaclav Havel—have argued, culture is not a secondary but fundamental dimension of society and politics. Moreover, they have all stated in different terms that politics follows culture in that it is the pedagogical baseline for how beliefs, identities, and personal attitudes are formed and inhabited. Furthermore, theorists such as

Paulo Freire and Stanley Aronowitz rightly argued that questions regarding agency, subjectivity, and culture should be a starting point for understanding both the politics that individuals inhabit and how the most repressive forms of authoritarianism become internalized and normalized. Havel was particularly prescient in recognizing that power in the twentieth century has been transformed, especially in light of the merging of culture and modern technologies such as the internet and social media. Given this transformation, he stated that power was inseparable from culture and that it was:

> ... grounded in an omnipresent ideological fiction which can rationalize anything without ever having to brush against the truth. [He states that] the power of ideologies, systems, apparat, bureaucracy, artificial languages, and political slogans [have reshaped] the horizons of our existence ... We must resist its complex and wholly alienating pressure, whether it takes the form of consumption, advertising, repression, technology, or cliché—all of which are the blood brothers of fanaticism and the wellspring of totalitarian thought depriv[ing] us—rulers as well as the ruled—of our conscience, of our common sense and natural speech and thereby, of our actual humanity.[43]

The role of culture as an educational force raises important, and often ignored, questions about the relationship between culture and power, politics, and agency. For instance, what ideological and structural mechanisms are at work in corrupting the social imagination, infantilizing a mass public, prioritizing fear over shared democratic values, and transforming robust forms of political agency into an abyss of depoliticized followers? What forces created the conditions in which individuals are willing give up their ability, if not will, to discern lies from the truth, good from evil? How are such pathologies produced and nourished in the public spaces, cultural apparatuses, and modes of education that shape meaning, identities, politics, and society in the current historical moment? What role does a culturally produced civic illiteracy play as a depoliticizing force and what are the institutions that generate it? What forms of slow violence create the conditions for the collapse of democratic norms? Vital to such questions is the need to recognize not only the endpoint of the collapse of democracy into a fascist state but also what the tools of power are that make it possible. At the same time, important questions must be raised regarding the need for developing a language capable of understanding how these underlying paralyzing conditions work in the service of authoritarianism, and how they are being sustained even more aggressively today to the benefit of a totalitarian state in the making. Language in the interest of social change and justice must be reinvented and function as a mode of critique and militant possibility. In part, this suggests the necessity for a language of informed resistance in which education becomes central to politics and enables conditions for producing new and more democratic forms of agency and collective struggle.

It is important to note that we are not suggesting that language is the only basis for power. Power is more expansive than language and is also present in the institutions, economic forms, and material relations in which language is produced, legitimated, constrained, and empowered. It is important to note that language has a dialectical quality in that it is both the source of symbolic power and a product of material relations of power. In terms of its relationship to cultural politics, language is defined through notions of literacy, civic culture, and shifting symbolic and material contexts. Matters of language and civic literacy cannot be either instrumentalized or stripped of the power of self-determination, critical agency, or self-reflection. At its core and against the discourse of authoritarianism, cultural politics should be addressed from the point of view of emancipation—enabled through a discourse about education, power, agency, and their relationship to democracy. Cultural politics should be acknowledged and defended as a pedagogical project that is part of a broader political offensive in the fight for a radical democracy and its sustaining institutions.

What we are witnessing in the United States is not merely a threat to democracy but a modernized and dangerous expression of right-wing extremism that is a prelude to a full-blown version of fascist politics. One crucial starting point for mass resistance is articulated by Paul Morrow, who, referencing Hannah Arendt, argues that authoritarian societies do "everything possible to uncouple beliefs from action, conviction from action."[44] Any struggle for resistance must create the pedagogical conditions that address the connection between agency and action. The great Frederick Douglass understood this when he stated that "knowledge makes a man unfit to be a slave."[45] While it is generally accepted that power cannot be divorced from knowledge, it is often forgotten that agency is a central political category and that at the heart of authoritarianism is a uniformed individual and an often isolated and depoliticized subject who has relinquished their agency to the cult of the strongman. Consequently, to resist authoritarianism means acknowledging the power of cultural politics to connect one's ideas and beliefs to those vital human needs, desires, and hopes that will persuade people to assert their voices and actions in the building of a new mass movement and a democratic socialist society. This is more than a matter of hope, it is a matter of revolutionary necessity.

CHAPTER TEN

Politicizing January 6th, White Supremacy, and the Assault on Historical Memory

Chapter 9 examined the January 6th insurrection as a manifestation of authoritarian, fascist, and white supremacist violence that sought to overthrow a democratically elected president. In this chapter, we elaborate upon our discussion of January 6th and the specter of rising fascism in America, exploring evidence of how mass support for the failed insurrection is inextricably linked to white supremacist politics. January 6th has become a Rorschach test for Americans, with most Republicans viewing the insurrectionists sympathetically, as holding legitimate grievances, and seeing them as protecting democracy, and with most Democrats seeing them as criminal and as a threat to the republic and democracy.[1] The efforts to erase the white supremacist and fascist ideology that drive January 6th-style insurrection politics speak to the larger war on historical memory—particularly the erasure of Americans' understanding of how right-wing politics gels with white nationalism and fascist insurgency.

Our argument in this chapter engages three primary points. First, the Republican Party and its acolytes in right-wing media have consistently sought to mainstream white replacement theory and white supremacy, thereby conferring a sense of legitimacy on white nationalist politics that envisions growing ethnic diversity and immigration as a fundamental threat to the republic and its identity. This campaign involves significant gaslighting, as right-wing officials and ideologues adopt the language of white supremacy while denying that they support it, all the while claiming they are merely protecting the American people and democracy.

Second, the longstanding U.S. cultural practice of American exceptionalism means that serious and sustained discussions of rising fascism and white supremacy are beyond the pale in "mainstream" political and media discourse. This omission further contributes to the assault on historical memory. Numerous historians have identified how U.S. imperialism and Manifest Destiny, Jim Crow white supremacist politics, anti-miscegenation laws, and eugenics laws served as points of inspiration for the Nazi regime.[2] This dark history is almost entirely ignored in mass discourse, with the U.S. and Nazi Germany commonly portrayed as diametrically opposed powers in the Second World War, and with the U.S. and democracy prevailing over fascism, anti-Semitism, and white supremacy. The reality is anything but, considering the significant cross-pollination between the two countries in terms of their commitment to white supremacist politics, in the past and present.

Not only are U.S. historical ties to the Nazi regime omitted from mass political discourse, but American culture is notable for perpetuating the narrative that the U.S. has transcended racism, or at the very least that mass culture is not characterized by racist, white supremacist, and neofascist values. But the war on historical memory goes even further, now encompassing efforts to erase from existence Trump and the Republican Party's role in stoking white supremacist and fascist violence at the U.S. Capitol on January 6th.

Third, we argue that the whitewashing of America's history and contemporary indulgences in racism and white supremacy carry grave implications for democracy. This denialism saps the nation of the critical political agency that is needed to combat white supremacist and fascist politics. How can one fight a problem they do not recognize exists? In the war on critical agency, the Republican Party gains by perpetuating and mainstreaming fascist and white supremacist values, while preventing substantive discussions of its growing commitment to political extremism.

It is a tragedy that honest and lucid discussions of white supremacy are nearly impossible in U.S. political and social discourse. This trend is clearly at work in the U.S. intellectual, political, and journalistic response to January 6th. Numerous groups that participated in the Capitol attack have a history of indulging in white nationalism, male supremacist activism, anti-Semitism, and vigilantism, including The Proud Boys, the Oath Keepers, and the Groyper Army, among others.[3] The activists participating in January 6th were driven by a commitment to former President Trump, working on behalf of his "stop the steal" campaign to demonize the Democratic Party and to frame it as an existential threat to vote integrity in America.

In line with white replacement theory, the January 6th insurrection was driven by activists who saw former President Donald Trump as their best hope for staving off demographic transformation in the United States. Support for his return to political power was inextricably linked to Trump's white nationalist political agenda,[4] which was the centerpiece of his presidency between his fixation on a wall between the U.S. and Mexico and his preoccupation with shutting down immigration from Muslim-majority and LatinX countries.

Furthermore, right-wing Republicans were instrumental in directing public outrage toward Democratic cities that are disproportionately minority populated, as these are the primary locations under attack via claims about alleged voter fraud.[5] The focus on Democratic-leaning cities with large concentrations of people of color speaks to the racialization of the "stop the steal" movement, which implicitly frames racial minorities as a threat to the Republican Party and to democracy. This racial paranoia within the GOP is captured in recent polling, which finds that a large majority of Republicans believe the changing demographics in America away from a white majority represent a threat to white culture and values and that this transformation "is not a natural change but has been motivated by progressive and liberal leaders actively trying to leverage political power by replacing more conservative white voters."[6] The racialization of "stop the steal," between the Republican Party's targeting of people of color and immigrants is accompanied by an increasingly popular narrative in the GOP that the country is being stolen from good, hard working, white Americans.[7]

Despite the clear ties of the insurrectionists to white supremacist, misogynistic, and fascist politics, there is virtually no effort from the intellectual class to explore how deeply these values resonate with the public regarding how they look at January 6th. The Congressional January 6th report includes references to white supremacy, white nationalism, and specific extremist groups that participated in the attack on the Capitol. But it is notably silent in terms of any discussion of how these values might resonate with the mass public.[8] Journalists, similarly, have systematically avoided raising questions about the extent to which white supremacy and white nationalism may be linked to how Americans look at January 6th.[9] Furthermore, academics have almost entirely avoided discussion of the mass public, white supremacy, and January 6th in their published works since the insurrection.[10] This denialism is what one would expect to find in the face of American exceptionalist ideology, which maintains that the U.S. has transcended racism and that fascism is alien to American politics.

Despite the serial omission of discussions of white supremacy and the public in relation to January 6th, there is good reason to suspect that these values are integral to how tens of millions of Americans interpret the events of that day. A 2018 University of Virginia poll found that 31 percent of Americans agreed that the United States "must protect and preserve its White European heritage," while a 2019 Associated Press poll revealed that 51 percent of Republicans and 22 percent of Democrats felt that "a culture established by the country's early European immigrants" is "important" to "the United States' identity as a nation."[11] These polite, diplomatically worded questions are effective at eliciting responses that paint a clear picture of modern white supremacy. They allow respondents to avoid stark language that would require them to acknowledge their bigotry by explicitly identifying themselves as "white nationalists."

There is a dearth of analysis and evidence from the intellectual class suggesting that white supremacist and white Christian nationalist values are central to how the public understands January 6th. Some unpublished research has identified how individuals who accept white replacement theory are more likely to support the "stop the steal" movement and insurrectionist violence.[12] However, at the time of writing this chapter (early 2023), we found only one published academic study documenting how people with white Christian nationalist values were significantly more likely to adopt views that were sympathetic to the January 6th insurrectionists.[13]

To better understand the relationship between white supremacy and January 6th, we explore in detail polling evidence coinciding with the second anniversary of the insurrection. This data was collected by the Harris polling group, with the survey questions designed by one of the co-authors of this book (DiMaggio). The survey of more than 2,000 Americans, conducted in late October 2022, gauged public opinion in relation to two questions:

1 The extent to which people agreed or disagreed with the pro-European ethno-nationalist contention that "It is important to protect the culture established by America's early European immigrants from those who might try and diminish it."
2 Whether Americans feel that "Those who occupied the U.S. Capitol on January 6th had legitimate concerns about election fraud and about their democracy being stolen."

Our study avoided asking Americans directly if they identify with "white nationalism"—since previous polling finds that only 7 percent of Americans openly accept that label as applied to their political ideology.[14] Rather, the Harris poll is advantageous because it adopts more subtle, diplomatic language that is better suited to pick up white supremacist and white nationalist values that have been mainstreamed in American political culture. This subtlety is necessary in a country that still suffers from massive racial and economic inequalities where intellectuals, pundits, journalists, academics, and much of the public insist that we have entered the "post-racial" era or are "getting beyond race."[15]

Our survey questions are also useful because they capture in their wording a sense of *threat*, in references to those trying to "diminish" European culture, and to a democracy "being stolen" from Trump supporters via mass "election fraud." At issue here is whether there is a clear statistical link between being more likely to embrace a European-centric ethno-nationalist agenda, and increased sympathy for the January 6th insurrectionists. A significant link between these two attitudes would tell us a lot about how white supremacy and insurrection politics are inextricably linked in a Republican Party that is mainstreaming white replacement theory and that depicts people of color and immigrants as a threat to the nation's integrity and greatness.

Examining the Harris survey, 66 percent of respondents agreed with the sentiment that the U.S. must protect a European-centric culture from "those who would diminish it." Nearly half—49 percent—agreed that the January 6th insurrectionists hold "legitimate grievances" about the 2020 election and democracy being "stolen from them." Furthermore, a large majority of respondents favoring a European-centric culture—62 percent— expressed sympathy for the insurrectionists, compared to just 24 percent of those who did not idealize a European cultural identity. This is a large difference of 38 percentage points. Statistically, the relationship between European-centric identity and sympathy with the January 6th insurrectionists is significant, after taking into account other factors, including respondents' political party, ideology, income, age, education, race, and gender.[16] Of course, Republican Party identification and conservative ideology are also significant predictors of sympathy for the January 6th insurrectionists, speaking to the trend of the party and the contemporary far-right's success in mainstreaming the "stop the steal" movement, white ethno-nationalist values, and white replacement theory.[17]

The January 6th insurrection was a serious threat to representative government and democratic electoral integrity. Since this failed coup, political officials, journalists, and academics have abdicated any professional or ethical responsibility to spotlight or condemn the connection between white ethno-nationalist values and sympathy for the January 6th insurrection. The evidence that documented the connection between rising white supremacy and fascist values on the one hand, and support for insurgent politics on the other, is available for those who wish to see it. But American exceptionalism necessitates that open discussions of bigotry as a "mainstream" American value must be suppressed. In the face of a dominant exceptionalist ethos, American intellectuals remain committed to erasing the nation's collective historical memory of its long and disturbing record of idealizing white supremacist values. With academics refusing to take responsibility for spotlighting white supremacist insurrection politics, it is unrealistic to talk about any serious critical educational effort that will light the way to combat racism and right-wing extremism.

Recognizing the ugly faces of American white supremacy and fascist politics means raising uncomfortable questions. How can the country claim to be a democracy when it indulges in hatred against people of color and immigrants as part of its mass culture? How delusional are a country's people for such a large segment of them to elect and approve of a white nationalist as president, and for his supporters to insist for four years that he is neither a racist nor a bigot, as he normalizes and mainstreams hatred, white supremacy, and fascist values? What hope is there for a principled opposition to fascist politics when the intellectual class of journalists and academics, and the loyal Democratic opposition consistently refuse to articulate a sober understanding of the gravity of the threat to the nation and democracy? These questions are all suppressed in a denialist culture that celebrates American exceptionalism, while ignoring disturbing questions about a culture that embraces the politics of bigotry and hate.

The assault on historical memory seeks not only to eradicate recognition of America's white supremacist culture, but to erase basic facts such as Trump's role in stoking insurrection violence. The war on memory is a central element of fascist politics. With the cult of patriarchal politics, *The Leader* tells his followers what to think, how to act, and what is real. And when *The Leader* wants to erase his role in stoking insurgency, his followers respond in kind. We see this outcome as polls demonstrate that two-thirds of Trump voters admit there is nothing he can do to lose their support, and as the large majority of the former president's supporters exonerate him from blame for his role in the January 6th violence.[18]

Trump's war on history manifested itself via his claim of executive privilege to withhold from the public and the January 6th Congressional committee presidential documents that might shed added light on his role in stoking insurrection. As *The New York Times* reported in the fall of 2022, the question of whether he had the right to do so was unresolved: "President Biden is not backing Mr. Trump's attempt" to withhold presidential documents, "and many legal scholars and the Justice Department have argued that he is stretching the narrow executive privilege rights the Supreme Court has said former presidents may invoke. But there are few definitive legal guideposts in this area, and the fights could have significant ramifications."[19] Despite Trump's efforts, the Biden administration announced that it would not comply with his push to keep January 6th related presidential documents secret from the public. Reporting from early 2023 recounted that "President Biden has determined that an assertion of executive privilege is not in the best interests of the United States, and therefore is not justified."[20]

Separate from the legal questions at stake and Biden's denial of executive privilege, there is a deeper substantive concern here for democracy if one of the two major political parties and its leader feel empowered in their efforts to erase history. Trump may not have succeeded in keeping his documents secret, but he did succeed in constructing an alternate political reality for his supporters in which concern with, and attention toward the January

6th insurrection and his role in it was suppressed. And as Trump encouraged his followers to ignore disturbing questions about his role in stoking the failed coup, he continued to gaslight his critics by portraying the January 6th insurrectionists as "great patriots" who sought to overturn a fraudulent election, and as victims of government overreach and repression.[21]

Trump's war on history was reinforced by his media acolytes. The late Rush Limbaugh—when he was not celebrating the insurrectionists as revolutionary heroes,[22] was baselessly claiming that the events at the Capitol were fueled by Antifa and "Democratically-sponsored instigators."[23] Similarly, *Fox News*'s Tucker Carlson referred to the January 6th insurrection as a "wholly created myth," insisting that "The DOJ has been allowed to prosecute and jail hundreds of nonviolent protesters whose crime was having the wrong opinions." Carlson framed the insurrectionists—including Ashli Babbitt, who was killed by Capitol Police for participating in a violent assault on the Capitol—as victims. Carlson also construed the event as evidence for the federal government making "a mockery of our Bill of Rights" and trying "to steal our core freedoms."[24] The message was clear: Trump's supporters were intent on rewriting the history of a violent and criminal insurrection in line with the GOP's propaganda depicting January 6th as "legitimate political discourse."[25]

The attempt to lionize the insurrectionists is part of a larger narrative that seeks to validate Trump's attempts to undermine the integrity of the 2020 election, and romanticize his increasingly violent base and its participation in vigilante street fascism. Trump was incredibly successful in constructing an alternative reality for much of his base, which removed itself from factual discussions of what happened on January 6th and from Trump's responsibility for stoking mass anger about fictitious voter fraud. An examination of the polling and the GOP base reveals a party that is living in a fantasy world in which Trump is the victim of a Congressional January 6th inquiry witch hunt, in which the January 6th insurrectionists were peaceful patriots, and the government has declared a war on its own people by destroying the democratic integrity of U.S. elections.

On the election front, three-quarters of Republicans said in the wake of the 2020 election that widespread fraud had occurred,[26] with more than six-in-ten believing Biden did not win "fair and square."[27] Nearly seven-in-ten Republicans believed Trump was "just exercising his right to contest the election."[28] This is in the face of evidence that he engaged in a coordinated effort to pressure his vice president to illegally overturn the election results in a multi-point plan to turn certification back to Republican states that he hoped would install him as president,[29] despite his attempt to intimidate the Georgia Secretary of State to manufacture votes to help him carry the state,[30] despite his encouragement of insurrectionists to travel to the Capitol and to "fight like hell" or "you're not going to have a country anymore,"[31] and despite his reported joy when the insurrectionists invaded the Capitol, while he refused to mobilize the national guard or to deliver a television address calling on his supporters to stop, as requested of him by Republican House leadership.[32] A significant minority of Republicans have also rationalized the January 6th insurrection, with 46 percent of party members in early 2023 agreeing with the GOP that the events of January 6th were not an insurrection, but evidence of "legitimate political discourse."[33]

Most of Trump's base had walled itself off in its own echo chamber, safely insulated from inconvenient facts that would implicate Trump in stoking insurrectionist violence. The vast majority of his supporters—more than 9 in 10—indicated that they did not plan on following the January 6th Congressional inquiry—suggesting that they had already made up their minds about what happened that day independent of whatever critical facts the committee might uncover.[34] Only 36 percent of his base thought January 6th represented a crisis moment or a major problem for the nation, while nearly 8 in 10 believed Trump did not encourage insurrectionist violence.[35] Nearly three-quarters of Republicans felt "the GOP should be accepting of candidates who believe the 2020 election was stolen."[36] Two-thirds of the party opposed charging Trump with a crime for his involvement in the January 6th insurrection.[37] More than 8 in 10 Republicans in late 2022 indicated that they still held a positive view of Trump, a number that was essentially unchanged since late 2020.[38]

The GOP's Orwellian efforts to invert reality rely on weaponized rhetoric to undermine democracy. A large majority of Republicans cite concerns with an assault on democracy,[39] even as they continued to embrace a former president who led the charge to overturn American elections. Although more than 6 in 10 Americans did not want Trump to run again in 2024,[40] by late 2022 he polled far and away as the most popular candidate in hypothetical matchups for the presidential primaries over competitors like Ron DeSantis, Nikki Haley, and Mike Pence.[41] With Trump and other big lie Republicans clearly in control of the party, a majority popular vote against Trump was no longer a guarantee of stopping him from stealing the 2024 election. This point was most apparent by late 2022, at which time about a third of Republicans running for various state offices openly supported big lie election fraud propaganda,[42] and as 60 percent of Americans voted in midterm races where an election denier was running as a Republican.[43]

Although none of the big lie GOP candidates won major races for governor or secretary of state positions in the 2022 midterms, concerns remained that a party taken over by fictitious voter fraud claims may seek to nullify Democratic wins in swing states in the future. This concern was most acute with the possibility that state legislatures might spearhead this campaign by ignoring pro-Democratic majority votes, in line with the GOP's appeal to the Supreme Court to grant them this power.[44] Even if GOP legislatures fail to overturn enough electoral votes to hand a "victory" to a Republican candidate in 2024, they could still implode the electoral system by a single state setting the precedent of ignoring a Democratic-favoring majority of voters. If this is allowed to happen, it could prevent other states from following a majority of voters in the future.

For Americans looking forward with clear eyes, the stakes are increasingly clear in the wake of the failed 2021 insurrection, and in the run-up to the 2024 election. The GOP's war on truth and historical memory has a clear goal: the demise of political agency for any voting majority that seeks to hand it electoral defeats. White nationalist and fascist politics are central to their political campaign to take power, as they continue to portray the country as facing an existential threat from immigrants, people of color, liberals, women, and the Democratic Party.

The specter of fascism that haunts America includes a war on critical education, which is essential to blunting public recognition of the crisis of rising right-wing extremism. As the U.S. moved into the second decade of the twenty-first century, it desperately needed to reinvigorate its educational system to prioritize the teaching of information literacy, critical thinking, and evidence-based reasoning, and to elevate anti-racist, anti-sexist, anti-classist principles as cornerstones of a renewed democratic politics. But with record inequality, an ascending men's rights movement that treats women as second-class citizens, and mainstreamed white supremacy, it was simply not possible to talk about democracy in any meaningful way.

Respect for scientific and evidence-based reasonings has deteriorated under fascism. This system has been co-opted within the neoliberal political economic system—elevating worker training, vocation, credentialism, and the consumer society as ultimate ideals. This equation leaves little room for a commitment to a critical public education—one in which Americans prioritize critical pedagogy as part of an educational agenda that promotes critical thinking and the common good. A nation of atomized consumers. A corporate media driven by profiteering from mass consumerism. Academics who retreat to academic silos well-removed from the public sphere. A Democratic Party that abdicates on its responsibility to call out growing right-wing extremism. With this cast of actors, who is left to resist the rising threats of white supremacy and fascism? Without a mass movement to preserve the rule of law, to oppose bigotry and hate, and to fight for democratic principles, there is little reason to think that America can roll back the rising tide of fascist politics.

PART SIX
American Society and the Turn Towards Fascism

CHAPTER ELEVEN

The Nazification of American Society

Violence in America surpasses the unthinkable and increasingly resides in the space of apocalyptic rage, manufactured ignorance, and the normalization of a pervasive culture of ritualized barbarism. As civic culture collapses and truth succumbs to conspiracy theories, censorship, and the whitewashing of history, politics is emptied of democratic values, shared responsibilities, and a viable moral compass. Right-wing lawlessness—fueled by a diminishing lack of accountability in the political realm—leads to an upsurge in racism, domestic terrorism, mass shootings, and increasing threats of violence.[1] Acts of violence erupt in even the most protected and secure spaces extending from schools to supermarkets, engulfing every facet of American life. We live in a time marked by a politics of displacement, disappearance, erasure, patriotic frenzy, and political repression. Human suffering is turned into a spectacle of racist aggression and a politics that embraces anti-democratic values, ideas, and social relations.

Once hidden or proclaimed to be on the fringe of American society, violence is at the center of power and everyday life and is normalized. Violent threats are repeatedly lodged against election officials, public health workers, teachers, librarians, as well as almost any politician who refuses to accept the lie that the presidential election was stolen. The threats of violence by a political movement of white supremacists and election denying extremists have reached an all-time high, as have its insane accusations, threats, and hate mongering. For example, influential peddlers of hate, particularly QAnon members, now claim that the Democratic Party is filled with blood sucking Satanists who abduct and sexualize young children. The fallout from these kinds of threats is too extensive to document here. One example, as reported by *The Daily Beast*, captures the vicious lies mainstreamed by such groups and how they incentivize violence among their followers:

> On August 11, Libs of TikTok falsely claimed Boston's Children's Hospital was performing hysterectomies on children. On August 15, Matt Walsh falsely said the hospital was putting "every toddler … on a path to sterilization and butchery before they can even talk." Unsurprisingly, the hospital has since faced a deluge of threats, hate mail, and harassment ever since.[2]

Threats not only function as theatrical performance in the interests of political opportunism and the stoking of mass violence, but are also used by MAGA Republicans to conquer major societal institutions that extend from public schools and libraries to the courts. In addition, dark money increasingly drives such extremism and those laws aimed at repressing women's reproductive and transgender rights, banning books, the weakening of voting rights, among other attacks. Many of these attacks are driven by the modern Republican Party's central fear of living with difference.[3]

Across the globe, violence is marketed to further white supremacy, racial purity, and the notion that some groups do not deserve citizenship and are therefore "non human."[4] Politicians such as Orbán in Hungary talk openly about the dangers of "race mixing" in Europe, echoing the discourse of white supremacy that now dominates the modern Republican Party. National memory is corrupted in the name of fascist politics. As G. M. Tamas observes, this narrowing of inclusion and universal citizenship is a form of "civic death," often followed by "violent death."[5] As civic culture is undermined, it becomes easier for the GOP to market violence at a time when far-right extremists groups such as the Proud Boys, Oath Keepers, and QAnon are "rapidly mutating," particularly in America.[6] As the titular head of the GOP, Trump legitimizes the language of violence by locating it in the rhetoric of victimhood, retribution, and the call to eliminate enemies. How else to explain Trump's 2023 speech at the Conservative Political Action Conference (CPAC) in which he stated: "In 2016, I declared, 'I am your voice.' Today, I add: I am your warrior. I am your justice. And for those who have been wronged and betrayed, I am your retribution."[7] This is an undiluted summons to battle, a fight to the finish in which the call to action suggests punishing people whom Trump considers his enemies. There is more at work in Trump's speech than a sinister and menacing tone. There are echoes of the rhetoric used by demagogic strongmen in the past threatening violent behavior against perceived opponents. As Ruth Ben-Ghiat argues, "Trump's CPAC speech brings forth a century of rhetoric and agendas that have been used to destroy democracy, conjuring threats that are meant to build support for authoritarian action and leadership, starting with the idea of the head of state as a vengeful victim."[8]

Right-wing language reduces politics to theater and spectacle, while using a neo-fascist echo chamber to spread a logic of neoliberal precarity and cruelty, a racist politics of disposability, and a celebration of white, male, Christian nationalism and supremacy. Echoes of an earlier fascist past combine the language of deprivation and dehumanization with policies designed to eliminate, repress, and kill those considered marginal—that is, those considered a contaminating and contemptible force in the script of hard-core fundamentalisms. Cruelty is ingrained in the ideological DNA and structure of the Republican Party, and much of it is aimed at children.

Right-wing politicians attack poor youth by sinking child tax credit, plunging millions of kids into poverty. The war on youth continues in other ways.[9] In spite of the fact that firearm related injuries are the leading cause of death among youth, Republicans call for the elimination of even the most sanguine of gun restrictions.[10] Republican pundits and politicians regularly blame young people for killing children, which is simply not true. As the brilliant Mike Males has repeatedly shown, most of the killings of children under 12 are committed by adults older than 25. He writes: "FBI tabulations of age of killer by age of victim show 77% of children younger than 12 murdered by guns were shot by grownups age 25 and older—a consistent pattern for at least 40 years. More children are shot by murderers over age 50 than under age 18."[11]

Republicans too often depict Black youth as part of a criminal culture and support sentencing children to life without parole—a position reinforced by a reactionary Supreme Court. It should be noted that America incarcerates more of its youth than any other country in the world. Republicans do not simply fail children; they wage a war on them. Idaho and other state Republicans have moved to make gender affirming care for transgender children a crime, even for the parents of such children.[12] The punishing state and its policing and surveillance apparatuses are the default models for addressing economic, political, and social problems. The policing system is weaponized against poor youth of color, migrants, underprivileged families, and Indigenous people.

Republican governors in Texas, Florida, and Arizona inflict immeasurable pain on defenseless migrants by lying to them and by bussing them, often illegally, to other states. In red states, politicians have enacted draconian anti-abortion policies and are seeking to outlaw access to health services in states that have not banned women's reproductive rights. A number of Republicans have voted against a federal disaster relief package that is crucial to aiding people caught in the path of ecological disasters, except when such disasters hit their own states.

Former President Trump provides cover for domestic terrorists such as the Proud Boys and radical conspiracy groups such as QAnon. Governor Abbott of Texas rejects Biden's pardon of untold numbers of people convicted of simple marijuana charges, condemning thousands of people in his state's prisons to the further injustices of a race-based policy of incarceration. Liberal and mainstream language with its embrace of Biden's notion of "semi-fascism" obliterates the long history and breeding grounds of fascism produced through the history of racial slavery, Native American genocide, colonial dispossession, and racial terror in America. It also hides or under-emphasizes the full-fledged fascist politics now driving the current nightmarish flight from liberal democracy both globally and in America. And these examples barely touch on the ongoing intensification of cruelties that are increasingly inflicted on those Americans considered unfit to claim the mantle of human dignity and universal political, economic, and social rights.

Fascism is not a marginal force. It has a long history in America that predates the European model of fascism. It has a concrete history that defies the label of a static configuration. Far from being static, it is a process that takes on different forms under distinct conjunctures and relations of power. In its current form, it is a counter-revolutionary movement in which neoliberal capitalism, white Christian nationalism, and white supremacy function to suppress various democratic and radical insurgencies waged by minorities of class and color. As a mass political movement it now occupies the centers of power and employs the willingness and complicity of millions who indulge its cultish and racist fantasies such as the sinister belief that Jews are bringing in millions of migrants across the American border (and European borders) to displace and disempower whites.[13] When Donald Trump claimed that America should have more people emigrating from Norway, he was mainstreaming the fascist discourse of racial purity that historically led to the death of millions. As Ruth Ben-Ghiat has argued, white replacement theory has a long fascist pedigree that has surfaced once again without apology as was evident when neo-Nazis shouted "Jews will not replace us" while marching in 2017 in Charlottesville, Virginia at the notoriously violent "unite the right" rally.[14] It has also become a central theme at right-wing rallies and in the far-right ecosystem. Writing for the Foreign Policy Research Institute, Colin P. Clarke and Tim Wilson observe that far-right celebrities such as former *Fox News* host Tucker Carlson play a prominent role in mainstreaming white supremacy through their relentless endorsement of white replacement theory. Referring to his former role as a prominent commentator on Fox News, they write:

> Tucker Carlson's show on *Fox News*, which draws approximately 4.5 million viewers each night, has mentioned elements of the Great Replacement theory in more than 400 episodes. The Great Replacement theory suggests that "global elites" are replacing white Christians ("legacy Americans") with immigrants. To prevent this phenomenon from playing out, far-right extremists call for the use of political violence.[15]

Replacement theory is being spread not only by pundits such as Tucker Carlson, it is also promoted by extreme right-wing Republican politicians such as Marjorie Taylor Greene and Paul Gosar. Moreover, it is also endorsed by Rep. Elise Stefanik, the third highest ranking leader in the GOP. As reported in *The Daily Beast*, she not only promoted ads on Facebook endorsing white replacement theory, but she did so knowing that "it radicalized Robert Bowers, the terrorist who killed 11 people at the Tree of Life Synagogue because he wanted to punish Jews for helping the 'invaders' [and] radicalized Brenton Tarrant, the Christchurch terrorist who killed more than 50 Muslims, and who served as the direct inspiration for the Buffalo terrorist."[16]

As we have stressed throughout this book, the language of violence and white supremacy does more than invoke insidious meanings and racist stereotypes, it also incites threats that lead to violence, mass shootings, and untold deaths. The language of hate and bigotry presents enormous cause for alarm in a society in which fascism is becoming a habitualized part of the culture. Such threats are now endemic to a modern far-right Republican Party that hates equality, difference, and democracy itself. The language of violence, cruelty, and disposability are the political currency of a fascist past and have emerged in the current Nazification of the present.

With Republican Party fascism on the rise, right-wing social media floods American society with discourses and images of hate, white nationalism, nativism, and the disavowal of citizenship as a universal right.[17] Christian nationalism, with spokespersons such as retired lieutenant general and former national security adviser Michael Flynn, is dedicated to building a movement in which Christianity defines the governing principles of American life and institutions, all the while destroying the social bonds that provide meaning, dignity, and security to Americans. For instance, Flynn argues that America is in the midst of a religious crusade. He willingly attends and speaks at right-wing conferences filled with endless speeches about the "Great Awakening" and with reminders that Christians are in a "spiritual war [where] you can't win without attacking."[18] Like many GOP evangelicals Flynn "sees conspiracies in every corner of American life." According to Michelle R. Smith reporting for *Frontline*, his thinking fuels violence and is rooted in a mix of lies and falsehoods. She writes:

> He's repeated falsehoods about Black Lives Matter and said that so-called globalists created COVID-19. He tells the tens of thousands of people who have paid to see him speak that there are 75 members of the Socialist Party in Congress and has said the left and Democrats are trying to destroy the country. He asserts, above all else, that America was founded on Judeo-Christian values. The bedrock, he warns, is crumbling …. He says elementary schools are teaching "filth" and "pornography." He continues to assert, ignoring all evidence to the contrary, that elections can't be trusted. He says, over and over, that some of his fellow Americans are "evil."[19]

Once again, major GOP politicians now use the language of violence to condone egregious acts of lawlessness. Blake Masters, the failed Republican Senatorial candidate in Arizona, has come to symbolize the violent rhetoric now endemic to the modern Republican Party. For example, he opened his political campaign with a video in which he is pictured in the desert holding a gun. He states, "This is a short-barreled rifle. It wasn't designed for hunting. This is designed to kill people."[20] He is a firm supporter of Trump, denies he lost the 2020 presidential election, and claims that immigrants are invaders. Appearing on a conservative talk show, he stated that "Dr. Anthony Fauci 'will see the inside of a prison cell this decade.'"[21] Sam Adler-Bell reports that "In November, Masters tweeted, 'When a society celebrates Antifa looters, arsonists, and pedophiles as heroes, while turning brave people like Kyle Rittenhouse into villains, it is a society that is not long for this world.'"[22] His propensity for violence matches his militantly fundamentalist right-wing views. Like many of his Republican colleagues, he views "coercive state power as an indispensable tool for achieving conservative ends: mandating patriotic curriculums in schools, supporting the formation of 'native-born' families, banning abortion and pornography, and turning back the rights revolution for L.G.B.T.Q. Americans."[23]

In this age of growing fascism, language has become a central part of the microphysics of repression and everyday life. This is a language that celebrates white nationalism along with a regenerating cult of rage and aggression as a legitimate tool of political power. In this new era of violence, it is crucial to comprehend not only the political, institutional, and cultural conditions at work that turn politics into a form of civil war, but also to identify the sites, policies, and regimes of power that exploit the fears, anxieties, loneliness, and rage that have been produced by a society that has become synonymous with a culture of cruelty, greed, and aggression, and unbridled racism.

It is also important to address the rhetorical silences about the threat of fascism in America. For example, the mainstream press uses coded language to divert from public view both the crisis of capitalism and its morphing into a form of neoliberal fascism. It deals with the authoritarian politics of abduction and disposability suffered by migrants by wrongly focusing on the personal narratives of its victims. It focuses on the lies of the GOP while saying nothing regarding what Chris Hedges calls the false claim that America is a functioning democracy.[24] The corporate-controlled media calls insurrectionists, such as a number of the Republican nominees for office in November election deniers rather than dangerous fascists. It condemns Trump's ongoing claims to pardon criminals and thugs who attacked the Capitol if he is re-elected, while treating the insurrection as an isolated event that disappears from the news within a short period of time. Trump's mishandling of government documents is treated as a personal act of lawlessness rather than as symptomatic of how lawlessness is a characteristic of fascist regimes, whether in Nazi Germany, Pinochet's Chile, or Orbán's Hungary.

When the neo-fascist Giorgia Meloni was elected as prime minister of Italy, the mainstream press, as well as Hillary Clinton, "focused solely on her being Italy's first woman prime minister."[25] What is often forgotten in this depoliticized homage to gender is that women have played a prominent role in the "pursuit of fascist goals."[26] George Pendle, writing in *Air Mail*, wrote that Italy's Meloni "is the most spectacular example of a recent trend in European politics in which charismatic women have taken the reins of far-right political parties and led them to increasing legitimacy. Just look at Marine Le Pen in France, Alice Weidel in Germany, Pia Kjaersgaard in Denmark or Siv Jensen in Norway."[27]

The crisis of language in America is symptomatic of the death of one order, liberal democracy, and the emergence of another, which we call neoliberal fascism.[28] The GOP, with its mix of neo-Nazis, conspiracy theorists, religious fanatics, politically corrupt grifters and politicians, January 6th insurrectionists, and right-wing extremists, are not simply trying to remove Joe Biden from office, ban books, turn public and higher education into right-wing propaganda machines, eliminate women's reproductive rights, and define historical, cultural and national memory through the lens white replacement theory and a nostalgic longing for the age of Jim Crow. They are ushering in an updated form of fascism that threatens global existence, not simply the last vestiges of democracy. They are engaged in a project that represents a counter-revolutionary fascist takeover grounded in the death dealing logics of gangster capitalism, mass violence, and a politics of disposability, especially when it refers to migrants and trans people.[29]

The seeds of fascism never disappear in any society. They lie dormant waiting for the right political, economic, and social conjuncture to emerge. In the current neoliberal incarnation, politics has become infantilized, reduced to theater of cruelty, addicted to the individualization of all social problems, and receptive to the rise of cult politics with its celebration of demagogues and denial of any vestige of government and social responsibility. We live in an age of political and social decay. Chris Hedges artfully presents the mobilizing passions of fascism that have become a dominant political force in America—a fascist politics that embraces symbols that mimic elements of American society. He is worth quoting at length.

> [F]ascism ... wraps itself in the most cherished symbols of the nation, in our case, the American flag, white supremacy, the Pledge of Allegiance and the Christian cross. It celebrates hypermasculinity, misogyny, racism and violence. It allows disenfranchised people, especially disenfranchised white men, to regain a sense of power, however illusory, and sanctifies their hatred and rage. It embraces a utopian vision of moral renewal and vengeance to coalesce around an anointed political savior. It is militaristic, anti-intellectual and contemptuous of democracy, especially when the established ruling class mouths the language of liberal democracy but does nothing to defend it. It replaces culture with nationalist and patriotic kitsch. It sees those outside the closed circle of the nation-state or the ethnic or religious group as contaminants who must be physically purged, usually with violence, to restore the health of the nation. It perpetuates itself through constant instability, for its solutions to the ills besetting the nation are transitory, contradictory and unattainable. Most importantly, fascism always has a religious coloring, mobilizing believers around rites and rituals, using sacred words and phrases, and embracing an absolute truth that is heretical to question.[30]

If Americans want a real debate about violence in America and globally, it is crucial to understand it as part of a larger neoliberal fascist order that enacts the abandonment of public goods, declares welfare as a reckless handout and as sinful, views class and racial solidarity as dangerous, and replaces the idea of equality, justice, and freedom with notions of white nationalism, patriotic correctness, and racial cleansing.[31] In addition, any serious discourse about violence has to address the growth of the military-industrial-academic complex, the militarization of everyday life, the rise of the carceral state, the militarizing of the police and its culture of racism, and the rise of the national security surveillance state. Americans need a vocabulary and language in which human beings are not considered expendable; profits are not viewed as more important than human needs; and systemic inequality is viewed as the scourge of social justice, freedom, and any viable notion of individual agency and collective self-determination. Americans need a vocabulary, as Robin D. G. Kelly, Angela Davis, Ruth Gilmore, and others repeatedly remind us, that rejects liberalism's defense of capitalism, the priority of the market, and a weak and deracinated notion of the public, social, and common good.

Liberals fear fascism but they fear the end of capitalism even more in spite of the fact that neoliberal capitalism's endpoint in a time of crisis embraces the fundamental rudiments of fascist politics. Voting will not stop fascism and neoliberalism is not its antidote; moreover, elections are at a historical moment in which money-driven politics offers a weak depoliticizing prop for avoiding the ideological and structural elements of capitalism that breed massive inequality, suffering, repression, a culture of immediacy, civic dysfunction, the logics of disposability, and ecological devastation. Neoliberalism with its war-against-all mentality mainstreams hatred for those considered other, subjects Black and Brown people to systemic violence, and punishes those who believe in long-term investments designed to develop a radically democratic future.

Violence is fundamental to how neoliberal capitalism legitimates and reproduces itself. Capitalism is not part of the laws of nature and is the product of an ongoing effort to subvert the public imagination, undermine critical thinking, and decouple economic activity from social costs. Its massive right-wing propaganda machines have militarized culture and the educational apparatuses of persuasion. For the modern Republican Party, the struggle over ideas has become an accelerated war to depoliticize, infantilize, and destroy any vestige of a mass consciousness that has a passion for a socialist democracy.

The hard fascism of the Republican Party now functions as a form of domestic terrorism with its embrace of a global authoritarian politics. The Democratic Party is the muted underside of fascist politics. It is wedded to a capitalist society that breeds the inequalities, misery, suffering, uncertainties, and precarity that, as Toni Morrison once said, support a militarized and racist environment that allows fascism to grow, while rejecting equality as a central principle of both human relations and democracy itself.[32] It hides its fascist impulses in the hypocritical discourse of a compassionate capitalism, an oxymoron whose ultimate purpose is to protect the financial elite and its ideological and repressive state apparatuses. Once again, wedded to big money, its call for fair elections rings hollow given that "both rising right-wing movements, as well as corporate control of elections, are linked."[33] They are two sides of the same coin. This addiction to neoliberal capitalism represents a lethal connection between the two political parties. The broader context of American foreign policy highlights the role that the Democratic Party, along with the GOP, has and continues to play in supporting a range of fascist countries and their right-wing movements, all of whom are blithely defined as allies.

The threat of violence is used by right-wing politicians and extremist groups to threaten dissent and those who advocate for public health, basic social provisions, democratic values, and democracy itself. Language when stripped of any regard for civic culture, informed judgment, and an inclusive notion of citizenship becomes spectacularized, emotive, and bereft of reason and any sense of justice.

Any viable notion of resistance needs a politics which, as the late Ellen Willis argued, would give people "a voice in collective decision making, not only in government, but at home, at work, at school."[34] It would offer a vocabulary for replacing a politics of disconnection and the individualization of the social with a politics of connection; that is, a comprehensive politics that embraces the totality of a system and social order. Following Stanley Aronowitz, Angela Davis, and Barbara Epstein, such resistance needs a new language for rethinking theory, developing anti-capitalist politics, and a mass movement aimed at democratizing power. This notion of resistance would also embrace discourse that relates education to social change, a theory of institutional structures, a developed notion of public intellectuals in the age of digital media and tyranny, and the politics of critique and possibility.[35]

A language of resistance, especially when used by educators, activists, and cultural workers, needs to function as a force that both names and ruptures. It must name how politics mutates and works in new historical moments, make visible how different forms of oppression overlap and relate, and provide a comprehensive set of connections and a wider theoretical lens for engaging social problems. This language must be dialectical, driven by an understanding of how matters of power, agency, education, values, and politics are forged within both the discourses of domination and emancipation. Not only does such a language complicate relations of oppression, but it also opens up diverse modes of resistance. In the current post-Trump era, violent rhetoric works as an apocalyptic rage machine, as words lose their substance and meaning.

It has taken too long for the American media, analysts, educators, and cultural critics to connect Trump and his MAGA movement to fascism, regardless of the fact that their rhetoric, actions, and policies echo a dark and dangerous past. Underlying such silence was an inability to recognize that fascism comes in many shapes, elements, forms, and symbols. Holocaust scholar Leonard Grob argues that Trump and his MAGA followers have appropriated a mix of fascist elements and in doing so claims that Donald Trump has become the signpost of American fascism. He writes:

> Fascism, however, has many shapes and sizes. When Mussolini coined the term fascism, he adopted the ancient Roman fasces as its symbol—a bundle of rods, with an ax-head, bound together with unifying cords. Fascism bundles ideological ingredients such as: authoritarian, antidemocratic, and supremacist nationalism; xenophobic population and immigration policies; favored economic status for a few, suppressed rights for unions and labor; intentional and intensified political divisiveness; weaponizing courts and police to exact retributive punishment of internal enemies; disrespect for truth; political control of media and schools; religious legitimation ... Trump and MAGA Republicanism bundle such elements in 2020s America. Fascism is alive in the United States. So much so, that it is not hyperbole to say that American fascism's face is Donald Trump's.[36]

In many societies, violence is elevated to an organizing principle of power, increasingly valued as a form of political currency. The conditions for democracy are obliterated by extremists globally who embrace repressive forms of control, lies, and white supremacy as tools of political opportunism. America has a full-fledged fascist problem that must be addressed if it is to think its way to a different politics and future. But America is not alone. Fascist governments are emerging in Sweden, Italy, Hungary, Chile, and the other countries. What these countries share is a hatred of difference, equality, and egalitarian policies and practices.

Traditional political categories that often pit parties against each other seem irrelevant when it comes to addressing the emerging threats to global democracy itself. This is especially true with respect to the notion that power is global and politics is local. This formulation is no longer acceptable in the age of global capitalism. We need a new language for developing and understanding global politics and its distinctive formations, and what it takes to develop new international modes of resistance to fight them. Restricting social movements to ideological silos is as dangerous as restricting social movements to national boundaries. As suggested above, any viable mode of resistance in the age of global capitalism must unite the different social movements under the banner of struggling for radical socialist democracy while simultaneously crossing national boundaries to join with others across the globe to fight the savagery of neoliberal global politics. Central to such a task is the work of intellectuals, unions, artists, cultural workers, and others who can fashion new tools and a global social movement in the fight against anti-democratic threats all over the world.

Liberal democracy is no longer on life-support in America, it is a barely breathing corpse hidden behind the language of myth, misrepresentation, and social and historical amnesia. The process of Nazification has almost reached its endpoint and the planet hangs in the balance. Across the globe, the struggle over politics is less a rivalry between traditional political parties and movements than a struggle between an updated brand of fascism and the promise of a socialist democracy. As the ghost of fascism washes across the globe, maintaining hope and the need for massive collective resistance is a revolutionary act with no other option.

DeSantis and the GOP are doing more than attacking the welfare state, the social contract, and public goods. They are also waging a war on historical consciousness so that the unthinkable cannot be revealed. The corrosion of memory is part of a broader assault on both the capacity for moral witnessing and the formative cultures that make thinking possible—that is, the conditions that provide for critical forms of agency. What most educators miss about the

GOP assault on the public imagination is that at its core it is a depoliticizing project that undermines the capacities crucial to creating an informed and active citizenry. It is what Franco Berardi calls a form of "annihilating nihilism and capitalist absolutism," a recipe for a failed state and the potential for mass violence and murder.[37]

One of the central questions at stake here is this: What is the role of educators in a time of tyranny? What is the relationship between education and democracy? How might educators form a social movement in defense of the public good with other cultural workers and how might they become part of a broader international movement? Educators have a responsibility to not only defend education as a crucial public sphere, but also to develop a new language regarding theory, politics, power, agency, and the future. They need a theoretical language that makes education central to politics, fosters forms of radical refusal, rethinks the role of consciousness and memory as terrains in which agency and politics can be refigured, and that dissolves the mirage of capitalist ideology and individual autonomy. The language of social change cannot be frozen within the discourse of an alleged reformed capitalism. Capitalism cannot be reformed; it must be replaced by a sustainable form of democratic socialism. At the same time, educators should be on the forefront in acknowledging that socialism cannot be implemented simply by changing economic policies. Such change requires a new kind of critical agent, a new script for mobilizing desire, and a change of consciousness. Matters of agency, creativity, compassion, and community must be embraced as part of a radical restructuring of the subject and the grounds for creating a mass movement of resistance.

Educators and other cultural workers bear enormous responsibility as public intellectuals who must sustain and expand the values, knowledge, modes of thinking, and identities crucial to bringing democratic political culture back to life. As citizen educators, they need to help young people to become informed, active, creative, and socially responsible members of society and the larger world. They have a responsibility to educate young people to be not only knowledgeable and critically informed, but to also be compassionate and caring, refusing to allow the spark of justice to go dead in themselves and in the larger society.

As meaningful public intellectuals, educators must have control over the conditions of their labor, affirm and engage student experience, connect learning to social problems that bear down on the lives of young people, and inspire young people to take risks and combine a faith in reason, moral courage, the power of justice, and compassion for others and democracy itself. Educators must take active responsibility for raising fundamental questions about what they teach, how they are to teach, and what their larger goals are. This means that they must take a responsible role in shaping the purposes and conditions of schooling. That much has been evident over the past four years as educators fought in America, Canada, and in other countries with governments dedicated to narrowing education, increasing class sizes, imposing patriotic forms of education, banning books, and undermining public and higher education as democratic public spheres. The role of educators as public intellectuals is a huge undertaking, one that calls on them to look at their work as a political, civic, and ethical practice that combines critical reflection and action as part of a struggle to overcome economic, political, and social injustices. Moreover, educators cannot do this work alone, they must join with workers, social movements, youth groups, and unions in their fight against the terrorism wrought by neoliberal fascism. We get a glimpse of the success of such strategies as educators around the country go on strike and push their unions beyond traditional bargaining demands to argue for more inclusive curricula, staff support, and funds to create conditions for their students to overcome the rapidly increasing disparities around matters of class, race, and sexual identity that undermine their chances for learning how to live with dignity, hold power accountable, and how to govern rather than be governed.[38]

As fascism expands across the globe, and extremism is normalized by the Republican Party and its global allies, the crisis of education must be matched by a crisis of ideas and the urgent project of merging the movement for economic and social justice with a formative culture and educational project that places matters of morality, justice, compassion, care, and civic courage above a predatory neoliberal capitalism that is destroying the planet and ushering in a new age of fascist barbarism. Educators need to think on the edge of possibilities, develop an anti-capitalist vision, and learn how to make social change meaningful and just. These changes must highlight power relations, providing people with a sense of dignity and with access to crucial social supports. There is a need to abolish the institutions and toxic values and feed a predatory neoliberalism intent on the Nazification of American society.[39]

CHAPTER TWELVE

What Fascism Is (and Isn't): The White Working Class and White Supremacy

This chapter cuts to the core of what it means to talk about American fascism. We explore the idea that support for Trump, white supremacy, and fascism are the result of mass economic and financial insecurity and desperation. This thesis is weak and the evidence for it is exaggerated, despite GOP propaganda about Trumpism as a working-class phenomenon that permeates mass discourse. Instead, we argue that white supremacy and fascism are primarily driven by right-wing socio-cultural values that legitimate the politics of hate, bigotry, and cruelty. We will examine Trump's speeches, exploring the ways he demonizes immigrants, people of color, and Democrats in favor of white supremacist politics, and through dehumanizing rhetoric that compares "othered" groups to animals. This tactic is right out of the pages of Nazi Germany and the Third Reich's propaganda.

To draw attention away from the U.S. political system's plutocratic biases, the Republican Party has for decades adopted the propaganda claim that it is the real savior of the working class.[1] Trump promised to protect workers harmed by globalization and to "Make America Great Again." Mainstream reporters fell into this rhetoric, depicting Trump as rallying blue collar workers. *The New York Times* called his election a "stunning repudiation of the establishment," and Trump as running "an explosive, populist, polarizing campaign" that was "a decisive demonstration of power by a largely overlooked coalition of mostly blue-collar white and working-class voters who felt that the promise of the United States had slipped their grasp amid decades of globalization and multiculturalism."[2] Scholarly research concludes that this narrative about working-class populism was pervasive in the news, and was strongest in right-wing venues like *Fox News*.[3]

A closer investigation of available evidence, which we have been directly involved in collecting and analyzing, reveals that the white working-class insecurity thesis rests on shaky ground. The scholars and journalists putting forward this claim point to the fact that Trump supporters are disproportionately more likely not to have a college degree and to work in blue-collar jobs,[4] and that parts of the country that suffered more from drug abuse, poverty, unemployment, depressed economic activity, and suicide rates, were more likely to cut toward Trump, particularly in the 2016 election.[5] What these studies overlook is that Trump voting in depressed areas was not more likely to come from poorer or working-class whites. Rather, considering the longstanding relationship between poverty and non-voting, poorer areas of the country see depressed voter turnout, so the more privileged people in these depressed areas have an outsized impact on election outcomes, relative to the working class and poor, and tend to significantly favor Republican candidates.[6] Furthermore, individuals who self-identify as lower or lower middle class or as white and working class are *not* significantly more likely to support Trump. And just because individuals with lower education levels and blue-collar jobs are more likely to vote for Trump than a Democrat, does not mean they are more likely to be economically insecure, considering that the median Trump supporter earns more than $100,000 a year.[7]

An exhaustive review of dozens of polling questions centered on the economic background of Trump supporters and those supporting right-wing extremism reveals that they are not more likely to suffer from financial insecurity.[8] Those sympathetic to the contemporary militia movement, QAnon neofascism, and "alt-right" white supremacy and neofascism are not more likely to come from poorer economic backgrounds.[9] And Trump support is not more likely to come from white individuals who are suffering from lower incomes, depression, and drug abuse,[10] contrary to the "deaths of despair" thesis.[11] Rather, support for Trump appears to closely track partisan rhetoric. When Trump was running for office in 2016, Republican Americans were enamored with his claims that the country's greatest days were behind them, that people were suffering economically, and that the state of the nation and economy were not good.[12] Once he was in office, however, these opinions rapidly shifted, with Trump supporters becoming the most enthusiastic of Americans about the alleged Trump economic miracle, and believing that Trump had made good on his promise to "Make America Great Again."[13]

The different Republican opinions about the state of the nation had little to do with metrics like economic growth, changes in household income, and unemployment rates, but appeared instead to be a function of Republicans reacting positively to Trump's own rhetoric celebrating his role in saving America.[14] Unsurprisingly, Republicans went back to overwhelmingly howling about the sad state of the economy immediately after Biden took office, despite problems of depressed economic growth, high unemployment, and inflation persisting across the late Trump and early Biden terms.[15] The message here is simple regarding the U.S. economy: when Democrats are in power, America deteriorates and must be made "great again" by a Republican savior of the white working class. When Republicans are in power, it is imperative that they remain in power to keep America great.

None of these findings should be taken to suggest that Trump support is unrelated to economic factors. Available evidence suggests that economics is a significant underlying factor in fueling Trumpism in numerous ways:

1. Trump supporters appear relatively content (and certainly not discontent) with neoliberal politics. They are no more likely to support government efforts to reduce health care costs for those struggling to pay them, to endorse allocating increased funding to Social Security and Medicare, or to call for government to help in reducing inequality.[16] And they are significantly more likely to oppose raising taxes on the upper class, to oppose government helping the needy and regulating business, and increasing the minimum wage. They are also more likely to prefer a smaller government with fewer services, and to endorse classist notions that the poor have it too easy because they are lazy and receive government handouts.[17]

2. As previously mentioned, Trump support is strongest in parts of the country suffering from economic depression, which is evidence that the bi-partisan supported neoliberal economy has a devastating effect on working class and poor people, deeply suppressing voter turnout among

groups that are historically more likely to vote Democratic (when they do vote), and providing a significant advantage to Republicans in depressed parts of the country, which contributed to Trump's electoral victory in 2016.

3   Despite a large volume of data revealing that Trump supporters are not more likely to be lower income and economically insecure, some data do reveal a very weak relationship between whiteness, lower income, and Trump support.[18] This suggests that Trump support may in part be a function of economic insecurity, although if this is the case, it is a relatively weak factor contributing to his rise to political power.

4   Speaking to struggles to get ahead in a neoliberal era when Americans are working harder and harder, are seeing dwindling returns, and enduring rising inequality, white Americans (and Americans in general) who hold a second job or who work overtime are significantly more likely to support Trump.[19] It makes sense to speak of this group as occupationally stressed, in that they are putting in extra hours to "make ends meet" or to "get ahead" in an economy that is notorious for fostering worker insecurity. Importantly, occupationally stressed Trump supporters are more likely to agree with broad statements that immigrants are bad for the country and that people of color are lazy. A plausible interpretation of this data is that Trump supporters are frustrated at the considerable number of hours they must put in at work to make ends meet or get ahead, and that they are looking for a scapegoat (immigrants and poor people) on which to take out their frustrations.

5   Individuals suffering from moderate to high levels of economic strain related to job insecurity, steep health care bills, risks of home foreclosure, and other forms of financial insecurity are significantly more likely to embrace white Christian nationalist ideology.[20] This finding must be carefully qualified, however, considering that a closer examination of this data finds that only a very small number of people—a few percent of Americans—are suffering from moderate to high amounts of economic strain and gravitating toward white Christian nationalism.[21] More

broadly speaking, this research also finds that higher income Americans and more affluent individuals who identify as middle, middle-upper, and upper class are significantly more likely to identify with Christian white nationalism than are those with lower incomes and people identifying as lower or lower-middle class.[22]

These findings do not at all suggest that large numbers of Trump supporters are suffering from economic and financial desperation and insecurity. Rather, it is the neoliberal economy—which Trump supporters are more likely to support—that is working in the background to fuel Trumpism by demobilizing a potentially progressive working-class voter base that would otherwise favor the Democratic Party. When evidence does link Trump support to economic insecurity, it is quite weak and must be carefully qualified, since Trumpism as a plutocratic-neoliberal movement is fueled by middle to middle-upper income voters who are unlikely to suffer from financial insecurity.

If economic insecurity is not the primary driver of Trumpism, then what accounts for the rise of this movement and the mainstreaming of white supremacist and fascist politics? Our review of previous work demonstrates that identification with right-wing socio-cultural political values is a consistently reliable predictor of support for Trump and his reactionary brand of politics.[23] Trump support is significantly and often powerfully associated with support for authoritarianism,[24] opposition to abortion, distrust of Muslims and immigrants, support for cracking down on immigration (authorized and unauthorized) and the further militarization of the border, concerns with terrorist threats, homophobia, opposition to recognizing the persistence of racial inequality, sexist support for the notion that men are the real victims in America and that women are more powerful, opposition to the belief that racial and ethnic diversity make the U.S. a better place to live, opposition to gun regulation, opposition to government efforts to address climate change, and support for religious fundamentalism.[25]

Trumpism as a neoliberal top-down social movement is notable for its primary reliance on not only right-wing socio-cultural values, but also white nationalist and fascist politics. Much of the rhetoric from Trump's speeches has been central to the Nazification of American society and politics. This claim will be contentious for those who have not closely examined Trump's rhetoric, or who are seeking to obscure his support for extremism because they agree with him. But a closer look at this messaging reveals that Trump's radical politics are defined by the dehumanization of people of color and immigrants in ways that echo Nazi-fascist rhetoric. This includes the comparison of immigrants of color and people of color more generally to animals, and eliminationist efforts to depict the Democratic Party as a fundamental threat to society's survival.

That tens of millions of Americans looked past Trump's Nazi-esque rhetoric—or actively indulged it—is a sign of the ritualized barbarism that defines American politics in an era of rising right-wing extremism. White nationalism has become almost mundane, with the politics of cruelty part and parcel of Republican messaging. These efforts to dehumanize people of color through the rhetoric of fear are central to the campaign to normalize eliminationist politics. The "other" is depicted as representing a threat to the nation's security. Implicit in this messaging is the notion that someone ought to act to suppress or eliminate these threats—be it the government or vigilantes. When rhetoric reaches this level, we are talking about an ideology of fascism that echoes the politics established by the Third Reich.

With the Nazification of American political rhetoric, primary targets include immigrants, civil rights activists, and the Democratic Party—the last of which is seen as a potential ally to the former groups. Drawing on the University of California Santa Barbara's American Presidency Project and its database on presidential rhetoric, we looked at numerous speeches from President Trump during his time in office. Previous research utilizing this database, and looking at dozens of speeches from presidents George W. Bush, Barack Obama, and Donald Trump, finds that Trump routinely invoked eliminationist language, as applied to the Democratic Party, immigrants, and civil rights activists. Trump was two to six times more likely to emphasize belligerent and extremist rhetoric targeting the other political party, compared to Bush and Obama.[26] Eliminationist rhetoric and extremist language in general was 13 to 15 times more common in Trump's speeches, when contrasted with Bush's and Obama's.[27]

Trump's language routinely followed this path. One of his preferred tactics for attacking the Democrats was to frame their economic policies as a radical deviation from capitalism and as an existential threat to the republic and its people. His speeches are replete with dire warnings about impending doom, referencing the Democratic Party as "undemocratic," "dangerous," and imposing a "nightmare" vision of "socialism" and "communism."[28] Consider, for example, his promise of "defending our great Second Amendment" against the "radical Democrats" who want to limit gun ownership, "destroy our prosperity," and rollback "the biggest [economic] comeback [under Trump] in our history." As Trump warned in one of his rants: "You don't want your 401(k) being cut in half, and if you vote Democrat, that's what's going to happen. They want to erase our gains and plunge our country into a nightmare of gridlock, poverty, chaos, and frankly, crime."[29]

Invoking the specter of socialism, Trump predicted that the Democrats would turn the country into Venezuela, linking his celebration of neoliberal capitalism to racist and xenophobic attacks on people of color. This link between his economic messaging and reactionary attacks on Latin America was apparent when he claimed that the core of "The Democratic Party is radical socialism, Venezuela, and open borders."[30] In one of the former president's many non-sequiturs, Trump linked the Democratic Party and immigration to entitlement benefits and the impending destruction of the nation.

> And to pay for their socialism, which is going to destroy our country, Democrats want to raid Medicare and destroy Social Security. That's what's going to happen. Democrats want to completely destroy Medicare with so-called Medicare for All ... Robbing our seniors of the benefits they paid into for their entire lives, giving it to people that don't deserve it. Giving it, by the way, to illegal aliens who come into our country. OK? Republicans want to protect Medicare for our great seniors who have earned it, and paid for it. And I will always fight for and always protect patients with pre-existing conditions.[31]

Reinforcing Trump's Manichean rhetoric juxtaposing the major parties as forces of good and evil, the Republican Party was clearly positioned as the savior of hard-working, freedom-loving Americans. Trump's language was also deeply classist, romanticizing punishment via the denial of health care to individuals who have not "earned" it. This is the politics of sadism and cruelty, in the service of neoliberal plutocracy.

Trump's speeches depicted the rise of Black Lives Matter (BLM) in 2020 following the murder of George Floyd as a fundamental threat to American safety and national security. Playing on the common stereotypes of angry, loud, and dangerous Black people, Trump misrepresented the nature of the BLM movement, despite the vast majority of protests in 2020 and years earlier (98 percent) being non-violent.[32] Trump deplored the "rioting and looting" that "broke out in our Nation's Capital," celebrating his utilization of the National Guard.[33] He lamented that "our Nation has been gripped by professional anarchists, violent mobs, arsonists, looters, criminals, rioters, Antifa, and others," promising to put an end to the "chaos" and "to stop the violence and restore security and safety in America."[34]

Trump also called for the further militarization of protest policing. He "strongly recommended to every Governor to deploy the National Guard in sufficient numbers that we dominate the streets. Mayors and Governors must establish an overwhelming law enforcement presence until the violence has been quelled."[35] In condemning the "violence and mayhem," Trump attacked Democratic Presidential candidate Joe Biden, depicting him as a part of the chaos—as "controlled by the radical left," and as encouraging violence after his campaign staffers contributed to a non-profit group committed to ending the practice of cash bail.[36]

Numerous problems are apparent with Trump's rhetoric. First, it depicted the BLM movement as endangering America, as he sought to foment national hysteria and mass fear against civil rights activists who were overwhelmingly peaceful, based on the violent actions of a very small minority. Second, Trump was eliminationist in his agenda, seeking not only to portray BLM as an existential threat, but calling on the U.S. army to occupy American cities and shoot activists in the street.[37] He advocated police state-style violence, idealizing the "overwhelming" use of force and deadly violence to "dominate the streets." Finally, Trump tied the Democratic Party to rising "violence and mayhem," depicting it as under the control of radical leftist insurgents who endanger national security. In sum, Trump's behavior spoke to his aspirational police state politics, as he mainstreamed the notion that civil rights activists, people of color, and the Democratic Party are menaces that endanger the well-being of freedom-loving, law-abiding Americans.

A central pillar of Trump's fascist-eliminationist politics is his assault on immigrants and the Democratic Party. Trump picked as one of his favorite targets the Salvadoran street gang MS-13, which originated in Los Angeles and has a presence in various cities. He depicted the gang and immigrants as engaged in violence, as "vicious" "killers" and "predators" who are "endangering" the country, as "ruthless animals" and "criminals" guilty of "kidnapping, drugging and raping" their victims, "stabbing," "murdering," and "decapitating" people, and leaving a trail of "slaughter" in "sanctuary cities" where these "violent criminals hide."[38]

Trump framed law enforcement as the antidote to a pandemic of street gang violence gripping a nation paralyzed by fear. This obscured the reality that U.S. violence in 2018—at the time that Trump delivered these speeches, was 28 percent of what it had been two decades earlier in the 1990s, when violent crime spiked (23.2 victims per 1,000 Americans in 2018 versus 79.8 victims per 1,000 in 1993).[39] Violence continued to decline (to less than 20 victims per 1,000) in 2020, while Trump stoked fear and paranoia about a pervasive crime wave.[40]

Trump began his presidency promising to end a plague of rising violence and "American carnage" at a time when violent crime was near a historic low.[41] He valorized the militarization of policing as a means of targeting immigrants, whom he portrayed as a dire threat to the nation's security. One should not forget that he kicked off his 2016 campaign by depicting Mexican immigrants as "bringing drugs," "bringing crime," and being "rapists," with only "some" being "good people."[42] The demonization of immigrants meant growing calls for violent suppression. The solution to "horrible and weak immigration laws" that Trump claimed fostered a crisis of violence, was to empower the "tough people" in law enforcement, including border patrols and ICE, the latter of which he celebrated for "liberating towns" from gang violence.[43]

Trump's rhetoric was Nazi-esque in his use of dehumanizing metaphors to refer to immigrants and people of color. Bemoaning towns that he claimed were "infested" with gang violence,[44] Trump portrayed ICE as courageously taking on the scourge of gang terror, and prevailing despite the Democratic Party's alleged support for American carnage:

They go into these MS-13 nests, nests of bad, bad people, killers, in many cases. And they go in there fearless, and they do an incredible job. And they get them out. They [gang members] either go to jail, or they get out of the country. So I want to just take my hat off to ICE and the brave people that have really been maligned by the Democrats.[45]

Trump supporters and apologists will likely claim Trump's comments were qualified, focusing on gang violence, rather than depicting people of color as a whole as violent and criminal. These defenses ring hollow considering Trump's history of referring to most all Mexican immigrants as criminals. Trump apologetics are also undermined by his rhetoric about cities disproportionately populated by people of color as "disgusting" and "rat and rodent infested,"[46] and by his call for Democratic women of color in Congress to "go back" to the "crime infested places from which they came."[47] These attacks were against women who are U.S. citizens, some of whom were not born in another country. Implicit in Trump's message, but clear, is the assumption that women of color are not real Americans. The use of words like "infestation" and references to "nests" of crime and violence are a powerful example of the dehumanization of immigrants, be it (alleged) gang members or women in Congress. This is the rhetoric of fascism—a page taken straight from the playbook of the Nazis in their efforts to demonize Jewish people and to justify their extermination.

Immigrants and citizens of color were not the only targets of Trump's Nazi-esque propaganda. He decried Democratically controlled "sanctuary cities" as the primary point "where crime pours in" to the country.[48] Democrats, Trump announced, were not merely soft on crime, they were the party *of* crime. Trump mourned, "Every day, innocent lives are stolen because of Democratic-supported immigrant policies" that are "dangerous" to the nation and its people. "The Democrats will open our borders to deadly drugs and ruthless gangs ... They are the party of crime."[49]

Trump's use of animal metaphors, his depiction of LatinX immigrants as criminals, and his contention that immigrants bring with them "tremendous infectious disease,"[50] are for all intents and purposes indistinguishable from eliminationist Nazi propaganda, which described Jews as "rats," as a "poison," as "filthy" and "infected" peoples, as a "plague," and as a criminal "arsonist" and "serpentine" threat to public order and safety.[51] That these damning fascist parallels have been almost entirely omitted in America's denialist discourse reveals the tremendous power of the propaganda of silence to erase history and to decontextualize the Republican Party's fascist efforts to dehumanize people of color. That Trump's supporters accept his fascist rhetoric, fearmongering, and white supremacy without criticism reveals the extent to which ritualized barbarism has taken hold in America.

PART SEVEN

Education and the Mobilizing Passions of Fascism

CHAPTER THIRTEEN

The Nazification of American Education

The crisis of education in America presents not only a danger to democracy, but also advances the ideological and structural foundations for the emergence of a fascist state. Repressive and dystopian educational policies, wedded to social control and the death of the social imagination, accelerate the slide towards lawlessness and authoritarianism. Such forms of education are crucial to propagate elements of fascism. An unimagined catastrophe now characterizes how American education is being shaped by far-right Republican Party politicians. Nowhere is this more evident than in the policies of Republican Governor Ron DeSantis, who is at the forefront of transforming American education into a propaganda tool for producing and legitimating what is euphemistically called "patriotic education." Coercion, conformity, and toxic forms of religious, political, and economic fundamentalism now threaten to destroy education as a democratic public sphere, however weak it may already be. Institutions of learning at all levels in the red states are becoming laboratories for what we term the Nazification of American education, replicating pedagogies of repression that were at work in Germany in the 1930s.

DeSantis and his Republican allies have inverted an insight taken from the renowned, late educator John Dewey, who recognized that politics required informed judgments, public dialogue, dissent, critical exchange, judicious discrimination, and the ability to discern the truth from lies. Instead of embracing these democratic elements of education as central to creating citizens with an open mind and with a willingness to engage in a culture of questioning, DeSantis and the GOP are doing everything they can to remove such practices both from schools and other cultural apparatuses that function as teaching machines. Under such circumstances, DeSantis and the GOP are producing what Dewey claimed amounted to the "eclipse of the public," which he considered the most serious threat to the fate of democracy.[1]

DeSantis is putting into place a range of reactionary educational policies. These include banning books and Critical Race Theory, barring majors in gender studies, limiting the use of trans pronouns, and eroding tenure protections for faculty.[2] He is requiring educators to sign what amounts to loyalty oaths and forcing them to post their syllabuses online. He has also instituted legislation that would allow students to film faculty classes without consent. In addition, he is initiating legislation that allows politically appointed trustees to determine what faculty get hired, completely removing faculty from the process. At the heart of this attempt to turn Florida into a laboratory for fascism is a series of policies that feed into and put into practice his white supremacist ideology.[3]

DeSantis's enactment of House Bill 999 is modeled after the right-wing educational policies of Hungarian Prime Minister Viktor Orbán, who not only drove the prestigious liberal Central European University out of Hungary but also waged a reactionary ideological assault against gender studies, trans students, and critical thinking in general, while amassing political control over public and higher education in Hungary. DeSantis's attack on public and higher education is even more ruthless. As Michelle Goldberg writes in *The New York Times*, Bill 999 "is a shocking piece of legislation that takes a sledgehammer to academic freedom."[4] Not only does it ban majors and minors that deal with race, sexual orientation, and intersectionality issues, it forbids core education courses from presenting "a view of American history 'contrary to the creation of a new nation based on universal principles stated in the Declaration of Independence,' creating obvious limits on the teaching of subjects like slavery and the Native American genocide."[5]

Along with GOP legislators, DeSantis is waging a major effort both to end academic independence for good and destroy freedom of speech. In addition to destroying free speech in public schools, DeSantis now has an additional target: to destroy freedom of the press and the right of individuals to criticize Florida's public officials. As Trevor Timm notes in *The Guardian*, "Florida's right-wing governor and legislature want to gut one of America's more important first amendment rulings." He writes:

The proposed law, authored by state legislator Jason Brodeur, would—I kid you not—compel "bloggers" who criticize the governor, other officers of the executive branch, or members of the legislature to register with the state of Florida. Under the bill, anyone paid to write on the internet would have to file monthly reports every time they utter a government official's name in a critical manner. If not, they'd face potentially thousands of dollars in fines. It's a policy so chilling that it would make Vladimir Putin proud, and I wish that was hyperbole.[6]

Not only are DeSantis's policies aimed at minorities of class and color, but this GOP attack on education is part of a larger war on the very ability to think, question, and engage in politics from the vantage point of being critical, informed, and willing to hold power accountable. More generally, it is part of a concerted effort to destroy not only public education, but the very foundations of political agency.[7] DeSantis poses a dangerous threat to higher education, which he would like to turn into "a dead zone for killing the social imagination, a place where ideas that don't have practical results go to die, and where faculty and students are punished through the threat of force or harsh disciplinary measures for speaking out, engaging in dissent and holding power accountable."[8] In this case, the attempt to undermine schooling as a public good and a democratic public sphere is accompanied by a systemic campaign to destroy the capacity for critical thinking, compassion for others, critical literacy, moral witnessing, support for the social compact, and the habits of democracy.

DeSantis justifies these policies by claiming that "Florida schools have become socialism factories" and that students at all levels of education should not be subjected to classroom material that would make them uncomfortable.[9] This leads to a repressive education system that revels in deception, kills the social imagination, depoliticizes students, and transforms schools into militarized punishing machines, propaganda factories, and components of the security-surveillance state. In many ways, the GOP's and DeSantis's approach to education is not unlike what Putin is doing in Russia. As a senior Kremlin bureaucrat, Sergei Novikov, recently put it, Putin's goal is to "impart state ideology to schoolchildren … We need to know how to infect them with our ideology. Our ideological work is aimed at changing consciousness."[10] Indeed!

Max Boot, writing in *The Washington Post*, argues that DeSantis's educational policies represent "one of the most alarming assaults on free speech and academic freedom [and reveal] a troubling pattern of authoritarianism and vindictiveness that would be extremely dangerous in the Oval Office."[11]

What is often ignored regarding DeSantis's attack on public and higher education is the utter fear, anxiety, and chilling effect it has on teachers, librarians, and school board members. Many teachers are leaving the profession because of the imposed censorship, the threats they receive from right-wing parents, and also because of the fear of criminal prosecution for, let's say, teaching that slavery was wrong, studying excerpts from Christopher Columbus's journal which reveals his cruelty toward Indigenous groups, or using historical material on the vindication of women's rights.[12] Others are being forced from their jobs because of the right-wing culture wars. Hannah Natanson and Moriah Balingit writing in *The Washington Post* provide some revealing examples:

> A Florida teacher lost her job for hanging a Black Lives Matter flag over her classroom door and rewarding student activism. A Massachusetts teacher was fired for posting a video denouncing Critical Race Theory. A teacher in Missouri got the ax for assigning a worksheet about privilege—and still another, in California, was fired for criticizing mask mandates on her Facebook page. They were among more than 160 educators who resigned or were fired from their jobs in the past two academic years due to the culture wars that are roiling many of the nation's schools ... On average, slightly more than two teachers lost their jobs for every week that school remained in session.[13]

DeSantis's policies have been particularly vindictive with respect to punishing youth who are marginalized by way of their race, religion, and sexual orientation. He has expanded his attack on Black people by pushing policies that translate "hate speech into proposed laws that would make societal pariahs out of transgender kids," and has made homophobia a driving force of his politics.[14] He shares the disgraced legacy of Trump and other far-right Republican politicians who believe that the threat of violence, if not its actual use, is not only the best way to resolve issues in the name of political opportunism, but also amounts to a display of patriotism.[15] DeSantis's policies reek of fear, intimidation, and the threat of violence against his critics, especially those educators, teachers, parents, youth, and community groups that reject his attacks on public education and his anti-gay legislation. His policies are also in line with the violence expressed by right-wing Christians such as Joe Ottman, founder of Faith, Education, and Commerce United who, as Paul Rosenberg remarked, "stated on his podcast, *Conservative Daily*, that teachers are 'recruiting kids to be gay' and that LGBTQ+ teachers should be 'dragged behind a car until their limbs fall off'."[16] There is little doubt that such measures echo the infamous anti-communist hysteria reminiscent of the dark days of the McCarthyite period in the 1950s, when thousands of people were banned from their jobs for holding left-wing views, and in some cases jailed. DeSantis's model of politics and reactionary education are closely related to the attacks on education and history that took place in Nazi Germany, a point that is almost completely missed in the mainstream and progressive press when analyzing DeSantis's war on education.

Education in Nazi Germany

Education under the Third Reich offers significant insights into how repressive forms of pedagogy become central to shaping the identities, values, and worldviews of young people. Nazi policies also made visible how education is always political in that it is a struggle over agency, ideology, knowledge, power, and the future. For Hitler, matters of indoctrination, education, and the shaping of the collective consciousness of young people was an integral element of Nazi rule and politics. In *Mein Kampf*, Hitler stated that "Whoever has the youth has the future." According to Lina Buffington and her co-authors, he viewed this battle to indoctrinate youth as part of a wider strategy of Nazi control over education. As Hitler wrote in *Mein Kampf*, Germany needs an "educational regime [where] young people will learn nothing else but how to think German and act German … And they will never be free again, not in their whole lives."[17] Under this regime, education was reduced to a massive propaganda machine whose purpose was to indoctrinate young people with "robot-like obedience to Nazi ideologies," while privileging physical strength, racial instruction, and nationalist fanaticism.[18] At the same time, the most valued form of knowledge under the Nazi educational system emphasized a pedagogy of racial purity.

Race consciousness was crucial. It was used to both unify young people and elicit political loyalty based on national honor and a "budding nationalistic fanaticism."[19] To achieve this goal and reduce resistance to fascist ideology, history books were censored, banned, destroyed, and rewritten to align with Nazi ideology. Any knowledge or information deemed dangerous was not only eliminated from books and the curricula, but also purged "from libraries and bookstores."[20]

Nazi education was designed to mold children rather than educate them. Races deemed "inferior" and "less worthy" were banned from schools while any positive reference to them and their history was expunged from history books and other curricular materials. The Nazi educational system was deeply anti-intellectual and created modes of teaching that undermined the ability of students to think for themselves. As stressed by the writers of *The Holocaust Explained*, the Nazis "aimed to de-intellectualize education: they did not want education to provoke people to ask questions or think for themselves. They believed this approach would instill obedience and belief in the Nazi worldview, creating the ideal future generation."[21] The turning of Nazi schools into propaganda factories functioned through a massive pedagogical machinery of conformity, censorship, repression, and indoctrination. The attack on teachers also took place through Nazi efforts to encourage students and loyal faculty to spy on those considered politically unreliable. Even worse, teachers who did not support either Nazi ideology or the restructuring of education were dismissed along with Jewish educators who were banned from teaching in the Nazi educational system.[22]

What critics often fail to acknowledge is that the open glorification of "Aryan" races in Nazi Germany has its counterparts in a range of policies now pushed by Republican politicians such as DeSantis. This is not only visible in white replacement theory and the rise of white supremacy in America, but also in voter suppression laws, the elimination of the history of oppressed groups from school curricula, the banning of books, and the assault on educators who do not agree with the transformation of American education into right-wing propaganda factories. Nazi education exhibited a contempt for critical thought, open dialogue, provocative books, intellectual ability, and those youth considered unworthy, and we are seeing this in America. The comparisons are particularly evident under the leadership of DeSantis with his deeply anti-intellectual view of schooling, whitewashing of history, outlawing of books, support for "patriotic education," advocacy of anti-LGBTQ+ bills, and the use of perpetual fear and intimidation directed at teachers, parents, and youth of color. A particularly egregious echo of the fascist past can be seen in the current attack on librarians, who are harassed, threatened, and called pedophiles by far-right extremists because they have books on their library shelves that deal with LGBTQ+ rights and racial equality. Some book censors have gone as far as claiming that librarians who refuse to remove banned books are "grooming" children to be sexually exploited and to "seek criminal charges against" them.[23]

The model of Nazi Germany's educational system has a great deal to teach us about the ideologies that produced a society wedded to the related doctrines of racial purity, book banning, the suppression of historical memory, ultra-nationalism, and the cult of the strongman.[24] Under DeSantis, white supremacy, systemic racism, and the inculcation of youth have the official power of the state on their side. DeSantis's attacks on youth considered unworthy (LGBTQ+ youth), his embrace of lower academic standards, subjection of faculty to political litmus tests through "viewpoint diversity surveys" aimed to "gather evidence" on non-compliant faculty, censorship of books that do not follow his ideological proclivities, racializing of knowledge, support for textbooks as crucial tools for spreading propaganda to students, and control of teachers' classroom actions are all closely related to the Nazi playbook for making education a tool for indoctrination.

The horrors of authoritarianism have returned with support from white supremacists like DeSantis.[25] The long simmering mobilizing passions of fascism are evident not only in a range of reactionary GOP policies that extend from undoing women's reproductive rights and the right to vote, but also in a more insidious and less acknowledged attack on America's educational institutions. These attacks amount to a counter-revolution against essential public institutions, critical agency, informed consciousness, engaged citizenship, and the capacity of individuals and the public to govern themselves. At its core, it is an attack on both the promise of democracy and the social imagination.

Critical education is the scourge of white supremacists because it offers a counterpoint to right-wing educational practices that seduce people into inhabiting the ecospheres of hate, bigotry, and racism. Such anti-racist pedagogies are especially important because of the threat posed by white supremacists to white youths, who are especially vulnerable given how many of them are alienated and isolated, lacking a sense of purpose, and in need of some sense of community. Racism is learned and white supremacists have enlisted several educational tools, particularly online video games, chat groups, TikTok, and other social platforms, to promote and enlist white youths. Ibram X. Kendi rightly raises the question of how "white children are being indoctrinated with white supremacist views, what causes them to hate, and how they have become the prime target of white supremacists."[26] He points to a 2021 Anti-Defamation League report which states: "An estimated 2.3 million teens each year are exposed to white-supremacist ideology in chats for multiplayer games [and] that 17 percent of 13-to-17-year-olds … encounter white-supremacist views on social media."[27] In response to this, there is a need to acknowledge the political importance of anti-racist education in teaching young people how to recognize the threats posed by white supremacy, how to resist racism in all of its forms, how to turn away from hate, and how to discern truth from falsehoods and right from wrong.[28] In reference to the ongoing threat of white supremacy to white kids, with its broad cultural reach and presence in the social media, Kendi stresses the importance of anti-racist teaching. He writes:

> But how can white kids—or any kids—guard against this threat if they can't recognize it? How can kids repel ideas of hierarchy if they haven't been taught ideas of equality? How can kids distinguish right from wrong if they haven't been shown what's right and wrong? Recognizing that "an increasing number of U.S. teens are getting 'radicalized' online by White supremacists or other extremist groups," an article published by the National Education Association concluded: "The best place to prevent that radicalization is U.S. classrooms."[29]

Republicans such as DeSantis reproduce and accelerate the adoption of white supremacist views among many vulnerable white youths.

They do this by censoring critical ideas, eviscerating history of its genocidal and racist past, banning books, and imposing degrading constraints on teachers. In doing so, they undermine the critical capacities crucial to teaching about systemic racism and its Jim Crow history. DeSantis's attack on the teaching of history in schools draws much of its energy from a nostalgic rendering of the past, when whites could be proud of a society in which whiteness was an unapologetic mark of privilege, inequality, and state violence. For DeSantis and his Republican Party allies, this right-wing rendering of the past is now threatened by people of color, justifying a "political programme that indicts the present as a crime against the past."[30] His attacks on public and higher education constitutes a form of apartheid pedagogy.

DeSantis's educational policies thrive on a mix of ignorance and racial hatred. The consequences, while indirect, are deadly, as we have witnessed from a number of mass shootings, including the massacre of ten Black shoppers in a Tops grocery store in Buffalo by a young hate-filled racist and self-proclaimed fascist. As historical consciousness and critical knowledge and skills disappear in schools under DeSantis's policies, young people are not merely misinformed, but are incapable of recognizing how white supremacists are using history for their own toxic purposes in the realm of popular culture. For instance, Jeffrey St. Clair writes about how far-right groups such as the Proud Boys and the Oath Keepers have appropriated the image of the late Chilean fascist dictator Augusto Pinochet, printing and circulating his image on "shirts, stickers, and flags."[31] In the educational world being produced by DeSantis and his Republican Party zombies, Pinochet would be erased from history, leaving young people ignorant of how history can be used for fascist goals. In this instance, educational repression is directly connected to the violence of organized forgetting.

Let's be clear about what is at stake in the forms of education promoted by the Republican Party currently in place in over 36 states.[32] This is an attack on the very possibility of thinking critically, along with the pedagogies and institutions that support the capacity for analytical thought and informed judgment as a foundation for creating informed individuals. It constitutes a full-fledged attack not just on Critical Race Theory, but also critical pedagogy in general. Of course, critical pedagogy is not just about anti-racist education, it is also part of a much broader project. It is a moral and political pedagogical theory whose purpose is to equip students with the vital knowledge, skills, values, and sense of social responsibility that enable them to be critical and engaged agents. In this sense, it is the essential foundation, regardless of where it takes place, for creating knowledgeable and socially responsible citizens capable of combating all elements of fascism and authoritarianism while envisioning a social order that deepens and extends power, democratic values, equitable social relations, collective freedom, economic rights, and social justice for everyone. This is precisely why it so dangerous to the white supremacists, fascists, and extremist forces now driving politics in America.

While the times we live in seem dire, it is worthwhile to take heed from Helen Keller, who, in a letter to Nazi youth, stated: "History hasn't taught you anything if you think you can kill ideas. The tyrants tried to do so often in the past, but the ideas revolted against them and destroyed them."[33] For Keller, history without hope is lost and opens the door to fascism, while ideas that draw upon history and combine with mass movements can serve to offer a model for fighting it. Ellen Willis builds upon Keller's sense of hope when she once urged the left to become a movement again. In doing so, she called for a new language, a new understanding of education, and a cultural politics that spoke to people's needs. Most importantly, she called for a "new vision of what kind of society we want," along with a mass movement capable of "creating institutions ... and new ways of living to figure out how our vision might work."[34] Not only were Willis's insights prescient for the times, but they are even more urgent now given the increasing danger of a fascism that threatens to engulf and destroy the last vestiges of an already weakened American democracy. The struggle for socialist democracy is more urgent than ever.

CHAPTER FOURTEEN

Orwell, Totalitarian Politics, and the War on Anti-Racism in Education

In the last chapter, we discussed the Nazification of U.S. education, with a focus on Governor Ron DeSantis's authoritarian reform agenda. This chapter provides an extensive analysis of the war on "Critical Race Theory" across the nation—and particularly in red states—charting out the rising opposition to critical education as a function of the right-wing backlash against Black Lives Matter (BLM) and anti-racism. The chapter provides a framework for understanding opposition to anti-racism, as we draw on George Orwell's writing about the rise of totalitarianism and Big Brother monitoring regimes, which represent an eliminationist assault on critical thought.

George Floyd's murder functioned as a catalyst that drove BLM forward, drawing a massive turnout in protest against institutional racism in policing. The movement, after struggling for years to break into the American mainstream and facing significant resistance from both the Obama and Trump administrations, was successful in appealing to the public. An estimated one-in-ten adult Americans reportedly attended a protest to challenge racial injustice in the summer of 2020—with an estimated 26 million people taking to the streets.[1] As *The New York Times* explained, BLM looked like it was becoming "the largest movement in U.S. history."[2]

The massive turnout was a remarkable opportunity for intellectuals to better understand social movements' centrality to empowering the people and promoting direct democracy in ways that undermine the plutocratic biases in U.S. political and economic institutions.[3] The 2010s and 2020s saw the rapid mainstreaming of protest, from pro-corporate movements like the Tea Party and

Trumpism, to progressive, bottom-up, democratic movements, like the 2011 Wisconsin labor protests, Occupy Wall Street, the Fight for $15, Black Lives Matter, environmentalism, the anti-Trump protests, and #MeToo. With movement after movement demanding massive political, social, and economic transformation, protests occurred with a consistency unseen since the activism of the 1950s, 1960s, and 1970s involving civil rights, women's rights, consumer rights, anti-war, and environmental activism. The mainstreaming of social movements was apparent in one national survey, which found in 2018 that 57 percent of Americans were so upset about an issue that they were willing to protest.[4]

Democrats again embraced neoliberal politics under the Biden administration. They also continued to demobilize working-class Americans, thereby strengthening the foundation for fascist politics that is fueled by the GOP's heavily middle-to-upper income base. The Democrats historically campaign on empowering the poor, needy, workers, and people of color, promising to raise the minimum wage, protect the environment, better fund health care, and fight for student loan debt relief. But under Biden, the Democratic Party's neglect and abuse of organized labor continued.[5] There has been no observable commitment to passing universal health care via a Medicare-for-All reform or a public option to provide health insurance for the uninsured. Biden's modest commitment to student loan forgiveness has languished due to legal challenges. The minimum wage continues its long slide, intensified by Democratic inaction and high inflation. Even the Democrats' biggest success in environmental action, funding hundreds of billions in tax credits for private businesses to shift toward renewable energy production, was projected to cut U.S. climate emissions by 40 percent by 2030 (from 2005 levels)—less than the 50 percent in cuts climate scientists insist is necessary.[6]

Biden continues the long slide of neoliberal Democrats disenfranchising disadvantaged groups of Americans. Barack Obama promised "hope" and "change" and progressive political reforms to aid working Americans and the poor. Instead, his administration saw little by way of substantive reforms to combat corporate power and inequality, while Obama actively admonished anti-racist activists.[7] Hillary Clinton's 2016 presidential campaign was also lackluster compared to the progressive policy proposals offered by the Bernie Sanders campaign. With the Democratic

Party's neoliberal politics, voter turnout for the party between 2012 and 2016 saw significant declines for young Americans, union households, low-income Americans, and people of color.[8]

Disenchantment with the Democratic Party continues into the 2020s, with Biden supporters being sober in their assessment of his platform. National polls in the run-up to election day 2020 found that nearly two-thirds of Democratic voters saw their choice for Biden as more of a vote "against Trump."[9] A modest majority of Democrats—57 percent—said they were "happy" with Biden's election in November of 2020, compared to a large majority—73 percent—who were more "happy that Trump lost."[10] Such sentiments contrasted dramatically with the attitudes of Trump supporters when he was in office, with nearly two-thirds of his base expressing a cult-like attachment and saying there was nothing he could do that would cause them to reconsider supporting him.[11]

While the Democratic Party under Biden has been busy losing support from disadvantaged groups, the Republican Party has ramped up its support for authoritarian policies that stimulate their base along reactionary gender and color lines. To roll back the successes of BLM, state and national Republicans have gone on the offensive, portraying the movement and educators as an existential threat to American children. Nowhere has this been clearer than in the sustained attack on "Critical Race Theory." In Iowa, Republicans passed House Bill 802, an Orwellian Big Brother attack on critical education, seeking to censor educators who discuss and analyze how U.S. political, social, and economic institutions are biased against women and people of color. The Iowa law explicitly prohibits public school teachers and college professors from assigning or discussing works examining how "the United States of America and the state of Iowa are fundamentally or systematically racist or sexist."[12]

Iowa is one of many states imposing a dystopian censorship and surveillance regime to punish teachers who are insufficiently committed to erasing discussions of white supremacy or racial inequality from the historical consciousness. Tennessee passed Senate Act 493, which prevents "public charter school[s]," "LEA[s]" (Local Education Agencies), public school teachers and other employees from discussing "concepts as part of a course of instruction or in a curriculum or instructional program" positing that "this state or the United States is fundamentally or irredeemably racist or sexist," that "an individual, by virtue of the individual's race or sex, is inherently privileged, racist, sexist, or oppressive, whether consciously or subconsciously," or that fosters "division between or resentment of, a race, sex, religion, creed, nonviolent political affiliation, social class, or class of people."[13]

The language in the Tennessee bill leaves much to the imagination. What does it mean to say that a curriculum, by spotlighting racial inequality, racism, and white supremacy, is portraying the nation and its people as "irredeemably" racist? It is difficult to entertain the notion that principled anti-racist scholars and educators are so cynical as to accept that an entire country is irredeemably racist and that there is no hope for change. Why risk angering right-wing parents, administrators, and politicians, if the nation is so hopelessly and "fundamentally" racist that nothing can be done? This language, we believe, is written in a way that is disingenuous by design, as the goal of these bills is not to simply ban lessons portraying the U.S. as hopelessly and forever racist, but to ban *any* discussions of racism, racial inequality, and white supremacy. These bills provide administrators and political officials maximum freedom to decide which lessons they want to eliminate as "divisive," "harmful," or "un-American" in their quest to glorify nationalist indoctrination masquerading as education, and in their efforts to suppress anti-racist messages.

As with Iowa and Tennessee, Idaho's reform legislation has imposed an Orwellian war on historical memory, to suppress recognition of racial inequality and racism in America. Idaho's Bill 377 declares the "tenets" of "Critical Race Theory" are such that they "exacerbate and inflame divisions on the basis of sex, race, ethnicity, religion, color, national origin, or other criteria in ways contrary to the unity of the national origin, or other criteria in ways contrary to the unity of the nation and the well-being of the state of Idaho and its citizens."[14] Idaho's law dictates that "no public institution of higher education, school district, or public school," and "no course of instruction or unit of study" will compel students "to personally affirm, adopt or adhere to any of the tenets" of "CRT."[15]

The Idaho bill is also notable for its disingenuous portrayal of race studies in education. Prior to the GOP attacks, "CRT" was historically known only to a very small number of college professors and students working in the areas of legal studies and race and ethnic politics, and was defined by writers and thinkers such as Kimberlé Crenshaw, Derrick Bell, and Patricia Williams, while drawing on socialist critical theory and Gramscian principles.

Socialist theory—in general and as applied to critical race analysis—has never been a core part of mainstream elementary and secondary education curricula throughout the United States, and clearly not in modern times. So, to stir up passions and fears about the specter of "CRT" speaks to the propagandistic nature of GOP messaging. But the party's fearmongering over "CRT," framing it as responsible for the nation's ills, obscures a deeper truth—that the right-wing assault on education was never about a specific legal academic theory. Instead, "CRT" serves as a punching bag—a code word—signaling a commitment to a larger political campaign that seeks to eradicate *any* references to racism, racial inequality, or institutional racism at a time when BLM was directing mass attention to these problems. The GOP's attack on "CRT," at its core, is really about the death of social imagination, via an effort to destroy efforts to envision how America might chart an alternate path forward—one that seeks to not only spotlight, but combat structural inequalities, white supremacy, and fascist politics. Contrary to democratically oriented education, the anti-CRT campaign is McCarthyist in orientation, stoking public paranoia about indoctrination in the classroom and the destruction of young minds.

State efforts to destroy anti-racist educational content have been greatly aided and amplified by Donald Trump's continued attacks on BLM. As the leader of his party, he played a prominent role in mainstreaming racist efforts to suppress discussions of America's historical problems with racial inequality. In demagogic and authoritarian flair, Trump rails against "left-wing indoctrination" in schools, attacking teachers who expose America's history of racism. He demands a "pro-American curriculum that celebrates the truth about our nation's great history." Trump created his "1776 Commission" while in office, to promote "patriotic education," despite the organization having no basis in American historical scholarship and being widely recognized by scholars as a propaganda effort to impose nationalistic indoctrination.[16] Trump also denied federal funds to racial sensitivity training as applied to federal contract workers, sending a message to state educators that the federal government and the Republican Party are behind them as they initiate their backlash against BLM.[17]

Capitalizing on the rising wave of "anti-CRT" legislation, Trump published an essay in *RealClear Politics* (*RCP*), outlining a dystopian vision for the future of education straight from the pages of George Orwell's *1984*, and elevating lessons on systemic and institutional racism to the level of thought crime. Trump envisioned a national campaign against "CRT," writing that "every state legislature should pass a ban on taxpayer dollars going to any school district or workplace that teaches Critical Race Theory … and Congress should seek to institute a federal ban through legislation as well."[18] For such a ban to be effectively implemented, it would require a Herculean enforcement and surveillance effort, involving the recruitment of countless children and parents across the country, and mechanisms in place across states and school districts to punish anyone who challenges the law. In full Orwellian style, Republicans even called for the introduction of cameras in the classroom to monitor teacher–student communications and to identify and suppress forbidden content.[19]

The Republican base was happy to act as foot soldiers to intimidate school districts, showing up in full force and physically threatening and issuing death threats to school board members that maintained mask mandates during the pandemic and that Republicans alleged were perverting children's minds by teaching "CRT."[20] This campaign was a profoundly brownshirt phenomenon—with Republican officials stoking mass hysteria and fear, while privatizing and outsourcing the dirty work of intimidating, threatening, and terrorizing educators to the base—thereby maintaining plausible deniability in promoting outrage and fascist violence.

Trump clearly had authoritarian Big Brother methods in mind when he called on the nation to rollback anti-racist education. As he explained in his *RCP* essay:

> Parents have a right to know exactly what is being taught to their children. Last year [2020], many parents had the chance to routinely listen in on classes for the first time because of remote learning. As students return to the classroom, states need to pass laws requiring that all lesson plans have to be made available to parents—every handout, article, and reading should be posted on an online portal that allows parents to see what their kids are being taught. Furthermore, in many places, there are rules preventing students from recording what teachers say in class. States and school boards should establish a "Right of Record."[21]

For educators and professors who had the audacity to challenge the "CRT" ban, Trump had an answer: termination. As he announced in his *RCP* essay, "States need to break the tenure monopoly in public K-12 schools ... Educators who are alienating children from their own country should not be protected with lifelong tenure; they should be liberated to pursue a career as a political activist."[22] Trump's reference to "liberating" teachers through termination was classic Orwellian propaganda, framing the suppression of dissent in a dystopian surveillance state as a form of therapeutic empowerment for educators.

To sell his nationwide ban on "CRT", Trump embraced authoritarian rhetoric that imagined an apocalyptic state of affairs in education, defined by a pervasive and all-encompassing threat from teachers acting as a leftist bogeyman to destroy America. Trump announced:

> Make no mistake: The motive behind all of this left-wing lunacy is to discredit and eliminate the greatest obstacles to the fundamental transformation of America. To succeed with their extreme agenda, radicals know they must abolish our attachment to the Constitution, the Declaration of Independence, and most of all, Americans' very identity as a free, proud, and self-governing people. The left know that if they can dissolve our national memory and identity, they can gain the total political control they crave.[23]

This rhetoric was another example of the GOP's war on truth, as Trump sought to project onto the opposing party his own support for rolling back Constitutional protections like free speech in education and for imposing a nightmare state dedicated to crushing dissenting views through intimidation.

Trump's political messaging extended beyond traditional conservatism, which celebrates American heritage, traditions, and customs and looks suspiciously at progressive social change, but without depicting those with whom one disagrees as needing to be stamped out. Trump's language draws on a fascist and eliminationist ideology and style that depicts his political critics and "enemies" as a fundamental threat to the nation that must be uprooted and burned away—their actions and ideas erased from the national consciousness and memory. The eliminationist politics he advocates in relation to education does not involve concentration camps and gas chambers. Instead, it involves the imposition of an unconstitutional mass surveillance state that destroys freedom of thought and the right to disagree and declares war on critical inquiry and expression.

The assault on critical thought is an assault on democracy and an informed citizenry. Under these "anti-CRT" laws, individuals are simply not allowed to talk about issues such as racism, sexism, white supremacy, and the GOP's rising fascist politics. This is the sort of propaganda and indoctrination that is observed in totalitarian, goose-stepping fascist regimes, not free societies that value free thought. This is a full-frontal attack on the very idea of critical pedagogy. It is an assault on the nation's commitment to education as a public good and as integral to a democratic public sphere that promotes informed social and political discourse. It is an Orwellian hellscape, with suppression of thought idealized in the name of promoting "critical thinking" and "education." Left unasked is a simple question: How does one attain critical thinking when banning dissident views and deciding in advance for students what ideas they are and are not allowed to consider?

This brings us to Trump's political heir—and one of the frontrunners for the Republican 2024 presidential race—Ron DeSantis. The white supremacy that he has mainstreamed in Florida looks quite different than the old white supremacy of slavery and Jim Crow America, prior to the successes of the civil rights movement. As a nation and under the modern GOP, we have traded Klan robes and open celebrations of white supremacy for subtler, and more insidious efforts to erase discussions of racism from the public consciousness. Nowhere is this clearer than in DeSantis's Florida.

As part of his war on education and critical thought, DeSantis called for a "core curriculum" for the state's public universities, demanding changes that "would mandate courses in Western civilization, eliminate diversity programs and reduce the protections of tenure."[24] DeSantis supports reforms to challenge "woke ideology," "from gender-neutral bathrooms to diversity, equity, and inclusion (DEI) departments in schools," making it clear that Republicans are not so much concerned with "CRT" as they are with *any* ideology or pedagogical approach that spotlights and combats racism, sexism, homophobia, anti-trans bigotry, or classism in America.[25]

DeSantis claims that the changes he demanded would disrupt "ideological conformity" in the academy.[26] But promoting ideological pluralism is clearly not what these reforms are about. If they were, he and other Republicans would support introducing anti-racist perspectives and content that identify racial inequalities in America, and that prioritizes exploring these positions alongside right-wing claims that the country has transcended race and is not a racist country.[27]

DeSantis's politics reflect a larger eliminationist commitment to destroying the public imagination and efforts to envision what an anti-racist America might look like. This is not just about attacking "CRT" and "gender theories," which he targeted in his admonishing of concepts being taught at the New College of Florida.[28] It also entails K-12 education reforms that introduce a scorched earth assault on advanced placement curriculum for African American Studies, which "purged the names of many Black writers and scholars associated with Critical Race Theory, the queer experience and Black feminism," and eliminates subjects of discussion such as BLM, while elevating and idealizing the study of "Black conservatism."[29] DeSantis also proposed eliminating gender studies programs and intersectionality studies altogether, sending a message that misogyny, gender inequality, and gender identity are unacceptable topics of study in the academy.[30]

These changes represent a shameless whitewashing of African American Studies curricula, drawing on authoritarian principles that privilege white supremacy and the war on progressive thought. This is not about removing "bias" from the classroom and protecting "objectivity." DeSantis is happy to prioritize "Black conservatism" as a political idea, while prohibiting the exploration of progressive, anti-racist, anti-sexist, and anti-classist perspectives. This is the propaganda of omission, in the service of white supremacy.

The Republican war on anti-racism coincides with its big lie election propaganda and its coup politics, which are central to the party's ascending fascist ideology. An increasingly fanatical reactionary white minority—based largely in the GOP—is becoming more desperate in its efforts to hold onto power in a country that is steadily changing demographically as it shifts away from a white majority. For the Republican Party, the American right, and some independents and Democrats, white nationalist politics and mainstreamed white replacement theory are central to their worldview.[31] The prospect of a white minority for the first time in U.S. history scares them deeply, as it becomes clearer that whites, and white Republicans particularly, struggle to win presidential elections based on numbers alone. This is a dangerous and precarious situation in which we find ourselves as a nation.

The GOP base rationalizes authoritarian acts from their leaders, and from Trump supporters and other far-right activists, which seek to ensure whites are not cast into permanent minority status "in their own country." These include supporting a white nationalist President who promises to "Make America Great Again" by stomping out immigration, unauthorized and authorized alike, from Latin America, Africa, and the Middle East. It also entails supporting a president who mainstreams inane and baseless conspiracy theories about election fraud, while working to overthrow the U.S. commitment to republican government, electoral integrity, and the rule of law, and to impose de facto one-party state rule.

These actions should frighten those who still believe in democratic governance. But where have opposition actors been throughout this process—particularly intellectuals, who one would expect to lead the charge against white supremacy and fascist ideology? Sadly, academics abdicate on their responsibility to fight back against rising fascism. They have also refused to prioritize the study of progressive social movements at the center of democratically empowering a disillusioned citizenry. Put bluntly, there is little concern in the social sciences for the study of social movements that empower disadvantaged groups of Americans. U.S. social scientists—particularly political scientists—are notorious for privileging the study of formal democratic institutions, including elections, legislatures, political parties, presidents, courts, and constitutions.[32] Lost in the fixation on the claim that the "system works" is any recognition via the study of social movements that the political system may be failing large numbers of Americans, and that the U.S. is in a crisis period of mass disillusionment and distrust of government. The trend is not much better in Sociology—an allegedly left discipline—which also heavily neglects the study of social movements in its most established journals.[33]

Academics self-censoring to marginalize citizen power in social movements is nowhere near as heavy-handed a tactic of indoctrination as are authoritarian government efforts to legislate what students can and cannot learn. Still, inculcation via acceptance of elitist "professional" norms of scholarship within the academy is brutally effective as a method of sterilizing examinations of social movements that fight white supremacy and fascism in America. By remaining silent in the face of the onslaught on "CRT," and by marginalizing social movements, academics voluntarily abdicate their responsibility to understand mass movements that are central to democracy. In the process they contribute to the assault on critical consciousness, robbing students of critical pedagogical lessons about how citizens empower themselves in a society characterized by police brutality, white supremacy, and neoliberal plutocracy.

Whether it is a more Orwellian and totalitarian method of suppressing dissent and critical inquiry, or voluntary self-censorship by the neoliberal intellectual class, these are two sides of the same coin in the war on critical thought. Totalitarian politics and the Nazification of education entail a commitment to propaganda and the whitewashing of history. When much of the public cannot recognize the threat of rising right-wing extremism in front of them, we face the death of social imagination in service of fascist indoctrination.

Conclusion: Gangster Capitalism and the Politics of Fascism

We have argued throughout this book that capitalism has always been constructed on the basis of organized violence. Wedded to a political and economic system that consolidates power in the hands of a financial, cultural, and social elite, it construes profit-making as the essence of democracy and consuming as the only obligation of citizenship. Matters of ethics, social responsibility, the welfare state, and the social contract are viewed as enemies of the market, thus legitimating the subordination of human needs to a relentless drive for accumulating profits at the expense of vital social needs and the larger public.[1] Driven by a ruthless emphasis on privatization, deregulation, commodification, a sclerotic individualism, and ruthless model of competition—neoliberal capitalism has morphed into a machinery of death—an unabashed form of gangster capitalism now wedded to an upgraded form of fascism.

No longer able to live up to its promises of equality, improved social conditions, and rising social mobility, capitalism now suffers from a legitimation crisis. Unable to defend an agenda that produces staggering levels of inequality, decimated labor rights, provides massive tax breaks to the financial elite, bailouts to big capital, and wages an incessant war on the welfare state, neoliberalism needed a new ideology to sustain itself politically.[2]

As Prabhat Patnaik observes, the most radical fix to the potential collapse of neoliberalism "came in the form of neofascism."[3] Neoliberalism's failure resulted in its aligning itself with appeals to overt racism, white supremacy, white Christian nationalism, the politics of disposability, and a hatred of those deemed other. As an unapologetic form of gangster capitalism, violence is wielded as an honorable political discourse and education as a cultural politics has become both divisive and injurious. The flattening of culture, elevated to new extremes through social media and the normalization of manufactured ignorance, is a major educational weapon in the annihilation of the civic imagination, politics, and a sense of shared citizenship. Pete Dolack draws an instructive and mutually affirming relationship between industrialists and financiers or what he calls the capitalist ruling class and fascist politics. He writes:

> But what is crucial is that a significant percentage of a country's industrialists and financiers—its capitalist ruling class—backs the imposition of a [fascist] dictatorship with money and other support. This is the crucial commonality overriding the different forms of fascist takeovers ... Why is this so crucial? Because fascism is a dictatorship imposed for the benefit of large industrialists and financiers. At its most basic level, fascism is a dictatorship established through and maintained with terror on behalf of big business. It has a social base, which provides the support and the terror squads, but which is badly misled since the fascist dictatorship operates decisively against the interest of its social base. Militarism, extreme nationalism, the creation of enemies and scapegoats, and, perhaps the most critical component, a rabid propaganda that intentionally raises panic and hate while disguising its true nature and intentions under the cover of a phony populism, are among the necessary elements.[4]

The American public lives in an age of fragmentation, psychic numbing, declining critical functions, and the loss of historical memory, all of which allow for the domestication of the unimaginable. Gangster capitalism thrives on the silence of the oppressed and the complicity of those seduced by its power. It is a politics of subjugation and denial, relentlessly aiming for a public that internalizes its own oppression as second nature. As an educational project, it trades in moral blindness, historical amnesia, and racial and class hatred. It boldly embraces white Christian nationalism, violence as a crucial element of politics, and uses state power to crush dissent and all forms of critical education, especially those pedagogical practices related to sexual orientation, Critical Race Theory, and a critical rendering of history.

As we stress in this book with a great deal of urgency, the forces of fascism are once again on the march. Market mentalities, racial cleansing, and a politics of social and historical amnesia increasingly tighten their grip on all aspects of society. One consequence is that democratic institutions and public spheres are being downsized, if not altogether disappearing, along with educated citizens, without which democracy is doomed. At the same time, the rampant lawlessness of the Trump years has given the GOP and his followers, in light of his recent state and federal indictments, new reasons to repudiate the separation of powers, declare that he and his wealthy cohorts are above the law, and to claim the Justice Department is weaponized under by Joe Biden, "Merrick Garland, the deep state and the feds."[5] Without even reading the federal indictment, many of Trump's allies and even some of his Republican rivals echoed "Trump's all-cap assertion that the charges were merely part of the 'GREATEST WITCH HUNT OF ALL TIME.'" Ignorance in this instance becomes an "article of faith, a default tactic or both."[6] Not only have a range of neo-fascist GOP politicians attacked the law and vilified a criminal inquiry while spewing "lawless nonsense in [Trump's] defense"[7]—some of them have used incendiary language in the interest of provoking violence. For instance, Andy Biggs, a Republican from Arizona who sits on the House of Representatives' Judiciary committee "went on Twitter and used violent language to call for retribution." He tweeted, "We have reached a war phase, eye for an eye." The latter is ominous given that a recent survey the University of Chicago found that "Two and a half years after the January 6 attack on the Capitol, an estimated 12 million American adults, or 4.4 percent of the adult population, believe violence is justified to restore Donald Trump to the White House."[8] In light of the violence against the Capitol by Trump's thugs, the threat of far-right violence in the US represents a serious and threatening call to arms rooted in fascist politics.[9] As the United States spirals into the abyss of fascism, political violence coupled with the normalization of daily mass shootings moves right-wing extremism from the fringes to the center of power, daily life, and political culture.

Against a fascism that draws much of its energy from a dark and horrific past, we argue that there is a need for progressives, workers, educators, and others to reclaim and advance the imperatives of a socialist democracy defined by visions, ideals, institutions, social relations, and pedagogies of resistance. Fundamental to such a call is the formation of a cultural politics that enables the public to imagine a life beyond capitalist society in which racial-class-and-gender-based violence produces endless assaults on the public and civic conscience, mediated through the elevation of war, militarization, violent masculinity, misogyny, and the politics of disposability to the highest levels of power. Neoliberal capitalism is a death-driven machinery that infantilizes, exploits, and devalues human life and the planet itself.

We live in a historical moment in which education has taken on a new role in the age of upgraded fascism. Cultural institutions rather than overt forces of repression are integral to a society mired in domination. This is a politics that, repeating Primo Levi, reduces social habits to silence and attempts to make a corpse out of everyone who does not accept the GOP's upgraded version of fascist politics.[10] A colonizing culture of education, with its wide array of indoctrination practices, is the principal instrument used by the right to create a culture of misinformation, implement and expand the politics of social abandonment, and align power and consciousness with the forces of fascism.[11] According to Historians for Peace and Democracy, right-wing culture wars are a dangerous assault on academic freedom and democracy. They write:

> The multifaceted culture wars against education constitute attacks on how history and social studies are taught and written. They are attempts to severely restrict or eliminate teaching about race, ethnicity, gender, sexuality, and LGBTQ issues. They are an assault on academic freedom in higher education and on professional autonomy and responsibility in K-12 schools. They reveal political efforts to undermine public education in the United States on all levels.[12]

Additionally, the current authoritarian force of irrationalism reverses the enlightenment tendency to view citizenship as a universal right. Instead, as G. M. Tamas argues, one of fascism's main characteristics is its hostility to universal citizenship, derided for its appeal to equality and human dignity.[13] In this new historical moment, the relationship between cultural institutions, power, and everyday life increasingly uses education to destroy the public imagination and dismantle an array of educational institutions fundamental to democracy itself.

Given the multiple crises that haunt the current historical conjuncture, educators need a new language for addressing the changing contexts and issues facing a world in which there is an unprecedented convergence of resources—financial, cultural, political, economic, scientific, military, and technological—that are increasingly used to concentrate powerful and diverse forms of control and domination. Such a language needs to be political without being dogmatic and needs to recognize that pedagogy is always political because it is connected to the struggle over agency. In this instance, making the pedagogical more political means being vigilant about those very "moments in which identities are being produced and groups are being constituted, or objects are being created."[14]

We believe that any viable pedagogy of resistance needs to create the educational visions and tools to produce a radical shift in consciousness among the public. It must be capable of recognizing both the scorched earth policies of neoliberalism and the twisted fascist ideologies that support it. This shift in consciousness cannot occur without pedagogical interventions that speak to people in ways that enable them to recognize themselves, identify with the issues being addressed, and place the privatization of their troubles in a broader systemic context. Otherwise, there will be no shift in the far-right's use of violence, its language of dehumanization, and its use of the state as an agent of force, indoctrination, and conquest. Under gangster capitalism, convenient fictions keep existing pillars of inequality in place, confirming its strangulation of democracy and its normalization of a vanishing future.

Education has become dangerous in the age of gangster capitalism. Not only because it is a public good, but also because it is subject to the question of what education should accomplish in a democracy. What is dreaded by GOP authoritarians is the question regarding what work educators have to do to create the conditions necessary to endow young people with the capacities to think, question, imagine the unimaginable, and defend education to inspire and energize citizens to promote a robust socialist democracy. Put differently, the danger of a liberating education lies in addressing a world in which there is an increasing abandonment of egalitarian and democratic impulses. A liberating education means contemplating what it will take to educate young people to challenge authority. It means resisting the notion that education and training are the same thing. And it means redefining public and higher education as democratic public spheres, rather than as sites of white Christian, white supremacist ideology.

What role might education and critical pedagogy have in a society in which the social has been individualized, emotional life collapses into the therapeutic, and education is relegated to either a kind of algorithmic mode of regulation or sites of state indoctrination? It is crucial for educators and progressives to remember that "education has always been foundational to politics, but it is rarely understood as a site of struggle over how identities are shaped, values are legitimated, and the future defined."[15]

Education in the broadest sense takes place not only in schools but permeates a range of corporate-controlled apparatuses that extend from the digital airways to print culture. Under the GOP reign of terror, these apparatuses have become updated sites of apartheid pedagogy. As one of us has noted elsewhere, "what is different about education today is not only the variety of spaces in which it takes place, but also the degree to which it has become an element of organized irresponsibility and a prop for white supremacy, the crushing of dissent, and a corrupt cultural and political order."[16] This is clear in the policies of Florida Governor Ron DeSantis, Texas Governor Greg Abbott, and others whose attack on public and higher education sanctions civic illiteracy, codifies whiteness as a tool of domination, and censors the past to abolish the future. This is a fascist model of education in which book burning, censorship, and the racial cleansing of history merge with an attempt to turn public and higher education into right-wing, white supremacist indoctrination centers operating under state control.

At work in this mode of fascist education are pedagogies of repression that assault rather than enlighten. These often employ modes of instruction that are not only wedded to white supremacist and exclusionary practices but are also punitive and mean-spirited and are principally driven by regimes of memorization and conformity. Pedagogies of repression are largely disciplinary and have little regard for analysing contexts, history, making knowledge meaningful, or expanding upon what it means for students to be critically engaged agents.

Culture as an educational force has been poisoned and plays a key role in normalizing fascist politics in America and around the globe. Mass media has turned into a flame thrower of hate and bigotry, stylized as spectacle. Alienating misery, social atomization, the death of the social contract, the militarization of public space, concentrations of wealth and power in the hands of the financial and ruling elite, all fuel a fascist politics. The signs of fascism no longer hide in the shadows. This is especially clear as modern-day politics draws much of its energy from a culture of fear, resentment, bigotry, political fundamentalism, and a state of mind in which the distinction between truth and falsehoods collapses into alternative realities.

As we stress throughout this book, we live in an age in which it would be wise for educators and others to be reminded of the importance of critical education, historical memory, civic literacy, and collective resistance as a counterweight to the current language of nativism, ultra-nationalism, bigotry, and violence. There is an urgent need on the part of educators and other cultural workers to resist the erasure of history and the attack on education by the far right in several states. This is particularly important at a time when America moves closer to a looming fascist abyss as thinking becomes dangerous, language is emptied of any substance, politics is driven by the financial elite, and institutions that serve the public good begin to vanish.

At the current moment, education is increasingly defined as an animating space of repression and violence and weaponized as a tool of censorship, state indoctrination, and terminal exclusion. The examples are too numerous to address. A short list would raise questions about how to explain a Florida school district banning a graphic novel version of Anne Frank's Diary, the firing of a Florida principal for showing her class an image of Michelangelo's *David*, and the publishing of a textbook that removed any hint of racism from Rosa Park's refusal to give up her bus seat in Montgomery, Alabama in 1955. It gets worse and appears to be updated with each passing day. For instance, Governor Ron DeSantis in his run for the presidency wants to model the U.S. after Florida, what author David Pepper labels as a laboratory of autocracy.[17]

DeSantis has signed one of the most restrictive abortion laws in the United States, waged a war against transgender youth, rolled back policies designed to ameliorate global warming, and claims that as president he would make the Justice Department and FBI an instrument of presidential control. This is a particularly revealing and frightening notion given that his goal rests on revising the constitution, destroying democracy, and crushing all institutions and individuals who dare to hold power accountable. The latter is clear in his ongoing feud with Disney, his disparaging comments regarding medical experts who oppose his anti-vax, anti-science stance, his removal of elected officials who disagree with him, and his war against teachers, librarians, and school board members who reject his attack on public and higher education. There is a decidedly anti-communist tone in the discourse of MAGA politicians that echoes the notion that all members of the opposition are enemies of the state and should be destroyed, a notion never far removed from the threat of state violence with deep roots in a violent racist past.

DeSantis's embrace of an older anti-communist rhetoric was revealed in an interview on *Fox News* in which the Florida governor stated that if elected president "I will be able to destroy leftism in this country and leave woke ideology in the dustbin of history."[18] Destroying leftism is code for his attack on critical education, his embrace of censorship, and for legitimating what Margaret Sullivan calls his "tireless campaign against supposed wokeness (read: egalitarian portrayals or treatment of Black, gay, and transgender people)."[19] Disparaging alleged enemies with Cold War McCarthyism rhetoric provides DeSantis, Trump, and other fascist politicians a legitimating cover to embrace white supremacy in terms that James Baldwin labeled in *No Name in the Street* "as a masturbatory delusion."[20] The editors of the prestigious journal *Scientific American* provide an illuminating commentary on the far-right politics that DeSantis and other MAGA politicians are promoting. They write:

> What Ron DeSantis has done in Florida mirrors efforts in other states, including Texas. He is among a new class of conservative lawmakers who speak of freedom while restricting freedom ... [He is] running for president of the United States on a record of anti-diversity, pro-censorship, white nationalist measures. He has targeted education, LGBTQ rights and access to health care, and should he prevail, his anti-science candidacy stands to harm millions of Americans. DeSantis has banned books in school libraries, restricted teachers' classroom discussions about

diversity, prohibited high school classes that focus on Black history and people, politicized college curricula, limited spending on diversity programs, ignored greenhouse gas reduction in climate change policy, diminished reproductive rights and outlawed transgender health care.[21]

At the heart of MAGA politics is not only a fear of individuals that embrace the ideals of democracy, but also those institutions, especially schools and other cultural apparatuses, where people can be made into informed and critical citizens.[22] The current age of barbarism and the crushing of dissent points to the need to emphasize how the cultural realm and pedagogies of closure operate as educational and political forces in the service of fascist politics. Under such circumstances, educators and others must question not only what individuals learn in society, but what they must unlearn, and what institutions provide the conditions for them to do so. Against apartheid pedagogies of repression and conformity—rooted in censorship, racism, and the killing of the imagination—there is the need for critical pedagogical practices that value a culture of questioning, view critical agency as a fundamental condition of public life, and reject indoctrination in favor of the search for justice in educational spaces and institutions that function as democratic public spheres.

An education for empowerment that embraces itself as the practice of freedom should provide a classroom environment that is intellectually rigorous, imaginative, and allows students to give voice to their experiences, aspirations, and dreams. It should be a protective space in which students speak, write, and act from a position of agency and informed judgment. It should be a place where education does the bridging work of linking schools to wider society, connecting the self to others, and addressing important social and political issues. A pedagogy for the practice of freedom is rooted in a broader project of a resurgent and insurrectional democracy—one that relentlessly questions the kinds of labor practices and forms of production that are enacted in public and higher education. Such a pedagogy does not offer guarantees. But it does recognize that particular modes of authority, values, and ethical principles must be constantly debated in relation to how they both open up and close down democratic relations, values, and identities.

Critical pedagogy that functions as a practice of freedom should provide the conditions for students to learn how to make connections with an increased sense of social responsibility coupled with a sense of truth. At the heart of such an education, one that is so dangerous to the far right—is the fundamental question of what role education must play in a democracy. At issue is what role education should play as a crucial institution that acknowledges the importance of providing the conditions for shaping critical consciousness and informed citizens. That is, recognizing that matters of agency and the subject are the grounds of politics, and that education is at the heart of critical literacy, learning, and the essence of civic education.

It is worth repeating that as a practice of freedom, education rejects the right-wing claim that education is about self-interest, training, teaching for the test, memorization, and naked forms of indoctrination and repression. As an empowering practice, it is about teaching students to embrace the common good and making young people into citizens willing to struggle over and for a democratic society—as well as against fascism. Education should educate young people to say no, imagine what it means to live in a better world, address systemic violence, develop a historical consciousness, and imagine a different and more equitable future.[23]

What becomes clear under the current regime of gangster capitalism is that its embrace of fascist politics functions to cancel out the teaching of democratic values, impulses, and practices of a civil society. It does this by either devaluing or absorbing these values within the logic of the market and a curriculum rooted in censorship, book banning, and attacks on Black, Brown, and trans students. It also does so within a language of violence that boldly displays the nativism, bigotry, lawlessness, and systemic racism so central to its upgraded version of fascist politics. For example, in the final stages of 2023, with four indictments hanging over his head, Trump has seized upon a language of violence that echoes a vocabulary reminiscent of fascist regimes in the 1930s. He has called for the shooting of shoplifters, raised the issue of shooting migrants crossing the southern border, and mimics Hitler's *Mein Kampf* by stating that "immigrants are poisoning the blood of our country." Hitler's use of words such as "poison" and "blood" were central to promoting the toxic rhetoric of racial purity that legitimized the killing machines that produced the concentration camps.

In the face of these incessant threats of vengeance and violence that inspire the rise of right-wing extremists such as the Proud Boys, encourage extremists in the Republican Party, and attack all vestiges of democracy, educators need a critical language to address these fascistic challenges to public and higher education. But they also need to join with other groups outside of the spheres of public and higher education to create broad national and international social movements that share a willingness to defend education as a civic value and public good and to engage in struggle for a socialist democracy.

The poisonous culture of fascism has become a model embraced by MAGA politicians and it does so in the name of American patriotism. This is more than a cause for alarm, it is a moment in which democracy, in its most fragile state, may be eliminated. How else to explain mass support for a former president who claims that if he wins the 2024 election, he will use the federal government to punish critics and opponents. In addition, he has pledged to root out and eliminate what he calls "radical thugs that live like vermin within the confines of our country"—code for targeting anyone he deems is a socialist. He also threatened to use the Insurrection Act to use the military to curb demonstrations against him and his policies. This is unapologetic fascism. In an age of emerging fascism, democracy has turned dark and speaks to a moment when educators must address what an anti-fascist education might look like, what it means to join with other groups to build a multicultural working-class movement, and how to connect elements of critique and hope with a vision in which a socialist democracy becomes not only plausible but necessary.

NOTES

Introduction

1. Alberto Toscano, "The Long Shadow of Racial Fascism," *Boston Review*, October 27, 2020, http://bostonreview.net/race-politics/alberto-toscano-long-shadow-racial-fascism
2. Geoff Mann, "Is Fascism the Wave of the Future," *The New Statesman*, February 11, 2022, https://www.newstatesman.com/ideas/2022/02/is-fascism-the-wave-of-the-future
3. Angela Y. Davis, Gina Dent, Erica R. Meiners, and Beth E. Richie, *Abolition. Feminism. Now* (Chicago: Haymarket Press, 2022); Angela Y. Davis, *Abolition Democracy: Beyond Empire, Prisons, and Torture* (New York: Seven Stories Press, 2005); Angela Y. Davis, *The Meaning of Freedom* (San Francisco: City Lights Books, 2012).
4. G. M. Tamás, "On Post-Fascism," *Boston Review*, June 1, 2000, https://bostonreview.net/articles/g-m-tamas-post-fascism/
5. Ibid.
6. Ibid.
7. Cited in Ruth Ben-Ghiat, "What Is Fascism?" *Lucid*, December 7, 2022, https://lucid.substack.com/p/what-is-fascism
8. Paul Gilroy, "The 2019 Holberg Lecture, by Laureate Paul Gilroy: Never Again: Refusing Race and Salvaging the Human," *Holbergprisen*, November 11, 2019, https://holbergprisen.no/en/news/holberg-prize/2019-holberg-lecture-laureate-paul-gilroy
9. Roger Sollenberger, "Trump Wanted to 'Maim' and 'Tear Gas' Migrants at US-Mexico Border, Former DHS Official Claims," *Salon*, August 27, 2020, https://www.salon.com/2020/08/27/trump-wanted-to-maim-and-tear-gas-migrants-at-us-mexico-border-former-dhs-official-claims/
10. Michel Martin and Tinbete Ermyas, "Former Pentagon Chief Esper Says Trump Asked About Shooting Protesters," *National Public Radio*, May 9, 2022, https://www.npr.org/2022/05/09/1097517470/trump-esper-book-defense-secretary

11 Jason Hoffman, "Trump Baselessly Claims Doctors are Inflating Coronavirus Death Counts for Money as Cases Again Hit Record Levels," CNN, October 31, 2020, https://www.cnn.com/2020/10/30/politics/trump-doctors-covid/index.html; Rebecca Falconer, "Trump Says if Biden's Elected, 'He'll Listen to the Scientists,'" *Axios*, October 18, 2020, https://www.axios.com/2020/10/19/trump-warns-lockdowns-if-biden-elected-scientists

12 Kyle Cheney, "'Where Are All of the Arrests?': Trump Demands Barr Lock Up His Foes," *Politico*, October 7, 2020, https://www.politico.com/news/2020/10/07/trump-demands-barr-arrest-foes-427389

13 Ben Zimmer, "What Trump Talks About When He Talks About Infestations," *Politico*, July 29, 2019, https://www.politico.com/magazine/story/2019/07/29/trump-baltimore-infest-tweet-cummings-racist-227485/; Julie Hirschfeld Davis, "Trump Calls Some Unauthorized Immigrants 'Animals' in Rant," *The New York Times*, May 16, 2018, https://www.nytimes.com/2018/05/16/us/politics/trump-undocumented-immigrants-animals.html; William Cummings, "Trump Tells Congresswomen to 'Go Back' to the 'Crime Infested Places From Which They Came,'" *USA Today*, July 14, 2019, https://www.usatoday.com/story/news/politics/2019/07/14/trump-tells-congresswomen-go-back-counties-they-came/1728253001/

14 Tina Nguyen, "Trump Isn't Secretly Winking at QAnon. He's Retweeting its Followers," *Politico*, July 12, 2020, https://www.politico.com/news/2020/07/12/trump-tweeting-qanon-followers-357238; David Klepper and Ali Swenson, "Trump Openly Embraces, Amplifies QAnon Conspiracy Theories," *Associated Press*, September 16, 2022, https://apnews.com/article/technology-donald-trump-conspiracy-theories-government-and-politics-db50c6f709b1706886a876ae6ac298e2

15 Caitlin Oprysko, "Trump Criticizes NASCAR Ban on Confederate Flags and Attacks Black Driver, NFL, and MLB Teams," *Politico*, July 6, 2020, https://www.politico.com/news/2020/07/06/trump-nascar-bubba-wallace-confederate-flag-349730

16 Brandon Tensley, "The Dark Subtext of Trump's 'Good Genes' Compliment," CNN, September 22, 2020, https://www.cnn.com/2020/09/22/politics/donald-trump-genes-historical-context-eugenics/index.html

17 Nurith Aizenman, "Trump Wishes We Had More Immigrants From Norway. Turns Out We Once Did," *National Public Radio*, January 12, 2018, https://www.npr.org/sections/goatsandsoda/2018/01/12/577673191/trump-wishes-we-had-more-immigrants-from-norway-turns-out-we-once-did

Chapter 1

1. Chris Hedges, "The Return of Fascism," *Scheer Post*, September 26, 2022, https://scheerpost.com/2022/09/26/chris-hedges-the-return-of-fascism/; Paul Street, *This Happened Here: Amerikaners, Neoliberals, and the Trumping of America* (New York: Routledge, 2022); Anthony DiMaggio, *Rising Fascism in America* (New York: Routledge, 2022).

2. Kenny Stancil, "210+ GOP Candidates Who Spread Doubt and Lies About 2020 Election Won Their Races," *Common Dreams*, November 9, 2022, https://www.commondreams.org/news/2022/11/09/210-gop-candidates-who-spread-doubt-and-lies-about-2020-election-won-their-races; Karen Yourish, Danielle Ivory, Aaron Byrd, Weiyi Cai, Nick Corasaniti, Meg Felling, Rumsey Taylor and Jonathan Weisman, "Over 370 Republican Candidates Have Cast Doubt on the 2020 Election," *The New York Times*, October 13, 2022, https://www.nytimes.com/interactive/2022/10/13/us/politics/republican-candidates-2020-election-misinformation.html

3. Rosalind S. Helderman and Yasmeen Abutaleb, "Biden Warns GOP Could Set Nation on 'Path to Chaos' as Democratic System Faces Strain," *The Washington Post*, November 2, 2021, https://www.washingtonpost.com/politics/2022/11/02/biden-warning-democracy-midterms-election-gop/

4. Tom Nichols, "Democracy Was on the Ballot—And Won," *The Atlantic*, November 9, 2022, https://www.theatlantic.com/newsletters/archive/2022/11/democracy-won/672061/?utm_source=newsletter&utm_medium=email&utm_campaign=atlantic-daily-newsletter&utm_content=20221109&utm_term=The%20Atlantic%20Daily

5. Michael Tomasky, "Looming Questions for the Democrats," *New York Review of Books*, December 22, 2022, https://www.nybooks.com/articles/2022/12/22/looming-questions-for-the-democrats-michael-tomasky/

6. Robert Reich, "Is Ron DeSantis a Fascist?," *Robert Reich*, August 23, 2022, https://robertreich.substack.com/p/is-ron-desantis-a-fascist#details; Eric Alterman, "Altercation: Ron DeSantis Is an Honest-to-God Semi-Fascist," *The American Prospect*, September 2, 2022, https://prospect.org/politics/altercation-ron-desantis-is-an-honest-to-god-semi-fascist/; Thom Hartman, "Did the Fascist Mantle Just Pass to Ron DeSantis?" *Common Dreams*, November 9, 2022, https://www.commondreams.org/views/2022/11/09/did-fascist-mantle-just-pass-ron-desantis

NOTES

7   Michelle R. Smith, "Former Trump Adviser Michael Flynn 'At the Center' of New Movement Based on Conspiracies and Christian Nationalism," *Associated Press*, September 7, 2022, https://www.pbs.org/newshour/politics/former-trump-adviser-michael-flynn-at-the-center-of-new-movement-based-on-conspiracies-and-christian-nationalism

8   Philip Bump, "Scott Adams and the Right-Wing Insistence on White Victimhood," *The Washington Post*, February 27, 2023, https://www.washingtonpost.com/politics/2023/02/27/dilbert-scott-adams-racism/

9   Jamele Hill, "What Does Kyrie Irving See in Anti-Semitic Conspiracy Theories?" *The Atlantic*, November 3, 2022, https://www.theatlantic.com/ideas/archive/2022/11/kyrie-irving-anti-semitism-kanye-conspiracy-theories/671979/

10 Dan Rosenzweig-Ziff, "'People are Afraid': Antisemitic Fliers Found in Atlanta Suburbs," *The Washington Post*, February 5, 2023, https://www.washingtonpost.com/nation/2023/02/05/antisemitism-flyers-atlanta-jewish-hate/; see also, Elisha Fieldstadt, "Antisemitic Flyers Found in Neighborhoods in at Least Three Cities Over the Weekend," *NBC News*, January 25, 2022, https://www.nbcnews.com/news/us-news/antisemitic-flyers-found-neighborhoods-least-3-cities-rcna13500

11 Bump, "Scott Adams and the Right-Wing Insistence on White Victimhood."

12 Jason Stanley and Federico Finchelstein, "White Replacement Theory is Fascism's New Name," *Los Angeles Times*, May 24, 2022, https://www.latimes.com/opinion/story/2022-05-24/white-replacement-theory-fascism-europe-history; David Bauder, "Explainer: White 'Replacement Theory' Fuels Racist Attacks," *AP News*, May 16, 2022, https://apnews.com/article/great-white-replacement-theory-explainer-c86f309f02cd14062f301ce6b9228e33

13 Michelle Boorstein and Isaac Arnsdorf, "Overt U.S. Antisemitism Returns with Trump, Kanye West: 'Something is Different'," *The Washington Post*, October 27, 2022, https://www.washingtonpost.com/religion/2022/10/27/antisemitism-kanye-trump-adidas-jews/

14 Vera Bergenruen, "Trump Attacks on Prosecutors and Judges Heighten Security Concerns," *Time*, August 15, 2023, https://time.com/6303523/trump-prosecutors-violent-threats/#:~:text=Prosecutors%20and%20judges%20across%20the,to%20overturn%20the%202020%20election

15 The essay also appears in Leo Lowenthal, "Atomization of Man," *False Prophets: Studies in Authoritarianism* (New Brunswick, NJ: Transaction Books, 1987), pp. 181–91.
16 Chauncey DeVega, "America's Epidemic of Loneliness: The Raw Material for Fascism," *Salon*, January 3, 2023, https://www.salon.com/2023/01/03/americas-epidemic-of-loneliness-the-raw-material-for-fascism/; Noreena Hertz, *The Lonely Century: How to Restore Human Connection in a World That's Pulling Apart* (New York: Currency, 2021).
17 See, especially, Jonathan Crary, *Scorched Earth: Beyond the Digital Age to a Post-capitalist World* (London: Verso Books 2022).
18 Chris Hedges, "The Plague of Social Isolation," *Scheerpost*, January 23, 2023, https://scheerpost.com/2023/01/23/chris-hedges-the-plague-of-social-isolation/
19 John Steppling, "Falling Out of Love," *John Steppling Journal*, February 22, 2023, https://john-steppling.com/journal/
20 This issue is brilliant analyzed in Heather Gautney, *The New Power Elite* (New York: Oxford University Press, 2023).
21 Crary, *Scorched Earth*, p. 2.
22 Amy Goodman and Denis Moynihan, "Make America Great, At Last," *Democracy Now*, November 3, 2022, https://www.democracynow.org/2022/11/3/make_america_great_at_last
23 Umberto Eco, "Ur-Fascism," *The New York Review of Books*, June 22, 1995, http://www.nybooks.com/articles/1995/06/22/ur-fascism/?pagination=false&printpage=true
24 Reprinted in *Truthout*. See Henry A. Wallace, "The Dangers of American Fascism," *Truthout*, February 28, 2011, https://truthout.org/articles/the-dangers-of-american-fascism/
25 Ibid.
26 Ibid.
27 See, for instance, Henry A. Giroux, *American Nightmare: Facing the Challenge of Fascism* (San Francisco: City Lights, 2018); Jason Stanley, *How Fascism Works: The Politics of Us and Them* (New York: Random House, 2018); Carl Boggs, *Fascism Old and New* (New York: Routledge, 2018); Sarah Churchwell, "American Fascism: It Has Happened Again," *The New York Review of Books*, May 26, 2020, https://www.nybooks.com/daily/2020/06/22/american-fascism-it-has-happened-here/; Bill V. Mullen and Christopher Vials, eds., *The U.S. Anti-Fascism Reader* (London: Verso, 2020); Chris Hedges, "The Rise of American Fascism,"

Common Dreams, June 27, 2022, https://www.commondreams.org/views/2022/06/27/rise-american-fascism
28 Mike Ellis, "Squeezed by Investigations, Trump Escalates Violent Rhetoric," *The Hill*, March 25, 2023, https://thehill.com/homenews/house/3917300-squeezed-by-investigations-trump-escalates-violent-rhetoric/
29 Maya Yang, "Florida Couple Unable to Get Abortion Will See Baby Die After Delivery," *The Guardian*, February 18, 2023, https://www.theguardian.com/world/2023/feb/18/florida-abortion-law-couple-birth
30 Ibid.
31 Cited in David Badash, "A 'Benefit to Society': Alaska GOP Lawmaker Touts 'Cost Savings' When 'Child Abuse is Fatal'," *AlterNet*, February 22, 2023, https://www.alternet.org/alaska-gop/
32 This would also include the historical roots of fascism and the modes of resistance that challenged it. See Helmut-Harry Loewen, "History Lessons for Antifascists," *CounterPunch*, February 20, 2023, https://www.counterpunch.org/2023/02/20/history-lessons-for-antifascists/
33 Pierre Bourdieu and Gunter Grass, "The 'Progressive' Restoration: A Franco-German Dialogue," *New Left Review* 14 (March–April, 2002), p. 66.
34 James Baldwin, *The Price of the Ticket* (Boston: Beacon Press, 2021), p. 417.
35 Henry A. Giroux, *The Violence of Organized Forgetting* (San Francisco: City Lights, 2014).
36 Cited in Greg Sargent, "The Trump-DeSantis Feud Just Got Worse. A Hidden Factor Is Driving It," *The Washington Post*, November 7, 2022, https://www.washingtonpost.com/opinions/2022/11/07/donald-trump-ron-desantis-feud-christian-nationalism/
37 Elie Mystal, "'It Could Have Been Worse' Is the Wrong Response to the Midterms," *The Nation*, November 11, 2022, https://www.thenation.com/article/politics/gerrymandering-republican-victories-midterms/?custno=&utm_source=Sailthru&utm_medium=email&utm_campaign=Daily%2011.10.2022&utm_term=daily
38 Will Bunch, "The Day Young Voters Lined Up to Keep the American Republic for 2 More Years," *The Philadelphia Inquirer*, November 9, 2022, https://www.inquirer.com/opinion/2022-midterms-young-voters-abortion-20221109.html; Jessica Corbett, "Young People Saved This Election' for Democrats, Say Progressives," *Common Dreams*, November 9, 2022, https://www.commondreams.org/news/2022/11/09/young-people-saved-election-

democrats-say-progressives?utm_source=daily_newsletter&utm_medium=Email&utm_campaign=daily_newsletter

39 Ruth Ben-Ghiat, "Instead of a Red Wave, The Midterms Produced a Wave of Historic Firsts in American Politics," *Lucid*, November 9, 2022, https://lucid.substack.com/p/instead-of-a-red-wave-the-midterms?utm_source=post-email-title&publication_id=300941&post_id=83526168&isFreemail=false&utm_medium=email

Chapter 2

1 Anthony DiMaggio, *Rising Fascism in America: It Can Happen Here* (London: Routledge, 2022).
2 Jenny Gross, "Far-Right Groups Are Behind Most U.S. Terrorist Attacks, Report Finds," *The New York Times*, January 20, 2021, https://www.nytimes.com/2020/10/24/us/domestic-terrorist-groups.html
3 Erica Chenoweth and Jeremy Pressman, "Black Lives Matter Protesters Were Overwhelmingly Peaceful, Our Research Finds," *The Spokesman-Review*, October 20, 2020, https://www.spokesman.com/stories/2020/oct/20/erica-chenoweth-and-jeremy-pressman-black-lives-ma/
4 Eric Litke, "Fact Check: Police Gave Kyle Rittenhouse Water and Thanked Him Before Shooting," *USA Today*, August 29, 2020, https://www.usatoday.com/story/news/factcheck/2020/08/29/fact-check-video-police-thanked-kyle-rittenhouse-gave-him-water/5661804002/
5 Jane C. Timm, "Trump Says Democrats are 'The Party of Crime.' We Fact Checked his Campaign-Trail Claims," *NBC News*, November 2, 2018, https://www.nbcnews.com/politics/donald-trump/trump-says-democrats-are-party-crime-we-fact-checked-his-n920451
6 Toni Morrison, "Racism and Fascism," *The Journal of Negro Education* (Summer 1995), https://www.leeannhunter.com/gender/wp-content/uploads/2012/11/Morrison-article.pdf
7 Federico Finchelstein, *A Brief History of Fascist Lies* (Oakland, CA: University of California Press, 2020), pp. 1, 18.
8 Rebecca Matoska-Mentink, "State of Wisconsin v. Kyle H. Rittenhouse: Instructions to the Jury," State of Wisconsin Circuit Court, November 15, 2021, https://int.nyt.com/data/documenttools/rittenhouse-trial-jury-instructions/0b78a521e19f369d/full.pdf

NOTES

9   Odette Yousef, "For Far-Right Groups, Rittenhouse's Acquittal is a Cause for Celebration," *National Public Radio*, November 19, 2021, https://www.npr.org/2021/11/19/1057478725/far-right-groups-rittenhouse-acquittal-celebration-violence

10 Andrew Buncombe, "Kyle Rittenhouse Cheered as 'Hero to Millions' as He Claims Homicide Trial Attempt to Come After 2nd Amendment," *The Independent*, December 21, 2021, https://www.independent.co.uk/news/world/americas/kyle-rittenhouse-speaks-hero-trial-b1979817.html

11 Associated Press, "Prosecutors Want to Show Rittenhouse Video at Trial," *Associated Press*, August 19, 2021, https://apnews.com/article/trials-f19acb6b4f1e4128610d2078105db1ce

12 Wilson Wong, "Kyle Rittenhouse, Out on Bail, Flashed White Power Signs at a Bar, Prosecutors Say," *NBC News*, January 14, 2021, https://www.nbcnews.com/news/us-news/kyle-rittenhouse-out-bail-flashed-white-power-signs-bar-prosecutors-n1254250

13 DiMaggio, *Rebellion in America*.

14 Megan O'Leary, "Competing Visions of America: An Evolving Identity or a Culture Under Attack?" *Public Religion and Research Institute*, November 1, 2021, https://www.prri.org/press-release/competing-visions-of-america-an-evolving-identity-or-a-culture-under-attack/

15 UVA Center for Politics, "New Poll: Majority of Americans Believe Race Relations Have Worsened Under President Trump," *University of Virginia*, August 9, 2018, https://centerforpolitics.org/crystalball/articles/new-poll-majority-of-americans-believe-race-relations-have-worsened-under-president-trump/; Anita Snow and Hannah Fingerhut, "AP-NORC Poll: Americans Agree on Many Aspects of US Identity," *Associated Press*, October 21, 2019, https://apnews.com/article/immigration-donald-trump-ap-top-news-politics-united-states-466e86ac67ef4c609b6ee28e5eb151d9?fbclid=IwAR1IcTka69MwkWoZKUC1ROu671U3rYx9eUXlA8lLOXjUiw29RZDAIyKYA4g

16 O'Leary, "Competing Visions of America."

17 Caitlin Dickson, "Poll: Two-Thirds of Republicans Still Think the 2020 Election was Rigged," *Yahoo News*, August 4, 2021, https://news.yahoo.com/poll-two-thirds-of-republicans-still-think-the-2020-election-was-rigged-165934695.html?guccounter=1; Andrew Solender, "Poll Finds Most Americans Think an Election Will Be Overturned over Partisan Sour Grapes," *Forbes*, September 15, 2021, https://www.forbes.com/sites/andrewsolender/2021/09/15/poll-finds-

most-americans-think-an-election-will-be-overturned-over-partisan-sour-grapes/?sh=52d7cd231710

18 Caitlin Dickson, "'Alarming Finding': 30 Percent of Republicans Say Violence May Be Needed to Save U.S., Poll Shows," *Yahoo News*, November 1, 2021, https://news.yahoo.com/prri-poll-republicans-violence-040144322.html

19 Adam Gabbatt, "Almost One in Three of Republicans Say Violence May Be Necessary to 'Save' US," *The Guardian*, November 1, 2021, https://www.theguardian.com/us-news/2021/nov/01/republicans-violence-save-us-poll

20 O'Leary, "Competing Visions of America."

21 Ibid.

22 New York Times, "Cross-Tabs for October 2022 Times/Siena Poll of Registered Voters," *The New York Times*, October 18, 2022, https://www.nytimes.com/interactive/2022/10/18/upshot/times-siena-poll-registered-voters-crosstabs.html

23 Fadel Allassan, "Poll: 62% of Trump Supporters Say Nothing He Could Do Would Change Opinion," *Axios*, https://www.axios.com/2019/11/05/monmouth-poll-trump-approval

24 Nurith Aizenman, "Trump Wishes We Had More Immigrants from Norway. Turns Out We Once Did," *National Public Radio*, January 12, 2018, https://www.npr.org/sections/goatsandsoda/2018/01/12/577673191/trump-wishes-we-had-more-immigrants-from-norway-turns-out-we-once-did

25 Tommy Beer, "Majority of Republicans Believe the QAnon Conspiracy Theory is Partly or Mostly True, Survey Finds," *Forbes*, September 2, 2020, https://www.forbes.com/sites/tommybeer/2020/09/02/majority-of-republicans-believe-the-qanon-conspiracy-theory-is-partly-or-mostly-true-survey-finds/?sh=2a0a457b5231

26 New York Times, "Cross-Tabs for October 2022."

27 Gallup, "Presidential Approval Ratings—Donald Trump," *Gallup*, 2023, https://news.gallup.com/poll/203198/presidential-approval-ratings-donald-trump.aspx

Chapter 3

1 See, for example, Victor Klemperer, *I Will Bear Witness 1933–1941* (New York: Modern Library 1999); Primo Levi, *The Drowned and the Saved* (New York: Simon and Schuster, 1986).

NOTES

2. Etienne Balibar, "Outline of a Topography of Cruelty: Citizenship and Civility in the Era of Global Violence," *We, the People of Europe? Reflections on Transnational Citizenship* (Princeton: Princeton University Press, 2004), p. 127.
3. Ibid., p. 117.
4. Henry A. Giroux, *Twilight of the Social: Resurgent Publics in the Age of Disposability* (New York: Routledge, 2012).
5. Primo Levi, *Survival in Auschwitz* (New York: Touchstone, 1958).
6. Bard Evans and Henry A. Giroux, *Disposable Futures: The Seduction of Violence in the Age of the Spectacle* (San Francisco: City Lights Books, 2015); Judith Butler, *Precarious Life: The Powers of Mourning and Violence* (London: Verso, 2006).
7. Balibar, "Outline of a Topography of Cruelty," p. 128.
8. Adam Serwer, "The Cruelty is the Point," *The Atlantic*, October 3, 2018, https://www.theatlantic.com/ideas/archive/2018/10/the-cruelty-is-the-point/572104/
9. See for instance Henry A. Giroux, *Hearts of Darkness: Torturing Children in the War on Terror* (New York: Routledge, 2010); Robert J. Lifton, "American Apocalypse," *The Nation*, December 22, 2003, https://www.thenation.com/article/archive/american-apocalypse/
10. Eric Alterman, "Altercation: Ron DeSantis Is an Honest-to-God Semi-Fascist," *The American Prospect*, September 2, 2022, https://prospect.org/politics/altercation-ron-desantis-is-an-honest-to-god-semi-fascist/
11. Martin Pengelly, "Outrage After DeSantis Says He'd 'Start Slitting Throats' If Elected President," *The Guardian*, August 4, 2023, https://www.theguardian.com/us-news/2023/aug/04/ron-desantis-slitting-throats-federal-jobs-president-campaign
12. Ibid.
13. Mona Charen, "Greg Abbott: Scrooge," *The Bulwark*, December 27, 2022, https://www.thebulwark.com/greg-abbott-scrooge/
14. Editorial Board, "Vaccines Saved Lives. DeSantis Threatens that Progress," *The Washington Post*, December 18, 2022, https://www.washingtonpost.com/opinions/2022/12/18/ron-desantis-vaccine-covid-threaten-progress/
15. Michael Sainato, "'It's Just Crazy': Republicans Attack U.S. Child Labor Laws as Violations Rise," *The Guardian*, February 11, 2023, https://www.theguardian.com/us-news/2023/feb/11/us-child-labor-laws-violations
16. Ibid.

17 Daniel Villarreal, "28 House Republicans Vote Against Bill to Protect Child Sex Abuse Victims," *AlterNet*, December 22, 2022, https://www.alternet.org/28-house-republicans-abuse-victims/

18 Stuti Mishra, "Trump says Federal Government will Directly Oversee Discipline in Schools If He is Re-elected," *The Independent*, February 21, 2023, https://www.independent.co.uk/news/world/americas/us-politics/trump-2024-school-discipline-crime-rate-b2286274.html

19 For an informative series of interviews on violence, see Brad Evans and Adrian Parr, *Conversations on Violence: An Anthology* (London: Pluto Press, 2021). Also, for a brilliant discussion of violence, Brad Evans, *Ecce Humanitas: Beholding the Pain of Humanity* (New York: Columbia University Press, 2021).

20 See Gun Violence Archive 2022. https://www.gunviolencearchive.org/

21 Jonathan Schell, "Cruel America," *The Nation*, September 28, 2011, http://www.thenation.com/article/163690/cruel-america

22 Lutz Koepnick, "Aesthetic Politics Today—Walter Benjamin and Post-Fordist Culture," *Critical Theory—Current State and Future Prospects*, ed. Peter Uwe Hohendahl and Jaimey Fisher (New York: Berghahn Books, 2002), pp. 94–116.

23 Evans and Giroux, *Disposable Futures*; Butler, *Precarious Life*.

24 There are numerous books and articles addressing neoliberalism, a selected few include: Pierre Bourdieu, *Acts of Resistance: Against the Tyranny of the Market* (New York: The New Press, 1998); Pierre Bourdieu, et al., *The Weight of the World: Social Suffering in Contemporary Society* (Stanford: Stanford University Press, 1999); Alain Touraine, *Beyond Neoliberalism* (London: Polity Press, 2001); David Harvey, *A Brief History of Neoliberalism* (New York: Oxford University Press, 2005); Henry A. Giroux, *Against the Terror of Neoliberalism: Politics Beyond the Age of Greed* (New York: Routledge, 2008); Thomas Piketty, *Capital and Ideology* (Cambridge: Belknap, 2020); Noam Chomsky, *The Precipice: Neoliberalism, the Pandemic and the Urgent Need for Radical Change* (New York: Penguin, 2021); and Alexander Cockburn and Jeffrey St. Clair, *An Orgy of Thieves: Neoliberalism and Its Discontents* (Petrolia: CounterPunch Books, 2022).

25 Jeremy Gilbert, "What Kind of Thing Is 'Neoliberalism'?" *New Formations*, 80/81 (2013), p. 15.

26 Michael D. Yates, *Work Work Work: Labor, Alienation, and Class Struggle* (New York: Monthly Review Press, 2023), p. 173.

27 Edgar Cabanas and Eva Illouz, *Manufacturing Happy Citizens* (London: Polity, 2018), p. 53.

28 I have developed this argument in detail in Henry A. Giroux, *Pedagogy of Resistance: Against Manufactured Ignorance* (London: Bloomsbury, 2022).
29 Rachel Kaadzi Ghansah, "The Mystic of Mar-a-Lago," *The New York Times*, November 20, 2022, https://www.nytimes.com/2022/11/18/opinion/trump-maga-fetish.html
30 Stuart Hall, "The Neo-Liberal Revolution," *Cultural Studies*, 25, no. 6 (November, 2011), p. 705.
31 Prabhat Patnaik, "Why Neoliberalism Needs Neofascists," *Boston Review*, July 13, 2021, https://bostonreview.net/class-inequality-politics/prabhat-patnaik-why-neoliberalism-needs-neofascists
32 See, for instance, Thomas Piketty, *Capital in the Twenty-First Century* (Cambridge: Belknap, 2017); Piketty, *Capital and Ideology*; Robert Kuttner, "Free Markets, Besieged Citizens," *The New York Review of Books*, July 21, 2022, https://www.nybooks.com/articles/2022/07/21/free-markets-besieged-citizens-gerstle-kuttner/
33 Pankaj Mishra, "The Incendiary Appeal of Demagoguery in Our Time," *The New York Times*, November 13, 2016, https://www.nytimes.com/2016/11/14/opinion/the-incendiary-appeal-of-demagoguery-in-our-time.html
34 Pankaj Mishra, "The New World Disorder: The Western Model is Broken," *The Guardian*, October 14, 2014, https://www.theguardian.com/world/2014/oct/14/-sp-western-model-broken-pankaj-mishra
35 Alex Honneth, *Pathologies of Reason* (New York: Columbia University Press, 2009), p. 188.
36 Pascale-Anne Brault and Michael Naas, "Translators Note," in Jean-Luc Nancy, *The Truth of Democracy* (New York: Fordham University Press, 2010), p. ix.
37 Mishra, "The Incendiary Appeal of Demagoguery in Our Time."
38 See, for instance, Elisabeth R. Anker, *Ugly Freedoms* (Durham: Duke University Press, 2022).
39 Michael Tomasky, "Looming Questions for the Democrats," *The New York Review of Books*, December 22, 2022, https://www.nybooks.com/articles/2022/12/22/looming-questions-for-the-democrats-michael-tomasky/
40 Josh Shapiro's speech can be found on Politico: https://www.politico.com/video/2022/11/09/pennsylvania-governor-shapiro-gives-victory-speech-a-womans-right-to-choose-won-765444
41 Friedrich Hayek, *The Road to Serfdom* (London: Routledge, 1944).

42 Milton Friedman, "The Social Responsibility of Business is to Increase its Profits," *The New York Times Magazine*, September 13, 1970, http://umich.edu/~thecore/doc/Friedman.pdf

43 Caleb Crain, "Is Capitalism a Threat to Democracy?" *The New Yorker*, May 14, 2018, https://www.newyorker.com/magazine/2018/05/14/is-capitalism-a-threat-to-democracy

44 Liz Theoharis, "The Poverty of the Political Mind," *TomDispatch*, October 27, 2022, https://tomdispatch.com/the-quality-or-inequality-of-life/

45 Ibid.

46 Thomas Piketty, *Time for Socialism: Dispatches from a World on Fire, 2016–2021*(New Haven: Yale University Press, 2021).

47 William J. Astore, "One Peculiar Form of American Madness," *LA Progressive*, December 2, 2022, https://www.laprogressive.com/defense/american-madness

48 See various books by Andrew J. Bacevich. Also, see "America's Militarism Will Be Its Downfall," *The Nation*, April 18, 2022, https://www.thenation.com/article/world/america-militarism-ukraine-king/

49 David Leonhardt, "The Right's Violence Problem," *The New York Times*, May 17, 2022, https://www.nytimes.com/2022/05/17/briefing/right-wing-mass-shootings.html

50 Anthony DiMaggio, "Christian White Supremacy Rising: The Fascist Connection," *CounterPunch*, September 28, 2022, https://www.counterpunch.org/2022/09/28/christian-white-supremacy-rising-the-fascist-connection/

51 Editorial, "World Military Spending Reaches All-Time High of $2.24 Trillion," *Al Jazeera*, April 24, 2023, https://www.aljazeera.com/news/2023/4/24/world-military-spending-reaches-all-time-high-of-2-24-trillion

52 Bill Blum, "Democracy on the Ballot," *Truthdig*, November 7, 2022, https://www.truthdig.com/articles/democracy-on-the-ballot/

53 Barbara Epstein, "Prospects for a Resurgence of the U.S. Left," *Tikkun*, 29, no. 2 (Spring 2014), p. 42.

54 David Harvey, "Neoliberalism Is a Political Project," *Jacobin*, July 23, 2016, https://www.jacobinmag.com/2016/07/david-harvey-neoliberalism-capitalism-labor-crisis-resistance/

55 See, for instance, Robert B. Reich, *Saving Capitalism: For the Many, Not the Few* (New York: Vintage, 2016).

56 See C. Wright Mills, "Letter to the New Left," *The New Left Review* (September–October, 1960), pp. 18–23. Also, see Stanley

Aronowitz, *Taking it Big: C. Wright Mills and the Making of Political Intellectuals* (New York: Columbia University Press, 2012).
57 James Baldwin, "As Much Truth as One Can Bear," *The New York Times*, January 14, 1962, p. BR38.

Chapter 4

1 On the issue of militarism and militarization, see Roberto J. Gonzalez, Hugh Gusterson, and Gustaaf Houtman, eds. *Militarization: A Reader* (Durham: Duke University Press, 2019).
2 Will Bunch, "America Needs to Confront its 'Mussolini Moment'," *The Philadelphia Inquirer*, March 7, 2023, https://www.inquirer.com/columnists/attytood/cpac-trump-hitler-mussolini-transgender-daniel-ellsberg-20230307.html?outputType=default
3 Johanna Chisholm, "Robert Crimo 'Sized Up' Synagogue Months Before Highland Park Shooting, Security Officer Says," *The Independent*, July 6, 2022, https://www.independent.co.uk/news/world/americas/crime/robert-crimo-synagogue-highland-park-b2116893.html; Joe Tacopino and David Propper, "Highland Park Parade Shooting Suspect Robert Crimo Posted Pics of his 'Teen Sex Doll' Online," *New York Post*, July 6, 2022, https://nypost.com/2022/07/06/highland-park-parade-shooting-suspect-robert-crimo-posted-pics-of-his-teen-sex-doll/
4 Carl Boggs, *Fascism Old and New: American Politics at the Crossroads* (London: Routledge, 2018); Paul Street, *This Happened Here: Amerikaners, Neoliberals, and the Trumping of America* (London: Routledge, 2022).
5 Anthony DiMaggio, *Rising Fascism in America: It Can Happen Here* (London: Routledge, 2022).
6 Ibid.
7 Paul Street, *This Happened Here*, pp. 147–173.
8 Ibid., pp. 140–146.
9 DiMaggio, *Rising Fascism in America*, p. 73.
10 Citied in Paul Gilroy, "The 2019 Holberg Lecture, by Laureate Paul Gilroy: Never Again: Refusing Race and Salvaging the Human," *Holbergprisen*, November 11, 2019, https://holbergprisen.no/en/news/holberg-prize/2019-holberg-lecture-laureate-paul-gilroy
11 Kathyrn Joyce, "What is 'Ecofascism' – and What Does it have to Do with the Buffalo Shooting?" *Salon*, May 18, 2022, https://www.salon.

com/2022/05/18/what-is-ecofascism--and-what-does-it-have-to-do-with-the-buffalo-shooting/

12 Michael Starr, "'I Wish all Jews to Hell' – Buffalo Shooter was a Fascist White Supremacist," *Jerusalem Star*, May 26, 2022, https://www.jpost.com/diaspora/antisemitism/article-706727

13 Michael Edison Hayden, "New Zealand Terrorist Manifesto Influenced by Far-Right Online Ecosystem, Hatewatch Finds," *Southern Poverty Law Center*, March 15, 2019, https://www.splcenter.org/hatewatch/2019/03/15/new-zealand-terrorist-manifesto-influenced-far-right-online-ecosystem-hatewatch-finds; Julia Kupper, Tanya Karoli Christensen, Dakota Wing, Marlon Hurt, Matthew Schumacher, and Reid Meloy, "The Contagion and Copycat Effect in Transnational Far-Right Terrorism: An Analysis of Language Evidence," *Perspectives on Terrorism*, Vol. 16, no. 4 (August 2022), 4–26. https://www.universiteitleiden.nl/binaries/content/assets/customsites/perspectives-on-terrorism/2022/issue-4/kupper-et-al.pdf

14 Kupper et al., "The Contagion and Copycat Effect."

15 Anti-Defamation League, "Deplatform Tucker Carlson and the 'Great Replacement' Theory," *ADL.org*, May 25, 2022, https://www.adl.org/resources/blog/deplatform-tucker-carlson-and-great-replacement-theory

16 Mark Jovella, "Tucker Carlson has Most-Watched Show in Cable News as Fox Leads Basic Cable for 17 Straight Weeks," *Forbes*, June 15, 2021, https://www.forbes.com/sites/markjoyella/2021/06/15/tucker-carlson-has-most-watched-show-in-cable-news-as-fox-leads-basic-cable-for-17-straight-weeks/?sh=38b8bca9661c

17 David Smith, "'Replacement Theory' Still Republican Orthodoxy Despite Buffalo Shooting," *The Guardian*, May 22, 2022, https://www.theguardian.com/us-news/2022/may/22/great-replacement-theory-republicans

18 Ewan Palmer, "Matt Gaetz Agreeing with Tucker Carlson's 'Replacement' Claim Resurfaces," *Newsweek*, May 16, 2022, https://www.newsweek.com/matt-gaetz-great-replacement-tucker-carlson-buffalo-1706894

19 Shane Goldmacher and Luke Broadwater, "Republicans Play on Fears of 'Great Replacement' in Bid for Base Voters," *The New York Times*, May 16, 2022, https://www.nytimes.com/2022/05/16/us/politics/republicans-great-replacement.html

20 Olafimihan Oshin, "6 in 10 Trump Voters Agree with Core Tenet of Great Replacement Theory: Survey," *The Hill*, May 24, 2022, https://

thehill.com/homenews/state-watch/3499877-6-in-10-trump-voters-agree-with-core-tenet-of-great-replacement-theory-survey/

21 Smith, "'Replacement Theory' Still Republican Orthodoxy."
22 Anthony DiMaggio and Paul Street, "Highland Park, Buffalo, and Fascism Denial in U.S. Media Culture," *CounterPunch*, July 15, 2022, https://www.counterpunch.org/2022/07/15/highland-park-buffalo-and-fascism-denial-in-u-s-media-culture/
23 Bruce Kuklick, *Fascism Comes to America: A Century of Obsession in Politics and Culture* (Chicago, IL: University of Chicago Press, 2022).
24 Associated Press, "Services Begin for Highland Park Parade Shooting Victims," *Los Angeles Times*, July 8, 2022, https://www.latimes.com/world-nation/story/2022-07-08/services-begin-for-highland-park-parade-shooting-victims
25 Shaila Dewan, "What Are the Real Warning Signs of a Mass Shooting?" *The New York Times*, August 24, 2022, https://www.nytimes.com/2022/08/22/us/mass-shootings-mental-illness.html
26 Ibid.
27 Angel Saunders, "Robert 'Bobby' Crimo III Was Seen Wearing 'Where's Waldo?' Costume at Trump Rally," *Revolt TV*, July 6, 2022, https://www.revolt.tv/article/2022-07-06/178686/robert-bobby-crimo-iii-was-seen-wearing-wheres-waldo-costume-at-trump-rally/; Louis Keene, "'We Knew He Was Aggressive': Highland Park Activist Recalls Encounters with Alleged Shooter," *Forward*, July 8, 2022, https://forward.com/news/509582/highland-park-shooter-attended-trump-rally/
28 Chris Schiano, "Highland Park Shooter Decried 'Commies' in Discord Chat," *Unicorn Riot*, July 5, 2022, https://unicornriot.ninja/2022/highland-park-shooter-decried-commies-in-discord-chat/
29 William Quartermaine, "New Details Reveal Highland Park Shooter's Extensive Far-Right History," *World Socialist Website*, July 8, 2022, https://www.wsws.org/en/articles/2022/07/09/tvrn-j09.html
30 Ibid.
31 DiMaggio and Street, "Highland Park, Buffalo, and Fascism Denial in U.S. Media Culture."
32 Victoria Kim and Amanda Holpuch, "What We Know About the Shooting in Highland Park," *The New York Times*, July 7, 2022, https://www.nytimes.com/article/highland-park-shooting-facts.html
33 Dakin Andone, Steve Almasy, and Curt Devine, "What We Know About the Highland Park Shooting Suspect," *CNN*, July 7, 2022,

https://amp.cnn.com/cnn/2022/07/05/us/robert-e-crimo-highland-park-suspect/index.html?fbclid=IwAR1mUlzKfdwuBzBBLUxuef0CU3RDPpEenDoaLocF6tsi4ApFrjYMsb9d_d0

34. Kat Bouza, "Was the 4th of July Shooting Politically Motivated?" *Rolling Stone*, July 5, 2022, https://www.rollingstone.com/culture/culture-news/4th-of-july-shooting-highland-park-political-1377975/

35. Lois Beckett, "White Supremacists Behind Majority of US Domestic Terror Attacks in 2020," *The Guardian*, October 22, 2020, https://www.theguardian.com/world/2020/oct/22/white-supremacists-rightwing-domestic-terror-2020

Chapter 5

1. Holly Ellyatt, "'Pretty Surreal': How the Rest of the World Views the U.S. Stance on Masks," *CNBC*, July 22, 2020, https://www.cnbc.com/2020/07/22/us-coronavirus-masks-position-is-surreal-to-the-rest-of-the-world.html; Benjamin Mueller and Eleanor Lutz, "U.S. Has Far Higher Covid Death Rate Than Other Wealthy Countries," *The New York Times*, February 1, 2022, https://www.nytimes.com/interactive/2022/02/01/science/covid-deaths-united-states.html

2. Cited in Isabel Rosales, Holly Yan, Chris Boyette and Emma Tuck, "A Beloved High School Athlete Was Among 4 People Killed and 28 Injured at a Sweet 16 Birthday Party in Alabama," *CNN*, April 16, 2023, https://www.cnn.com/2023/04/16/us/dadeville-alabama-mass-shooting/index.html

3. David French, "There Is No MAGA Movement Without Threats and Violence," *Newsletters The Atlantic*, August 12, 2022, https://newsletters.theatlantic.com/the-third-rail/62f6811cc5c05500224fa5bf/trump-fbi-search-political-violence/

4. Ibid.

5. Andrew Solender, "Capitol Police Data Indicates Threats to Lawmakers Have Surged Since 2017," *Axios*, June 21, 2022, https://www.axios.com/2022/06/22/capitol-police-threats-congress

6. Ben Collins and Ryan J. Reilly, "After Mar-a-Lago Search, Users on Pro-Trump Forums Agitate For 'Civil War'—Including a Jan. 6 Rioter," *NBC News*, August 9, 2022, https://www.nbcnews.com/politics/justice-department/mar-lago-search-users-trump-forums-agitate-civil-war-jan-6-rioter-rcna42148

7. Kenny Stancil, "'Lock and Load': Trump-Loving Extremists React to FBI Search of Mar-a-Lago," *Common Dreams*, August 9, 2022,

https://www.commondreams.org/news/2022/08/09/lock-and-load-trump-loving-extremists-react-fbi-search-mar-lago

8   Cited in Alan Feuer, "As Right-Wing Rhetoric Escalates, So Do Threats and Violence," *The New York Times*, August 13, 2022, https://www.nytimes.com/2022/08/13/nyregion/right-wing-rhetoric-threats-violence.html

9   Ibid.

10 Ibid.

11 Kim Bellware, "There Will Be 'Riots In The Street' If Trump Is Prosecuted, Graham Says," *The Washington Post*, August 29, 2022, https://www.washingtonpost.com/politics/2022/08/29/lindsey-graham-riots/

12 Rex Huppke, "'DEATH WISH'? What Trump and His Wannabes Did in One Weekend Should Scare Us All," *USA Today*, October 3, 2022, https://www.usatoday.com/story/opinion/2022/10/03/donald-trump-death-wish-mitch-mcconnell-elaine-chao-marjorie-taylor-greene-killing-huppke/8164744001/

13 Asawin Suebsaeng and Patrick Reis, "Trump Privately Proposes Wave of High-Level Jan. 6 Pardons," *Rolling Stone*, March 8, 2023, https://www.rollingstone.com/politics/politics-features/donald-trump-pardons-jan6-maralago-raid-1234692667/

14 Robert Reich, "Trump's Latest Threat Is a Doozy and Requires Four Responses," *Common Dreams*, September 16, 2022, https://www.commondreams.org/views/2022/09/16/trumps-latest-threat-doozy-and-requires-four-responses

15 Laura Italiano, "'Civil War' Mentions Doubled in Extremist Online Spaces After the Mar-a-Lago Raid, Experts Say," *Insider*, August 18, 2022, https://www.businessinsider.com/civil-war-threats-double-dark-web-mar-a-lago-expert-2022-8?utm_medium=referral&utm_source=yahoo.com\

16 Ibid.

17 Kenny Stancil, "Violent Threats Against FBI Soar as Trump Lies About Mar-a-Lago Search," *Common Dreams*, August 14, 2022, https://www.commondreams.org/news/2022/08/14/violent-threats-against-fbi-soar-trump-lies-about-mar-lago-search

18 Robert A. Pape and Keven Ruby, "The Capitol Rioters Aren't Like Other Extremists," *The Atlantic*, February 2, 2021, https://www.theatlantic.com/ideas/archive/2021/02/the-capitol-rioters-arent-like-other-extremists/617895/; Phil Rogers, "Millions of Americans Hold Beliefs That Drove Jan. 6 Capitol Attack, Study Says," *5Chicago*,

January 6, 2022, https://www.nbcchicago.com/investigations/millions-of-americans-hold-beliefs-that-drove-jan-6-capitol-attack-study-says/2723149/

19   Martin Pengelly, "Nearly Half of Republicans Think US Has to Live With Mass Shootings, Poll Finds," *The Guardian*, January 6, 2022, https://www.theguardian.com/us-news/2022/jun/06/us-mass-shootings-republicans-poll

20   Byung-Chul Han, *Topology of Violence* (Cambridge: MIT Press, 2018), p. 10.

21   Cited in Susan Sontag, "Fascinating Fascism," *New York Review of Books*, February 6, 1975, https://www.nybooks.com/articles/1975/02/06/fascinating-fascism/

22   Han, *Topology of Violence*, p. 121.

23   Anthony DiMaggio, "The Campus Thought Police: Faux Outrage, Intimidation, and the Threat to Free Speech," *CounterPunch*, October 30, 2020, https://www.counterpunch.org/2020/10/30/the-campus-thought-police-faux-outrage-intimidation-and-the-threat-to-free-speech/

24   Andy McLaverty-Robinson, "An A to Z of Theory | Walter Benjamin: Fascism and Crisis," *Ceasefire*, August 14, 2013, https://ceasefiremagazine.co.uk/walter-benjamin-fascism-crisis/

25   Ibid.

26   Pierre Bourdieu and Gunter Grass, "The 'Progressive' Restoration: A Franco-German Dialogue," *New Left Review*, Vol. 14 (March–April, 2002), p. 2.

27   Stanley Aronowitz, "What Kind of Left Does America Need?" *Tikkun*, April 14, 2014, http://www.tikkun.org/nextgen/what-kind-of-left-does-america-need; Angela Davis on Amy Goodman, "Angela Davis on Abolition, Calls to Defund Police, Toppled Racist Statues & Voting in 2020 Election," *Democracy Now*, July 3, 2020, https://www.democracynow.org/2020/7/3/angela_davis_on_abolition_calls_to; Barbara Epstein, "Prospects for a Resurgence of the US Left," *Tikkun*, Vol. 29, no. 2 (Spring 2014), pp. 41–4.

28   Ruth Ben-Ghiat, "Oath Keepers and the GOP." *Lucid*, October 7, 2022, https://lucid.substack.com/p/oath-keepers-and-the-gop-no-q-and

29   Toni Morrison, ed., *James Baldwin, Collected Essays: No Name in the Street* (New York: Library of America, 1998), p. 471.

30   Editors, "Now What?" *Jacobin*, No. 24 (Winter 2017), https://www.jacobinmag.com/2017/02/now-what

Chapter 6

1. Tyler Monroe and Rob Savillo, "Fox News has Attacked Black Lives Matter over 400 Times in a 6-Month Period," *Media Matters for America*, May 26, 2021, https://www.mediamatters.org/black-lives-matter/fox-news-has-attacked-black-lives-matter-over-400-times-6-month-period

2. Reuters, "Fact Check: Vote Spikes in Wisconsin, Michigan and Pennsylvania Do Not Prove Election Fraud," *Reuters*, November 10, 2021, https://www.reuters.com/article/uk-factcheck-wi-pa-mi-vote-spikes/fact-check-vote-spikes-in-wisconsin-michigan-and-pennsylvania-do-not-prove-election-fraud-idUSKBN27Q307

3. Joey Garrison, "Trump Baselessly Claims Voter Fraud in Cities, but Suburbs Actually Lost Him the Election," *USA Today*, November 16, 2020, https://www.usatoday.com/in-depth/news/politics/elections/2020/11/13/donald-trump-lost-election-suburbs-not-cities-despite-claims/6263149002/

4. Holly Otterbein, "Philly is the 4th Most Segregated Big City in the Country," *Philly Mag*, September 22, 2015, https://www.phillymag.com/citified/2015/09/22/philadelphia-segregated-big-city/; U.S. Census Bureau, "Quick Facts: Detroit City, Michigan; United States," *U.S. Census Bureau Quick Facts*, 2021, https://www.census.gov/quickfacts/fact/table/detroitcitymichigan,US/PST045221

5. Cassie Miller, "SPLC Poll Finds Substantial Support for 'Great Replacement' Theory and Other Hard-Right Ideas," *Southern Poverty Law Center*, June 1, 2022, https://www.splcenter.org/news/2022/06/01/poll-finds-support-great-replacement-hard-right-ideas

6. Rolinda S. Helderman, Jacqueline Alemany, Josh Dawsey, and Tom Hamburger, "New Evidence Shows Trump Was Told Many Times There Was No Voter Fraud—But He Kept Saying It Anyway," *The Washington Post*, May 3, 2022, https://www.washingtonpost.com/politics/2022/03/03/trump-election-jan-6/; Meridith McGraw, "Trump's Election Fraud Claims Were False. Here Are His Advisors Who Said No," *Politico*, June 13, 2022, https://www.politico.com/news/2022/06/13/trumps-election-fraud-claims-were-false-here-are-his-advisers-who-said-so-00039346

7. Gideon Taaffe and Zachary Pleat, "Fox News Knew It Was Pushing Lies About Dominion," *Media Matters for America*, September 2, 2022, https://www.mediamatters.org/fox-news/fox-news-knew-it-was-pushing-lies-about-dominion

8. Oliver Darcy, "Dominion Voting Systems Sues Newsmax and One America News for 'Barrage of Lies' Targeting the Company," *CNN*, August 10, 2021, https://www.cnn.com/2021/08/10/media/dominion-lawsuit-newsmax-oan/index.html
9. Anthony DiMaggio, *Rising Fascism in America: It Can Happen Here* (London: Routledge, 2021).
10. DiMaggio, *Rising Fascism in America*.
11. Media Matters Staff, "Tucker Carlson Claims 'Dead People Vote in Large Numbers,'" *Media Matters for America*, November 2, 2021, https://www.mediamatters.org/fox-news/tucker-carlson-claims-dead-people-vote-large-numbers
12. Casey Wexler, Kaila Philo, Cydney Hargis, Alex Walker, Sergio Munoz, and Julie Tulbert, "It Wasn't Just Signey Powell. Fox Repeated the Same Dominion Lies," *Media Matters for America*, March 26, 2021, https://www.mediamatters.org/fox-news/it-wasnt-just-sidney-powell-fox-repeated-same-dominion-lies
13. Katelyn Polantz, "Dominion Voting Wins Key Decision in Lawsuit Against Fox News," *CNN*, December 16, 2021, https://www.cnn.com/2021/12/16/media/fox-news-court-dominion/index.html
14. Ibid.
15. Richard Luscombe, "Fox News Hosts Thought Trump's Election Fraud Claims Were 'total BS', Court Filings Show," *The Guardian*, February 17, 2023, https://www.theguardian.com/media/2023/feb/17/fox-news-hosts-dominion-lawsuit-trump-election-fraud-tucker-carlson-sean-hannity-laura-ingraham. See also Heather Cox Richardson, "Letters from an American," Substack.com, February 27, 2023, https://heathercoxrichardson.substack.com/p/february-27-2023
16. David Folkenflik, "Fox News' Defense in Defamation Suit Invokes Debunked Election-Fraud Claims," *National Public Radio*, January 23, 2023, https://www.npr.org/2023/01/23/1150213311/fox-news-dominion-voting-system-election-fraud-claims
17. Anthony DiMaggio, "Fox News Could Be in Big Trouble: Dominion's Huge Defamation Lawsuit Makes a Strong Case," *Salon*, February 2, 2022, https://www.salon.com/2022/02/02/fox-news-could-be-in-big-trouble-dominions-huge-defamation-makes-a-strong-case/
18. Ibid.
19. Brennan Center for Justice, "The Myth of Voter Fraud," *Brennan Center for Justice*, 2023, https://www.brennancenter.org/issues/ensure-every-american-can-vote/vote-suppression/myth-voter-fraud

20 Federico Finchelstein, *A Brief History of Fascist Lies* (Oakland, CA: University of California Press, 2020), p. 31.
21 Ibid., p. 30.
22 Fox News Staff, "US Media's Inaccurate Reporting on Rittenhouse Had Real Consequences Internationally: Greenwald," *Fox News*, November 20, 2021, https://www.foxnews.com/media/kyle-rittenhouse-glenn-greenwald-media-consequences
23 Glenn Greenwald and Tucker Carlson, "Tucker Carlson Tonight," *Fox News*, November 19, 2021, 8pm EST.
24 Robby Soave, "Matt Taibbi: Media Stampede of Kyle Rittenhouse Reveals Rot in Modern Journalism," *The Hill*, November 23, 2021, https://www.youtube.com/watch?v=vMJqQLJCj7k
25 Ibid.
26 For a detailed review of decades of academic literature on the question of bias and liberal media bias in the media, and a review of evidence for an official source bias that varies depending on what party is in power, see: Anthony R. DiMaggio, *The Politics of Persuasion: Economic Policy and Media Bias in the Modern Era* (Albany, NY: State University of New York Press, 2017).
27 Carl Hulse, "Shut Out on Budget Bill, Republicans Take Shots From the Sidelines," *The New York Times*, October 27, 2021, https://www.nytimes.com/2021/10/27/us/politics/budget-bill-republicans.html
28 Caleb Ecarma, "Tucker Carlson Leans into White-Power Hour, Promotes Racist Replacement Theory," *Vanity Fair*, April 9, 2021, https://www.vanityfair.com/news/2021/04/tucker-carlson-promotes-racist-replacement-theory
29 Anthony DiMaggio, "The White Supremacy Lie: The Rittenhouse Trial and Rightwing Media Fabrication," *CounterPunch*, November 28, 2021, https://www.counterpunch.org/2021/11/28/the-white-supremacy-lie-the-rittenhouse-trial-and-rightwing-media-fabrication/
30 Ibid.
31 Ibid.
32 Ibid.
33 Ibid.
34 Ibid.
35 Ibid.
36 Ibid.
37 Ibid.
38 Ibid.

Chapter 7

1. Kelly Hayes, "Fascism Has Gone Mainstream," *Truthout*, September 9, 2022, https://truthout.org/audio/fascism-has-gone-mainstream/
2. Edgar Sandoval, Miriam Jordan, Patricia Mazzei and J. David Goodman, "The Story Behind DeSantis's Migrant Flights to Martha's Vineyard," *The New York Times*, October 2, 2022, https://www.nytimes.com/2022/10/02/us/migrants-marthas-vineyard-desantis-texas.html
3. Judd Legum, "The Smoking Gun in Martha's Vineyard," *Popular Information*, September 19, 2022, https://popular.info/p/the-smoking-gun-in-marthas-vineyard#:~:text=Several%20migrants%20told%20NPR%20they,receive%20%22expedited%20work%20papers.%22
4. See for instance, Elie Mystal, "Let's Talk About Ron DeSantis's 'Reason' for Kidnapping Migrants," *The Nation*, September 26, 2022, https://www.thenation.com/article/politics/ron-desantis-excuse-kidnapping-migrants/; Jonathan Chait, "DeSantis Tries to Prove Liberals Hate Immigrants as Much as He Does, Fails," *New York Magazine*, September 15, 2022, https://nymag.com/intelligencer/2022/09/desantis-tries-fails-to-prove-liberals-hate-migrants-too.html
5. Gabrielle Emanuel, "The Cruel Story Behind The 'Reverse Freedom Rides'," *NPR: Code Switch-Race in Your Face*, February 9, 2020, https://www.npr.org/sections/codeswitch/2020/02/29/809740346/the-cruel-story-behind-the-reverse-freedom-rides
6. Ibid.
7. Kate Storey, "Ron DeSantis Flew Immigrants to Martha's Vineyard, Echoing a Racist Stunt from Exactly 60 Years Ago," *Esquire*, September 16, 2022, https://www.esquire.com/news-politics/a41228853/desantis-marthas-vineyard/
8. Craig Graziosi, "DeSantis Claims It Was Only the American Revolution that Caused People to Question Slavery," *The Independent*, September 23, 2022, https://www.independent.co.uk/news/world/americas/us-politics/desantis-american-revolution-slavery-b2174224.html
9. Cited in Meaghan Ellis, "'Goes Beyond Ignorance' Historians Slam DeSantis' Claims about American Slavery," *Alter Net*, September 24, 2022, https://www.alternet.org/2022/09/ron-desantis-2658332899/
10. Ibid.

11 James Baldwin, "The White Man's Guilt," in *James Baldwin: Collected Essays*, ed. Toni Morrison (Washington, D.C.: The Library of America, 1998), p. 727.
12 Robert S. McElvaine, "A Short History of Fake History: Why Fighting for the Truth is Critical," *Salon*, September 17, 2022, https://www.salon.com/2022/09/17/a-short-history-of-fake-history-why-fighting-for-the-truth-is-critical/
13 Frank Bruni, "Ron DeSantis's God Complex," *The New York Times*, November 9, 2022, https://www.nytimes.com/2022/11/09/opinion/rnalson-desantis-god-complex.html
14 Jack Stripling, "Channeling Orwell, Judge Blasts Florida's 'Dystopian' Ban on 'Woke' Instruction," *The Chronicle of Higher Education*, November 17, 2022, https://www.chronicle.com/article/conjuring-orwell-florida-judge-blasts-dystopian-ban-on-woke-instruction?cid2=gen_login_refresh&cid=gen_sign_in
15 Michael Kunzelman, "Antisemitic Celebrities Stoke Fears of Normalizing Hate," *Politico*, December 4, 2022, https://www.politico.com/news/2022/12/04/antisemitic-celebrities-stoke-fears-of-normalizing-hate-00072073
16 Chloe Melas, "Exclusive: Kanye West has a Disturbing History of Admiring Hitler, Sources tell CNN," *CNN Entertainment*, October 27, 2022, https://www.cnn.com/2022/10/27/entertainment/kanye-west-hitler-album; Jeet Heer, "Kanye West, Elon Musk, Donald Trump, and the Mainstreaming of Nazism," *The Nation*, December 2, 2022, https://www.thenation.com/article/society/kanye-west-musk-trump-nazism/?custno=&utm_source=Sailthru&utm_medium=email&utm_campaign=Daily%2012.5.2022&utm_term=daily
17 AJC, "5 of Kanye West's Antisemitic Remarks, Explained," *AJC/Global Voice*, December 2, 2022, https://www.ajc.org/news/5-of-kanye-wests-antisemitic-remarks-explained
18 Nikki McCann Ramirez and Ryan Bort, "Kanye to Alex Jones: 'I Like Hitler'," *Rolling Stone*, December 1, 2022, https://www.rollingstone.com/politics/politics-news/kanye-west-alex-jones-i-like-hitler-1234639617/; Editorial, "GOP Committee Account Deletes 'Kanye'. Elon. Trump Tweets after Ye Praises Hitler," *USAMEDIACAP*, December 1, 2022, https://usamediacap.com/2022/12/01/gop-committee-account-deletes-kanye-elon-trump-tweets-after-ye-praises-hitler/
19 Dan Milmo, "Kanye West Suspended from Twitter after Posting Swastika Inside Star of David," *The Guardian*, December 2, 2022,

https://www.theguardian.com/music/2022/dec/02/kanye-west-suspended-from-twitter-after-posting-swastika-inside-the-star-of-david

20. Emma Brockes, "Why Was Kanye West Allowed to Air His Frothing Antisemitism in Public for So Long?" *The Guardian*, October 26, 2022, https://www.theguardian.com/commentisfree/2022/oct/26/kanye-westurday-antisemitism-ye-donald-trump-trolling

21. Mike Ludwig and Alana Yu-lan Price, "Right-Wingers Who Stoke the War on Trans People Have Club Q Blood on Their Hands," *Truthout*, November 22, 2022, https://truthout.org/articles/right-wingers-who-stoke-the-war-on-trans-people-have-club-q-blood-on-their-hands/

22. Matthew Chapman, "Watch: Trump-loving Nick Fuentes Gets into Food Fight with In-N-Out Patrons," *RawStory*, December 3, 2022, https://www.rawstory.com/nick-fuentes-in-and-out/

23. Jacob Crosse, "Trump Hosts Fascist Nick Fuentes and Anti-Semite Kanye West for Dinner at Mar-a-Lago Compound," *WSWS*, November 28, 2022, https://www.wsws.org/en/articles/2022/11/28/mdfd-n28.html

24. Stanley L. Cohen, "Words Ache, But Indifference Kills," *CounterPunch*, December 9, 2022, https://www.counterpunch.org/2022/12/09/words-ache-indifference-kills. We want to insert an important point articulated by Cohen in this article. He states that while the hate speech of West, Fuentes, and other white supremacist reflects both the rot of its speakers and an emerging fascist politics in the United States, it should not undermine or silence critics of the Israeli state. He writes:

> Today politicians, pundits, journalists and liberals alike express, as they should, outrage over the "recent" putrid outbursts spewed not just from West and Fuentes, but other equally failed and ignorant white supremacists who proudly target and deplore persons of different color, of different faith, of different sexual identity [yet] their silence about Israel ... speaks volumes of their discerning support of but certain faiths, certain ethnicities, certain cultures, certain histories to the exclusion of others. Nowhere is that more palpable than it is in the almost deafening silence about systemic human rights abuses perpetrated by Israel throughout Palestine.

25. Chris Walker, "Trump Hosts Mar-a-Lago Meeting with Kanye West, Holocaust Denier Nick Fuentes," *Truthout*, November 28, 2022, https://truthout.org/articles/trump-hosts-mar-a-lago-meeting-with-kanye-west-holocaust-denier-nick-fuentes/

26 Jamelle Bouie, "Republicans Hate Everything About Trump's Dinner with Ye and Fuentes Except Trump," *The New York Times*, November 29, 2022, https://www.nytimes.com/2022/11/29/opinion/trump-ye-fuentes-mar-a-lago.html

27 Michelle Boorstein and Isaac Arnsdorf, "Overt U.S. Antisemitism Returns with Trump, Kanye West: 'Something is Different'," *The Washington Post*, October 27, 2022, https://www.washingtonpost.com/religion/2022/10/27/antisemitism-kanye-trump-adidas-jews/

28 This issue has been explored by Zygmunt Bauman in a number of books. See, especially, *Wasted Lives* (London: Polity Press, 2004) and *Identity: Conversations with Benedetto Vecchi* (London: Polity Press, 2004).

29 Clarence Lusane, "The MAGAfication of America," *CounterPunch*, December 1, 2022, https://www.counterpunch.org/2022/12/01/the-magafication-of-america/

30 Ibid.

31 Geoff Mann, "Is Fascism the Wave of the Future?" *The New Statesman*, February 11, 2022, https://www.newstatesman.com/ideas/2022/02/is-fascism-the-wave-of-the-future

32 Lusane, "The MAGAfication of America."

33 David Graeber, *The Democracy Project: A History, A Crisis, A Movement* (London: Penguin, 2014), p. xviii.

34 Albert Einstein, "Why Socialism?" *Monthly Review*, Vol. 61, no. 01 (May 2009), https://monthlyreview.org/2009/05/01/why-socialism/; see also Alfredo Saad-Filho, "The Left Must Seize This Moment, or Others Will," *Jacobin Magazine*, April 23, 2020, https://www.jacobinmag.com/2020/04/coronavirus-crisis-covid-economy-recession-pandemic

35 See for instance, Michael Lerner's brilliant book *Revolutionary Love: A Political Manifesto to Heal and Transform the World* (Berkeley: University of California Press, 2019).

36 Audre Lorde, "Learning from the 60s," *BlackPast*, August 12, 2012 (originally delivered as a speech at Harvard University in February 1962), https://www.blackpast.org/african-american-history/1982-audre-lorde-learning-60s/#:~:text=As%20Black%20people%2C%20if%20there,forced%20to%20take%20into%20ourselves

37 Khalid Lyamlahy, "The Professional Stranger: On Abdelkebir Khatibi's 'Plural Maghreb'," *Los Angeles Review of Books*, December 3, 2019, https://lareviewofbooks.org/article/the-professional-stranger-on-abdelkebir-khatibis-plural-maghreb/

38 Stuart Hall and David Held, "Citizens and Citizenship," in *New Times*, ed. Stuart Hall and Jacques Martin (London: Verso, 1990), p. 175.

39 Robin D. G. Kelley and Deborah Chasman, "Fascism Never Disappears Because People Come to Their Senses," *Boston Review*, November 21, 2022, https://www.bostonreview.net/articles/fascism-never-disappears-because-people-come-to-their-senses/?utm_source=Boston+Review+Email+Subscribers&utm_campaign=0b0a11bd1a-roundup_november_22&utm_medium=email&utm_term=0_2cb428c5ad-0b0a11bd1a-41183853&mc_cid=0b0a11bd1a&mc_eid=2d6289191d

Chapter 8

1 Harriet Sherwood, "Nearly Two-Thirds of US Young Adults Unaware 6m Jews Killed in Holocaust," *The Guardian*, September 16, 2020, https://www.theguardian.com/world/2020/sep/16/holocaust-us-adults-study

2 Richard Luscombe, "US Libraries Face 'Unprecedented' Efforts to Ban Books on Race and Gender Themes," *The Guardian*, September 16, 2022, https://www.theguardian.com/us-news/2022/sep/16/us-libraries-book-ban-challenges-race-gender

3 Clarisa Diaz, "Book Bans are Spiking in the US. Here are the Most Targeted Titles," *Quartz*, September 22, 2022, https://qz.com/book-bans-are-spiking-in-the-us-here-are-the-most-targ-1849565948

4 Moms for Liberty, "Who We Are," *Moms for Liberty*, 2023, https://www.momsforliberty.org/about/

5 Ibid.

6 Ibid.

7 Elena Fishbein, "Our Origin," *No Left Turn in Education*, 2023, https://www.noleftturn.us/about-us/

8 Elena Fishbein, "Missions, Goals, and Objectives," *No Left Turn in Education*, 2023, https://www.noleftturn.us/mission-goals-objectives/

9 Erik Eckholm, "In Hillsdale College, a 'Shining City on a Hill' for Conservatives," *The New York Times*, February 1, 2017, https://www.nytimes.com/2017/02/01/education/edlife/hillsdale-college-great-books-constitution-conservatives.html

10 Fishbein, "Missions, Goals, and Objectives."

11 Varda Liberman, Julia A. Minson, Christopher J. Bryan, and Lee Ross, "Naïve Realism and Capturing the 'Wisdom of Dyads'," *Journal of Experimental Social Psychology*, Vol. 48, no. 2 (2011), pp. 507–512.

12 Anthony DiMaggio, "White Supremacy 2.0: DeSantis's Big Brother Assault on Higher Education," *CounterPunch*, February 10, 2023.

13 Jack Jenkins, "Republicans Mostly Mum on Calls to Make GOP 'Party of Christian Nationalism'," *The Washington Post*, August 19, 2022, https://www.washingtonpost.com/religion/2022/08/19/republicans-mostly-mum-calls-make-gop-party-christian-nationalism/

14 Elizabeth Dias, "The Far-Right Christian Quest for Power: 'We Are Seeing Them Emboldened'," *The New York Times*, July 13, 2022, https://www.nytimes.com/2022/07/08/us/christian-nationalism-politicians.html

15 Kathryn Joyce, "'Without the Bible, There is No America': Josh Hawley Goes Full Christian Nationalist at NatCon," *Salon*, September 13, 2022, https://www.salon.com/2022/09/13/without-the-bible-there-is-no-america-josh-hawley-goes-full-christian-nationalist-at-natcon/

16 Amy Eskind, "Ron DeSantis' Campaign Ad Says He Was Sent by God to 'Take the Arrows'," *People*, November 7, 2022, https://people.com/politics/ron-desantis-god-made-fighter-ad/

17 Chris Cillizza, "Yes Donald Trump Really Believes He is 'the Chosen One'," *CNN*, August 24, 2019, https://www.cnn.com/2019/08/21/politics/donald-trump-chosen-one/index.html; Darragh Roche, "Trump Responds to Meme Saying He's the 'Savior of Western Civilization'," *Newsweek*, February 10, 2023, https://www.newsweek.com/trump-meme-savior-western-civilization-1780370

18 Stella Rouse and Shibley Telhami, "Most Republicans Support Declaring the United States a Christian Nation," *Politico*, September 21, 2022, https://www.politico.com/news/magazine/2022/09/21/most-republicans-support-declaring-the-united-states-a-christian-nation-00057736

19 George Gao, "How Do Americans Stand Out from the Rest of the World," *Pew Research Center*, March 12, 2015, https://www.pewresearch.org/fact-tank/2015/03/12/how-do-americans-stand-out-from-the-rest-of-the-world/

20 Kelsey Dallas, "Many Americans Say God Inspired the Constitution … Except That Part About Guns," *Deseret News*, April 23, 2022, https://www.deseret.com/faith/2022/4/22/23036178/many-americans-

say-god-inspired-the-constitution-except-that-part-about-guns-pew-research-marist

21 PRRI Staff, "Dueling Realities: Amid Multiple Crises, Trump and Biden Supporters See Different Priorities and Futures for the Nation," *Public Religion Research Institute*, October 19, 2020, https://www.prri.org/research/amid-multiple-crises-trump-and-biden-supporters-see-different-realities-and-futures-for-the-nation/

22 Michael Lipka, "Half of Americans Say Bible Should Influence U.S. Laws, Including 28% Who Favor it Over the Will of the People," *Pew Research Center*, April 13, 2020, https://www.pewresearch.org/fact-tank/2020/04/13/half-of-americans-say-bible-should-influence-u-s-laws-including-28-who-favor-it-over-the-will-of-the-people/

23 Tom Jensen, "Republican Majority Would Support Christianity as 'National Religion'," *Public Policy Polling*, February 26, 2015, https://www.publicpolicypolling.com/news/republican-majority-would-support-christianity-as-national-religion/

24 Ibid.

25 Michel Martin and Tinbette Ermyas, "Former Pentagon Chief Esper Says Trump Asked About Shooting Protesters," *National Public Radio*, May 9, 2022, https://www.npr.org/2022/05/09/1097517470/trump-esper-book-defense-secretary; Fadel Allassan, "Poll: 62% of Trump Supporters Say Nothing He Could Do Would Change Opinion," *Axios*, November 5, 2019, https://www.axios.com/2019/11/05/monmouth-poll-trump-approval

26 PRRI Staff, "Dueling Realities."

27 Robert P. Jones, "Racism Among White Christians is Higher Than Among the Nonreligious. That's No Coincidence," *NBC News*, July 27, 2020, https://www.nbcnews.com/think/opinion/racism-among-white-christians-higher-among-nonreligious-s-no-coincidence-ncna1235045; Robert P. Jones, *White Too Long: The Legacy of White Supremacy in American Christianity* (New York: Simon & Schuster, 2021).

28 Olivia Rubin, Lucien Bruggerman, and Will Steakin, "QAnon Emerges as Recurring Theme of Criminal Cases Tied to US Capitol Siege," *ABC News*, January 19, 2021, https://abcnews.go.com/US/qanon-emerges-recurring-theme-criminal-cases-tied-us/story?id=75347445

29 Tiffany Hsu, "QAnon Accounts Found a Home, and Trump's Support, on Truth Social," *The New York Times*, August 31, 2022, https://www.nytimes.com/2022/08/29/technology/qanon-truth-social-trump.html

30 Zachary Cohen, "What We Know About Infamous Oval Office Meeting Held by Trump's Inner Circle in December 2020," *CNN*, July 12, 2022, https://www.cnn.com/2022/07/12/politics/trump-oval-office-meeting-december-2020/index.html

31 Axios Staff, "Trump Praises QAnon Supporters: 'I Understand They Like Me Very Much'," *Axios*, August 19, 2020, https://www.axios.com/2020/08/19/trump-praises-qanon-supporters-i-understand-they-like-me-very-much

32 Chris Cillizza, "Donald Trump's New Low on QAnon," *CNN*, October 16, 2020, https://www.cnn.com/2020/10/16/politics/donald-trump-qanon-pedophilia/index.html

33 David Gilbert, "Trump's Not Even Pretending to Hide His Support for QAnon Any More," *Vice*, September 13, 2022, https://www.vice.com/en/article/epzbya/trump-support-qanon

34 David Klepper and Ali Swenson, "Trump Begins Openly Embracing and Amplifying False Fringe QAnon Conspiracy Theory," *PBS News Hour*, September 16, 2022, https://www.pbs.org/newshour/politics/trump-begins-openly-embracing-and-amplifying-false-fringe-qanon-conspiracy-theory

35 John General and Richa Naik, "QAnon is Spreading Amongst Evangelicals. These Pastors are Trying to Stop it," *CNN*, May 23, 2021, https://www.cnn.com/2021/05/23/business/qanon-evangelical-pastors/index.html; Ari Shapiro, "How QAnon Conspiracy is Spreading in Christian Communities Across the U.S.," *National Public Radio*, August 21, 2020, https://www.npr.org/2020/08/21/904798097/how-qanon-conspiracy-is-spreading-in-christian-communities-across-the-u-s

36 Tal Lavin, "QAnon, Blood Libel, and the Satanic Panic," *The New Republic*, September 29, 2020, https://newrepublic.com/article/159529/qanon-blood-libel-satanic-panic

37 Ewan Palmer, "Nearly Half of QAnon Followers Believe Jews Plotting to Rule the World," *Newsweek*, June 28, 2021, https://www.newsweek.com/qanon-antisemitism-morning-consult-survey-1604752

38 Mike Rothschild, *The Storm is Upon Us: How QAnon Became a Movement, Cult, and Conspiracy Theory of Everything* (Brooklyn, NY: Melville House, 2021).

39 Rachel Scully, "Trump Calls Biden 'An Enemy of the State'," *The Hill*, September 4, 2022, https://thehill.com/homenews/state-watch/3628611-trump-calls-biden-an-enemy-of-the-state/; Kyle Cheney, "'Where are All of the Arrests?': Trump Demands Barr Lock

Up His Foes," *Politico*, October 7, 2020, https://www.politico.com/news/2020/10/07/trump-demands-barr-arrest-foes-427389

40 Paul Hanebrink, *A Specter Haunting Europe: The Myth of Judeo-Bolshevism* (Cambridge: Harvard University Press, 2020).

41 Richard Stengel, "It Can Happen Here: 8 Great Books to Read About the Decline of Democracy; Reading List," *The New York Times*, November 2, 2022; Hamilton Cain, "Alone Together," *The New York Times*, October 2, 2022, BR15; Hamilton Cain, "What Happens When Ex-Spouses Quarantine Together?" *The New York Times*, September 16, 2022.

42 Anthony DiMaggio, "Erasing QAnon Fascism: A Case Study in Black Comedy," *CounterPunch*, September 19, 2022, https://www.counterpunch.org/2022/09/19/erasing-qanon-fascism-a-case-study-in-black-comedy/

Chapter 9

1 Candice Bernd, "Red States Plot Use of Vigilantes to Restrict Abortion Seekers' Travel," *Truthout*, July 11, 2022, https://truthout.org/articles/red-states-plot-use-of-vigilantes-to-restrict-abortion-seekers-travel/

2 Kathryn Joyce, "Right-Wing 'American Birthright' Curriculum Pushes Christianity, Obscures Racism," *Truthout*, July 8, 2022, https://truthout.org/articles/right-wing-american-birthright-curriculum-pushes-christianity-obscures-racism/

3 Jason Stanley and Federico Finchelstein, "White Replacement Theory is Fascism's New Name," *Los Angeles Times*, May 24, 2022, https://www.latimes.com/opinion/story/2022-05-24/white-replacement-theory-fascism-europe-history

4 Clarence Lusane, "The GOP Has a Klan Problem That is Not Going Away," *TomDispatch*, September 17, 2023, https://tomdispatch.com/the-political-rise-of-a-new-white-nationalism/

5 Ishaan Tharoor, "Democracy is in Decline Around the World—and Trump is Part of the Problem," *The Washington Post*, March 5, 2020, https://www.washingtonpost.com/world/2020/03/05/democracy-is-decline-around-world-trump-is-part-problem/

6 Staff, "2020 Marked 15th Straight Year of Declining World Freedom: Report," *Aljazeera*, March 3, 2021, https://www.aljazeera.com/news/2021/3/3/2020-15th-straight-year-declining-global-freedom-report

7 Ibid.

8   Ibid.
9   Hazel Carby, "We Must Burn Them," *London Review of Books*, May 26, 2022, https://www.lrb.co.uk/the-paper/v44/n10/hazel-v.-carby/we-must-burn-them
10 Nikole Hannah-Jones, "'The 1619 Project,' Teaching Critical Race Theory & White Supremacy on Trial," *Democracy Now*, November 23, 2021, https://www.democracynow.org/2021/11/23/nikole_hannah_jones_1619_project
11 Amy Goodman, "Angela Davis: 'Forces of White Supremacy' Are Behind Attacks on Teaching Critical Race Theory," *Democracy Now!*, November 19, 2021, https://www.democracynow.org/2021/11/19/angela_davis_us_critical_race_theory
12 Paul Gilroy, "The 2019 Holberg Lecture, by Laureate Paul Gilroy: Never Again: Refusing Race and Salvaging the Human," *Holbergprisen*, November 11, 2019, https://holbergprisen.no/en/news/holberg-prize/2019-holberg-lecture-laureate-paul-gilroy
13 Thom Hartmann, "All the GOP Has Left is Racism & That's a Lie, Too," *Hartmann Report*, February 16, 2022, https://hartmannreport.com/p/all-the-gop-has-left-is-racism-and. For an analysis of the scope of racism in America and the struggle to resist it, some definitive sources include: Angela Davis, *Women, Race, and Class* (New York: Knopf Doubleday, 1983); Robin D. G. Kelley, *Race Rebels: Culture, Politics, and the Black Working Class* (New York: Free Press, 1996); David Theo Goldberg, *The Racial State* (New York: Wiley-Blackwell, 2001); Tyler Stovall, *White Freedom: The Racial History of an Idea* (Princeton: Princeton University Press, 2021); Ibram X, Kendi and Keisha N. Blain, *Four Hundred Souls* (New York: One World, 2021).
14 Hartmann, "All the GOP Has Left is Racism & That's a Lie, Too." See also, Deena Zaru, "The Symbols of Hate and Far-Right Extremism on Display in Pro-Trump Capitol Siege," *ABC News*, January 14, 2021, https://abcnews.go.com/US/symbols-hate-extremism-display-pro-trump-capitol-siege/story?id=75177671
15 Jonathan Chait, "Blake Masters, Nazi-Adjacent Arizona Republican Senate Candidate Another Sign of the GOP's Radicalization," *New York*, July 7, 2022, https://nymag.com/intelligencer/2022/07/blake-masters-nazi-adjacent-arizona-gop-senate-candidate.html
16 Ibid.
17 Tom Nichols, "Are the Last Rational Republicans in Denial?" *The Atlantic*, July 6, 2022, https://www.theatlantic.com/newsletters/archive/2022/07/are-the-last-rational-republicans-in-denial/661503/

18 Eliza Griswold, "A Pennsylvania Lawmaker and the Resurgence of Christian Nationalism," *The New Yorker*, May 9, 2021, https://www.newyorker.com/news/on-religion/a-pennsylvania-lawmaker-and-the-resurgence-of-christian-nationalism

19 Philip Rucker, "'A Blowtorch to the Tinder': Stoking Racial Tensions is a Feature of Trump's Presidency," *The Washington Post*, June 20, 2012, https://www.washingtonpost.com/politics/a-blowtorch-to-the-tinder-stoking-racial-tensions-is-a-feature-of-trumps-presidency/2018/06/20/e95e71dc-73d9-11e8-805c-4b67019fcfe4_story.html

20 See, for instance, Sam Fullwood III, "Trump Outdoes Himself with Latest Display of Rank Hatred and Rancid Bigotry," *Think Progress*, July 18, 2019, https://thinkprogress.org/the-stench-of-racism-envelops-trump-and-the-gop-45113a1f61c2/; Colbert I. King, "The Most Racist President in Modern History Revels in Violence," *The Washington Post*, June 12, 2020, https://www.washingtonpost.com/opinions/the-most-racist-president-in-modern-history-revels-in-violence/2020/06/12/c406fee4-ac1d-11ea-a9d9-a81c1a491c52_story.html; Peter Baker, "More Than Ever, Trump Casts Himself as the Defender of White America," *The New York Times*, September 6, 2020, https://www.nytimes.com/2020/09/06/us/politics/trump-race-2020-election.html; Eugene Robinson, "Trump is Shouting his Racism. He Must be Stopped," *The Washington Post*, September 7, 2020, https://www.washingtonpost.com/opinions/trump-is-shouting-his-racism-he-must-be-stopped/2020/09/07/06036768-f13a-11ea-bc45-e5d48ab44b9f_story.html

21 Gilroy, "The 2019 Holberg Lecture."

22 Wajahat Ali, "No, Our Institutions Didn't Hold After Jan. 6—Just Look at the GOP," *The Daily Beast*, June 23, 2022, https://www.thedailybeast.com/no-our-institutions-didnt-hold-after-jan-6just-look-at-the-gop

23 On the issue of inverted totalitarianism and economic sovereignty, see Sheldon S. Wolin, *Democracy Incorporated: Managed Democracy and the Specter of Inverted Totalitarianism* (Princeton: University Press, 2008).

24 Michael Gillespie, "Biden Visits Ukraine and Ignores East Palestine," personal email, February 21, 2023.

25 Cleve R. Wootson Jr., "Trump and Allies Try to Redefine Racism by Casting White Men as Victims," *The Washington Post*, February 5, 2022, https://www.washingtonpost.com/politics/2022/02/05/trump-redefine-racism/

26 Viktor Frankl, "Viktor Frankl on Reductionism," *Psychology & Spirituality*, January 7, 2018, https://www.thecontemplativelife.org/blog/victor-frankl-on-reductionism
27 Gilroy, "The 2019 Holberg Lecture."
28 George Yancy, "Robin Kelley: White Indifference is Normalizing Spectacular Acts of Violence," *Truthout*, May 5, 2022, https://truthout.org/articles/robin-kelley-white-indifference-is-normalizing-spectacular-acts-of-violence/
29 Rob Nixon, *Slow Violence and the Environmentalism of the Poor* (Cambridge: Harvard University Press, 2011), p. 2.
30 Ibid., p. 3.
31 James Baldwin, "A Talk to Teachers," *Zinn Education Project: Teaching People's History*, October 16, 1963, https://www.zinnedproject.org/materials/baldwin-talk-to-teachers (delivered in a speech first on October 16, 1963, as "The Negro Child—His Self-Image" and originally published in *The Saturday Review*, December 21, 1963, and then reprinted in *The Price of the Ticket, Collected Non-Fiction 1948–1985* (New York: Saint Martin's Press, 1985).
32 Kathleen Belew, *Bring the War Home: The White Power Movement and Paramilitary America* (Cambridge: Harvard University Press, 2019).
33 David Smith, "The January 6 Panel Said Trump Incited an 'Attempted Coup'. Will it Kill Him or Make Him Stronger?" *The Guardian*, June 11, 2022, https://www.theguardian.com/us-news/2022/jun/11/jan-6-hearings-capitol-attack-trump-coup-analysis. The final report of the January 6th committee can be found here: https://www.govinfo.gov/collection/january-6th-committee-final-report?path=/GPO/January%206th%20Committee%20Final%20Report%20and%20Supporting%20Materials%20Collection
34 January 6th Report.
35 Marshall Cohen, "Timeline of the Coup: How Trump Tried to Weaponize the Justice Department to Overturn the 2020 Election," *CNN Politics*, November 5, 2021, https://www.cnn.com/2021/11/05/politics/january-6-timeline-trump-coup/index.html; Ang Li and Rex Sakamoto, "Trump Leaned on Justice Dept. to Investigate Election Fraud Claims," *The New York Times*, June 23, 2022, https://www.nytimes.com/video/us/politics/100000008414289/jan-6-hearing-trump-doj.html?playlistId=video/jan-6-committee-hearing-video;

36 David A. Graham, "The Most Damning January 6 Testimony Yet," *The Atlantic*, June 28, 2022, https://www.theatlantic.com/ideas/archive/2022/06/january-6-hearings-trump-cassidy-hutchinson/661414/?utm_source=newsletter&utm_medium=email&utm_campaign=atlantic-daily-newsletter&utm_content=20220628&utm_term=The%20Atlantic%20Daily

37 Steve Benen, "Supreme Court: 2nd Amendment Guarantees Right to Carry Guns in Public," *MSNBC*, June 23, 2022, https://www.msnbc.com/rachel-maddow-show/maddowblog/supreme-court-2nd-amendment-guarantees-right-carry-guns-public-rcna34990

38 Peter Baker, "Trump Is Depicted as a Would-Be Autocrat Seeking to Hang Onto Power at All Costs," *The New York Times*, June 9, 2022, https://www.nytimes.com/2022/06/09/us/politics/trump-jan-6-hearing.html

39 Peter Wehner, "A Withering Indictment of the Entire GOP," *The Atlantic*, June 29, 2022, https://www.theatlantic.com/ideas/archive/2022/06/hutchinson-testimony-deranged-seditious-president/661424/

40 Maanvi Singh, "January 6 Hearing: Five Key Takeaways from the First Primetime Capitol Attack Inquiry," *The Guardian*, June 10, 2022, https://www.theguardian.com/us-news/2022/jun/09/january-6-hearing-five-key-takeaways-us-capitol-attack

41 Harry Enten, "Donald Trump has Become More Popular Since the January 6 Capitol Attack," *CNN Politics*, June 11, 2022, https://www.cnn.com/2022/06/11/politics/donald-trump-january-6-democrats-moderate/index.html

42 Ruth Ben-Ghiat, *Strongmen: Mussolini to the Present* (New York: W. W. Norton, 2021).

43 Vaclav Havel, "Politics and Conscience," translated into English by Erazim Kohák and Roger Scruton, *Salisbury Review*, No. 2 (Jan 1985), https://www.dadychery.org/2012/03/25/politics-and-conscience-an-essay-by-vaclav-havel/

44 Cited in Paul Morrow, "The Emperor's New Clothes and Pluralistic Ignorance," *Hannah Arendt Center*, May 27, 2014, https://hac.bard.edu/amor-mundi/the-emperors-new-clothes-and-pluralistic-ignorance-2014-05-27

45 Frederick Douglass, *Narrative of the Life of Federick Douglass, an American Slave* (Victoria, B.C.: Mint Editions, 2022), p. 31.

Chapter 10

1. Susan Milligan, "Three-Quarters of Republicans Sympathize with Jan. 6 Rioters: Poll," *US News and World Report*, January 4, 2022, https://www.usnews.com/news/politics/articles/2022-01-04/three-quarters-of-republicans-sympathize-with-jan-6-rioters-poll; Brittany Shepherd, "Majority of Americans Think Jan. 6 Attack Threatened Democracy: POLL," *ABC News*, January 2, 2022, https://abcnews.go.com/Politics/majority-americans-jan-attack-threatened-democracy-poll/story?id=81990555

2. Stefan Kuhl, *The Nazi Connection: Eugenics, American Racism, and German National Socialism* (New York: Oxford University Press, 1994); C. Kakel, *The American West and the Nazi East: A Comparative and Interpretive Perspective* (New York: Palgrave Macmillan, 2011); James Q. Whitman, *Hitler's American Model: The United States and the Making of Nazi Race Law* (Princeton: Princeton University Press, 2018); Timothy Snyder, *Black Earth: The Holocaust as History and Warning* (New York: Crown, 2016).

3. U.S. House of Representatives, "Final Report of the Select Committee to Investigate the January 6th Attack on the United States Capitol," *United States House of Representatives*, December 22, 2022, https://www.govinfo.gov/content/pkg/GPO-J6-REPORT/pdf/GPO-J6-REPORT.pdf

4. Anthony DiMaggio, "Jan. 6 as White Supremacy: New Research on the Toxic Spread of 'Great Replacement' Theory," *Salon*, December 8, 2022, https://www.salon.com/2022/12/08/jan-6-as-supremacy-new-research-on-the-spread-of-great-replacement-theory/

5. Brandon Tensley, "The Racist Rhetoric Behind Accusing Largely Black Cities of Voter Fraud," *CNN*, November 20, 2020, https://www.cnn.com/2020/11/20/politics/trump-giuliani-black-cities-analysis/index.html

6. Cassie Miller, "SPLC Poll Finds Substantial Support for 'Great Replacement' Theory and Other Hard-Right Ideas," *Southern Poverty Law Center*, June 1, 2022, https://www.splcenter.org/news/2022/06/01/poll-finds-support-great-replacement-hard-right-ideas

7. U.S. House of Representatives, "Final Report … to Investigate the January 6th Attack"; Lane Crothers and Grace Burgener, "Insurrectionary Populism? Assessing the January 6 Attack on the U.S. Capitol," *Populism*, Vol. 4, no. 2 (2021), pp. 129–145; Brandon Tensley, "The Racist Rhetoric Behind Accusing Largely Black Cities

of Voter Fraud," *CNN*, November 20, 2020, https://www.cnn.com/2020/11/20/politics/trump-giuliani-black-cities-analysis/index.html

8 Anthony DiMaggio, "White Supremacy and January 6: What's Missing from the Congressional Report," *CounterPunch*, December 30, 2022, https://www.counterpunch.org/2022/12/30/white-supremacy-and-january-6-whats-missing-from-the-congressional-report/

9 Ibid.

10 Ibid.

11 Kyle Kondik, J. Miles Coleman, and Larry J. Sabato, "New Poll: Some Americans Express Troubling Racial Attitudes Even as Majority Oppose White Supremacists," *UVA Center for Politics*, September 14, 2017, https://centerforpolitics.org/crystalball/articles/new-poll-some-americans-express-troubling-racial-attitudes-even-as-majority-oppose-white-supremacists/; Anita Snow and Hannah Fingerhut, "AP-NORC Poll: Americans Agree on Many Aspects of US Identity," *Associated Press*, October 21, 2019, https://apnews.com/article/immigration-donald-trump-ap-top-news-politics-united-states-466e86ac67ef4c609b6ee28e5eb151d9

12 Robert Pape, "Understanding American Domestic Terrorism: Mobilization Potential and Risk Factors of a New Threat Trajectory," *Chicago Project on Security and Threats*, April 6, 2021, https://d3qi0qp55mx5f5.cloudfront.net/cpost/i/docs/americas_insurrectionists_online_2021_04_06.pdf?mtime=1617807009

13 Philip S. Gorski and Samuel L. Perry, *The Flag and the Cross: White Christian Nationalism and the Threat to American Democracy* (New York: Oxford University Press, 2022).

14 Reuters/IPSOS/UVA Center for Politics, "Race Poll," *UVA Center for Politics*, September 14, 2017, https://www.ipsos.com/sites/default/files/ct/news/documents/2017-09/2017%20Reuters%20UVA%20Ipsos%20Race%20Poll%209%2014%202017_0.pdf

15 Tim Elfrink, "Tucker Carlson Says White Supremacy is a Hoax," *The Washington Post*, August 7, 2019, https://www.washingtonpost.com/nation/2019/08/07/tucker-carlson-white-supremacy-hoax-lie-not-real-problem/; Media Matters Staff, "Rush Limbaugh: White Supremacists 'Are Such a Small Number You Could Put Them in a Phone Booth'," *Media Matters for America*, June 2, 2020, https://www.mediamatters.org/rush-limbaugh/rush-limbaugh-white-supremacists-are-such-small-number-you-could-put-them-phone-booth; Donna Brazile, "Obama a Marker on Post-Racial Path," *CNN*, February 21, 2013, https://www.

cnn.com/2013/02/21/opinion/brazile-black-history-crossroads/index.html; Daniel Schor, "A New, 'Post-Racial' Political Era in America," *National Public Radio*, January 28, 2008, https://www.npr.org/templates/story/story.php?storyId=18489466; William Julius Wilson, *The Declining Significance of Race: Blacks and Changing American Institutions* (Chicago: University of Chicago Press, 2022); Richard J. Payne, *Getting Beyond Race: The Changing American Culture* (New York: Basic Books, 1998).

16 Anthony DiMaggio, "Jan. 6 as White Supremacy: New Research on the Toxic Spread of 'Great Replacement' Theory," *Salon*, December 8, 2022, https://www.salon.com/2022/12/08/jan-6-as-supremacy-new-research-on-the-spread-of-great-replacement-theory/

17 Ibid.

18 Fadel Allassan, "Poll: 62 Percent of Trump Supporters Say Nothing He Could Do Would Change Opinion," *Axios*, November 5, 2019, https://www.axios.com/2019/11/05/monmouth-poll-trump-approval; Bradley Jones, "Fewer Americans Now Say Trump Bears a Lot of Responsibility for the Jan. 6 Riot," *Pew Research Center*, February 8, 2022, https://www.pewresearch.org/fact-tank/2022/02/08/fewer-americans-now-say-trump-bears-a-lot-of-responsibility-for-the-jan-6-riot/

19 Charlie Savage and Glenn Thrush, "Jan. 6 and Mar-a-Lago Inquiries Converge in Fights Over Executive Privilege," *The New York Times*, September 30, 2022, https://www.nytimes.com/2022/09/30/us/politics/trump-executive-privilege.html

20 Yamiche Alcindor, "White House Blocks Donald Trump from Withholding Documents on Jan. 6 Attack," *PBS*, October 8, 2021, https://www.pbs.org/newshour/politics/white-house-blocks-donald-trump-from-withholding-documents-on-jan-6-attack

21 Simone Carter, "Donald Trump Praises Jan. 6 Rioters. 'Great Patriots'," *Newsweek*, January 14, 2023, https://www.newsweek.com/donald-trump-praises-jan-6-rioters-great-patriots-1773808

22 Dominick Mastrangelo, "Limbaugh Dismisses Calls to End Violence After Mob Hits Capitol," *The Hill*, January 7, 2021, https://thehill.com/homenews/533236-limbaugh-dismisses-calls-to-end-violence-after-mob-hits-capitol/

23 Media Matters Staff, "Rush Limbaugh: Pro-Trump Mob 'Undoubtedly' Included 'Some Antifa Democrat-Sponsored Instigators'," *Media Matters for America*, January 7, 2021, https://www.mediamatters.org/january-6-insurrection/rush-limbaugh-pro-trump-mob-undoubtedly-included-some-antifa-democrat

24 Media Matters Staff, "Tucker Carlson Marks January 6 Anniversary by Calling it a 'Wholly Created Myth'," *Media Matters for America*, January 6, 2023, https://www.mediamatters.org/fox-news/tucker-carlson-marks-january-6-anniversary-calling-it-wholly-created-myth

25 Jonathan Weisman and Reid J. Epstein, "G.O.P. Declares Jan. 6 Attack 'Legitimate Political Discourse'," *The New York Times*, February 4, 2022, https://www.nytimes.com/2022/02/04/us/politics/republicans-jan-6-cheney-censure.html

26 Jon Greenberg, "Most Republicans Still Falsely Believe Trump's Stolen Election Claims. Here Are Some Reasons Why," *Poynter*, June 16, 2022, https://www.poynter.org/fact-checking/2022/70-percent-republicans-falsely-believe-stolen-election-trump/

27 Mark Murray, "Poll: 61% of Republicans Still Believe Biden Didn't Win Fair and Square in 2020," *NBCNews*, September 27, 2022, https://www.nbcnews.com/meet-the-press/meetthepressblog/poll-61-republicans-still-believe-biden-didnt-win-fair-square-2020-rcna49630

28 New York Times, "September 2022 Times/Siena Poll: Cross-Tabs for All Respondents," *The New York Times*, September 16, 2022, https://www.nytimes.com/interactive/2022/09/16/upshot/september-2022-times-siena-poll-crosstabs.html

29 CNN, "READ: Trump Lawyer's Memo on Six-Step Plan for Pence to Overturn the Election," *CNN*, September 21, 2021, https://www.cnn.com/2021/09/21/politics/read-eastman-memo/index.html

30 BBC, "Donald Trump: 'I Just Want to Find 11,780 Votes'," *BBC*, January 3, 2021, https://www.bbc.com/news/av/world-us-canada-55524676

31 Brian Naylor, "Read Trump's Jan. 6 Speech, A Key Part of Impeachment Trial," *National Public Radio*, February 10, 2021, https://www.npr.org/2021/02/10/966396848/read-trumps-jan-6-speech-a-key-part-of-impeachment-trial

32 Lexi Lonas, "Sasse Says Trump was 'Delighted' and 'Excited' by Reports of Capitol Riot," *The Hill*, January 8, 2021, https://thehill.com/homenews/senate/533403-sasse-says-trump-was-delighted-and-excited-by-reports-of-capitol-riot/; CNN, "'Chilling': GOP Lawmaker Describes Trump's Call with McCarthy on Jan. 6," *CNN*, July 22, 2022, https://www.cnn.com/videos/politics/2022/07/22/kevin-mccarthy-trump-calls-january-6-hearing-vpx.cnn

33 Anthony DiMaggio, "Qualtrics Survey of White Nationalism in America," February 2023.

NOTES

34 William A. Galston, "What Are Americans Thinking about the January 6 Hearings?" *Brookings*, June 23, 2022, https://www.brookings.edu/blog/fixgov/2022/06/23/what-are-americans-thinking-about-the-january-6-hearings/

35 Jennifer Agiesta, "CNN Poll: January 6 Hearings Haven't Changed Opinions Much, But Most Agree Trump Acted Unethically," *CNN*, July 26, 2022, https://www.cnn.com/2022/07/26/politics/cnn-poll-january-6-trump/index.html

36 Ibid.

37 Monmouth University, "Jan. 6 Hearings Have No Impact on Opinion," *Monmouth University*, August 9, 2022, https://www.monmouth.edu/polling-institute/reports/monmouthpoll_us_080922/

38 Ibid.

39 Nick Corasaniti, Michael C. Bender, Ruth Igielnik, and Kristen Bayrakdarian, "Voters See Democracy in Peril, But Saving It Isn't a Priority," *The New York Times*, October 18, 2022, https://www.nytimes.com/2022/10/18/us/politics/midterm-election-voters-democracy-poll.html

40 Matt Loffman, "Trump Should Not Run for President in 2024, Majority of Americans Say," *PBS*, September 7, 2022, https://www.pbs.org/newshour/politics/trump-should-not-run-for-president-in-2024-majority-of-americans-say

41 Michael C. Bender, "Half of G.O.P. Voters Ready to Leave Trump Behind, Poll Finds," *The New York Times*, July 12, 2022, https://www.nytimes.com/2022/07/12/us/politics/trump-approval-polling-2024.html

42 Nicholas Riccardi, "Nearly 1 in 3 Republican Candidates for Statewide Office Support False Election Claims," *PBS*, September 8, 2022, https://www.pbs.org/newshour/politics/nearly-1-in-3-republican-candidates-for-statewide-office-support-false-election-claims

43 FiveThirtyEight Staff, "60 Percent of Americans Will Have an Election Denier on the Ballot this Fall," *FiveThirtyEight*, November 8, 2022, https://projects.fivethirtyeight.com/republicans-trump-election-fraud/

44 Nina Totenberg, "Supreme Court to Hear Controversial Election-Law Case," *National Public Radio*, December 7, 2022, https://www.npr.org/2022/12/07/1140465909/supreme-court-independent-state-legislature-theory

Chapter 11

1. Robert O'Harrow Jr., Andrew Ba Tran and Derek Hawkins, "The Rise of Domestic Extremism in America," *The Washington Post*, April 12, 2021, https://www.washingtonpost.com/investigations/interactive/2021/domestic-terrorism-data/
2. Wajahat Ali, "It's Time to Call MAGA a National Security Threat," *The Daily Beast*, September 16, 2022, https://www.thedailybeast.com/its-time-to-call-maga-a-national-security-threat
3. Amy Goodman, "Historian of Radical Right: Biden Is Correct, Trump Poses Existential Threat to Future of Democracy," *Democracy Now*, September 9, 2022, https://www.democracynow.org/2022/9/2/biden_speech_maga_trump_democracy
4. G. M. Tamás, "On Post-Fascism," *Boston Review*, June 1, 2000, https://bostonreview.net/articles/g-m-tamas-post-fascism/
5. Ibid.
6. Cited in Blake Hounshell, "Warnings From Authors Who Track Domestic Extremism," *The New York Times*, September 16, 2022, https://www.nytimes.com/2022/09/16/us/politics/domestic-extremism-warnings.html
7. Cited in Maggie Haberman and Shane Goldmacher, "Trump, Vowing 'Retribution,' Foretells a Second Term of Spite," *The New York Times*, March 7, 2023, https://www.nytimes.com/2023/03/07/us/politics/trump-2024-president.html
8. Ruth Ben-Ghiat, "Victim and Avenger: The Fascist Roots of Trump's CPAC Speech," *Lucid*, March 7, 2023, https://lucid.substack.com/p/victim-and-avenger-the-fascist-roots?utm_source=direct&r=rls8&utm_campaign=post&utm_medium=web
9. For the war on youth, see Jeffrey St. Clair, "The Origins of America's Vicious War on Its Own Kids," *CounterPunch*, May 1, 2022, https://www.counterpunch.org/2022/05/01/the-origins-of-americas-vicious-war-on-its-own-kids-2/; Carl Suddler, *Presumed Criminal: Black Youth and the Justice System in Postwar New York* (New York: NYU Press, 2020); Henry A. Giroux, *America's Education Deficit and the War on Youth: Reform Beyond Electoral Politics* (New York: Monthly Review Press, 2013); Henry A. Giroux, *Youth in a Suspect Society* (New York: Palgrave, 2010); Mike Males, *The Scapegoat Generation: America's War on Adolescents* (Common Courage Press, 1996).

10 J. E. Goldstick, R. M. Cunningham, and P. Carter, "Current Causes of Death in Children and Adolescents in America," *New England Journal of Medicine*, 386 (2022), pp. 1955–1956.

11 Mike Males, "The Grotesque Lies That Keep America's Phony 'Gun Debate' Going," *LAP Progressive*, October 14, 2022, https://www.laprogressive.com/law-and-the-justice-system/phony-gun-debate

12 Dan Cassino, "Why Are Republicans So Focused on Restricting Trans Lives?" *The Washington Post*, March 21, 2022, https://www.washingtonpost.com/politics/2022/03/21/republican-trans-sports-texas-idaho-lgbtq/

13 See Henry A. Giroux, *American Nightmare: Facing the Challenge of Fascism* (San Francisco: City Lights Books, 2018); Carl Boggs, *Fascism Old and New: American Politics at the Crossroads* (New York: Routledge, 2018); Paul Street, *This Happened Here* (New York: Routledge, 2021); Anthony R. DiMaggio, *Rising Fascism in America: It Can Happen Here* (New York: Routledge, 2021).

14 Ruth Ben-Ghiat, "The Racist Demagoguery of Tucker Carlson and Trump Has a Fascist Lineage," *Lucid*, May 20, 2022, https://lucid.substack.com/p/the-racist-demagoguery-of-tucker

15 Colin P. Clarke and Tim Wilson, "Mainstreaming Extremism: The Legacy of Far-Right Violence from the Past to the Present," Foreign Policy Research Institute, October 11, 2022, https://www.fpri.org/article/2022/10/mainstreaming-extremism-the-legacy-of-far-right-violence-from-the-past-to-the-present/

16 Wajahat Ali, "Republicans Must Answer for 'Great Replacement Theory' Violence'," *The Daily Beast*, May 15, 2022, https://www.thedailybeast.com/republicans-must-answer-for-great-replacement-theory-violence

17 Anthony DiMaggio, "Christian White Supremacy Rising: The Fascist Connection," *CounterPunch*, September 28, 2022, https://www.counterpunch.org/2022/09/28/christian-white-supremacy-rising-the-fascist-connection/

18 Michelle R. Smith, "Michael Flynn: From Government Insider to Holy Warrior," *Frontline*, September 7, 2022, https://www.pbs.org/wgbh/frontline/article/michael-flynn-government-insider-holy-warrior/

19 Ibid.

20 Sam Adler-Bell, "The Violent Fantasies of Blake Masters," *The New York Times*, August 3, 2022, https://www.nytimes.com/2022/08/03/opinion/blake-masters-arizona-senate.html

21 Ibid.
22 Ibid.
23 Ibid.
24 Chris Hedges, "Let's Stop Pretending America Is a Functioning Democracy," *The Chris Hedges Report*, September 4, 2022, https://chrishedges.substack.com/p/lets-stop-pretending-america-is-a
25 Natasha Lennard, "It's a Girl (Fascist)!" *The Intercept*, September 26, 2022, https://theintercept.com/2022/09/26/giorgia-meloni-italy-fascist/
26 George Pendle, "They're with Her: Across Europe, a New Generation of Far-Right Female Politicians is Breaking Glass Ceilings (Among Other Things)," *Air Mail* 168, October 1, 2022, https://airmail.news/issues/2022-10-1/theyre-with-her
27 Ibid.
28 Henry A. Giroux, *Pedagogy of Resistance: Against Manufactured Ignorance* (London: Bloomsbury, 2022).
29 Henry A. Giroux, *Insurrections: Education in an Age of Counter-Revolutionary Politics* (London: Bloomsbury, 2023); see also Kelly Hayes, "Fascism Has Gone Mainstream," *Truthout*, September 9, 2022, https://truthout.org/audio/fascism-has-gone-mainstream/
30 Chris Hedges, "America's Theater of the Absurd," *The Chris Hedges Report*, January 8, 2023, https://chrishedges.substack.com/p/americas-theater-of-the-absurd
31 See especially Brad Evans's work on violence, especially his histories of violence site: https://www.historiesofviolence.com/conversations
32 Toni Morrison, "Racism and Fascism," *The Journal of Negro Education* (Summer 1995), pp. 384–385, https://www.leeannhunter.com/gender/wp-content/uploads/2012/11/Morrison-article.pdf
33 Benay Blend, "Biden's Battle for the 'Soul of America': On Calling out the Rising Fascism at Home but What About Abroad?" *The Palestine Chronicle*, September 12, 2022, https://www.palestinechronicle.com/bidens-battle-for-the-soul-of-america-on-calling-out-the-rising-fascism-at-home-but-what-about-abroad/
34 Ellen Willis, *Don't Think, Smile: Notes on a Decade of Denial* (Boston: Beacon Press, 1999), p. 13.
35 Stanley Aronowitz, "What Kind of Left Does America Need?" *Tikkun*, April 14, 2014, http://www.tikkun.org/nextgen/what-kind-of-left-does-america-need; Angela Davis on Amy Goodman, "Angela Davis on Abolition, Calls to Defund Police, Toppled Racist Statues & Voting in 2020 Election," *Democracy Now*, July 3, 2020, https://

www.democracynow.org/2020/7/3/angela_davis_on_abolition_calls_to; Barbara Epstein, "Prospects for a Resurgence of the US Left," *Tikkun*, Vol. 29, no. 2 (Spring 2014), pp. 41–44.

36 Chauncey Devega, "Holocaust Scholars Explain Why Trump Has Ramped Up His Nazi-style Rhetoric: 'Words Can Kill'," *Salon*, August 7, 2023, https://www.salon.com/2023/08/07/holocaust-scholars-explain-why-has-ramped-up-his-nazi-style-rhetoric-words-can-kill/

37 Franco 'Bifo' Berardi, *Heroes. Mass Murder and Suicide* (London: Verso, 2015), p. 9.

38 Henry A. Giroux and William Paul, "Educators and Critical Pedagogy: An Antidote to Authoritarianism," *Canadian Dimension*, October 16, 2022, https://canadiandimension.com/articles/view/educators-and-critical-pedagogy-an-antidote-to-authoritarianism?fbclid=IwAR1ynrqtPUZZiERwr8nioZC9BumB1s_T3TXup1a4F_2pYqwWeuePRjqdAto

39 Angela Y. Davis, Gina Dent, Erica R. Meiners and Beth E Richie, *Abolition. Feminism. Now* (Chicago: Haymarket, 2022).

Chapter 12

1 Anthony DiMaggio, "Rise of the Right: White Supremacy and the Myth of the 'White Working Class'," *CounterPunch*, July 23, 2021, https://www.counterpunch.org/2021/07/23/rise-of-the-right-white-supremacy-and-the-myth-of-the-white-working-class/

2 Ronald Brownstein, "The Billionaire Candidate and His Blue-Collar Following," *The Atlantic*, September 11, 2015, https://www.theatlantic.com/politics/archive/2015/09/the-billionaire-candidate-and-his-blue-collar-following/432783/; Matt Flegenheimer and Michael Barbaro, "Donald Trump Is Elected in Stunning Repudiation of the Establishment," *The New York Times*, November 9, 2016, https://www.nytimes.com/2016/11/09/us/politics/hillary-clinton-donald-trump-president.html

3 Anthony DiMaggio, *Rebellion in America: Citizens Uprising, the News Media, and the Politics of Plutocracy* (New York: Routledge, 2020), p. 194.

4 Joyce Tseng and Jennifer Agiesta, "The Anatomy of a White, Working-Class Trump Voter," *CNN*, September 23, 2016, https://www.cnn.com/2016/09/19/politics/trump-supporters-working-class-white-kaiser-family-foundation-infographic/index.html

5 For a comprehensive review of these studies, see chapter 4 of Anthony R. DiMaggio, *Rising Fascism in America: It Can Happen Here* (New York: Routledge, 2022).
6 Jacob Whiton, "Where Trumpism Lives," *Boston Review*, January 19, 2021, https://www.bostonreview.net/articles/jacob-whiton-where-sedition-rewarded/; Thomas Ogorzalek, Luisa Godinez Puig, and Spencer Piston, "White Trump Voters are Richer Than They Appear," *The Washington Post*, November 12, 2019, https://www.washingtonpost.com/politics/2019/11/13/white-trump-voters-are-richer-than-they-appear/; Philip Bump, "Places that Backed Trump Skewed Poor; Voters Who Backed Trump Skewed Wealthier," *The Washington Post*, December 29, 2017, https://www.washingtonpost.com/news/politics/wp/2017/12/29/places-that-backed-trump-skewed-poor-voters-who-backed-trump-skewed-wealthier/
7 DiMaggio, *Rebellion in America*, p. 205.
8 Ibid., pp. 207–213.
9 DiMaggio, *Rising Fascism in America*, pp. 206–207.
10 Ibid., pp. 203–204.
11 Maggie Fox, "Where 'Despair Deaths' Were Higher, Voters Chose Trump," *NBCNews*, September 5, 2018, https://www.nbcnews.com/health/health-news/where-despair-deaths-were-higher-voters-chose-trump-n906631
12 For a detailed summary of how Republicans' economic perceptions fluctuated radically between the late Obama, Trump, and early Biden years, independently of metrics for the state of the economy, see: DiMaggio, *Rising Fascism in America*, pp. 205–206.
13 Ibid.
14 Ibid.
15 Ibid.
16 DiMaggio, *Rebellion in America*, pp. 198–201.
17 Ibid.; Anthony R. DiMaggio, *Unequal America: Class Conflict, the News Media, and Ideology in an Era of Inequality* (New York: Routledge, 2021), p. 275.
18 DiMaggio, *Unequal America*, p. 272.
19 DiMaggio, *Rebellion in America*, p. 211.
20 The Marcon Institute, "America in Denial: Exposing the Religious, Racial, and Class Dimensions of Rightwing Extremism," *CounterPunch*, February 24, 2023, https://www.counterpunch.

org/2023/02/24/america-in-denial-exposing-the-religious-racial-and-class-dimensions-of-rightwing-extremism/
21 Ibid.
22 Ibid.
23 For a comprehensive review of these studies, see DiMaggio, *Rising Fascism in America*, p. 200.
24 Matthew Macwilliams, "The One Weird Trait That Predicts Whether You're a Trump Supporter," *Politico*, January 17, 2016, https://www.politico.com/magazine/story/2016/01/donald-trump-2016-authoritarian-213533/; David Norman Smith and Eric Hanley, "The Anger Games: Who Voted for Donald Trump in the 2016 Election, and Why?" *Critical Sociology*, Vol. 44, no. 2 (2018), https://journals.sagepub.com/doi/abs/10.1177/0896920517740615
25 DiMaggio, *Rebellion in America*, pp. 197–213; DiMaggio, *Unequal America*, pp. 271–275.
26 Anthony DiMaggio, "Fascism by Gaslighting: Trump's Coup and the Grassroots Insurrection Strategy," *CounterPunch*, January 8, 2021, https://www.counterpunch.org/2021/01/08/fascism-by-gaslighting-trumps-coup-and-the-grassroots-insurrection-strategy/; DiMaggio, *Rising Fascism in America*.
27 DiMaggio, "Fascism by Gaslighting"; DiMaggio, *Rising Fascism in America*.
28 DiMaggio, "Fascism by Gaslighting"; DiMaggio, *Rising Fascism in America*.
29 Donald J. Trump, "Remarks at a 'Make America Great Again' Rally in Rochester," *The American Presidency Project*, October 4, 2018.
30 Donald J. Trump, "Remarks at a 'Make America Great Again' Rally in Wheeling, West Virginia," *The American Presidency Project*, September 29, 2018.
31 Ibid.
32 Erica Chenoweth and Jeremy Pressman, "Black Lives Matter Protesters Were Overwhelmingly Peaceful, Our Research Finds," *The Spokesman-Review*, October 20, 2020, https://www.spokesman.com/stories/2020/oct/20/erica-chenoweth-and-jeremy-pressman-black-lives-ma/
33 Donald J. Trump, "Remarks at a Turning Point Action Students for Trump Rally in Phoenix, Arizona," *The American Presidency Project*, June 23, 2020.

34 Donald J. Trump, "Remarks on the Nationwide Demonstrations and Civil Unrest Following the Death of George Floyd in Minneapolis, Minnesota," *The American Presidency Project*, June 1, 2020.

35 Donald J. Trump, "Remarks at a 'Make America Great Again' Rally in Tulsa, Oklahoma," *The American Presidency Project*, June 20, 2020.

36 Ibid.

37 Michel Martin and Tinbete Ermyas, "Former Pentagon Chief Esper Says Trump Asked About Shooting Protesters," *National Public Radio*, May 9, 2022, https://www.npr.org/2022/05/09/1097517470/trump-esper-book-defense-secretary

38 DiMaggio, "Fascism by Gaslighting"; DiMaggio, *Rising Fascism in America*.

39 Lois Beckett, "US Violent Crime and Murder Down After Two Years of Increases, FBI Data Shows," *The Guardian*, September 24, 2018, https://www.theguardian.com/us-news/2018/sep/24/fbi-data-violent-crime-murder-us; John Gramlich, "Violent Crime is a Key Midterm Voting Issue, But What Does the Data Say?" *Pew Research Center*, October 31, 2022, https://www.pewresearch.org/fact-tank/2022/10/31/violent-crime-is-a-key-midterm-voting-issue-but-what-does-the-data-say/

40 Gramlich, "Violent Crime is a Key Midterm Voting Issue,"; Jake Horton, "Are US Cities Seeing a Surge in Violent Crime as Trump Claims?" *BBC*, September 1, 2020, https://www.bbc.com/news/world-us-canada-53525440

41 BBC, "Trump Inauguration: President Vows to End 'American Carnage'," *BBC*, January 21, 2017, https://www.bbc.com/news/world-us-canada-38688507

42 Time Staff, "Here's Donald Trump's Presidential Announcement Speech," *Time*, June 15, 2015, https://time.com/3923128/donald-trump-announcement-speech/

43 Donald J. Trump, "Remarks at the 'Salute to Service' Dinner in White Sulphur Springs, West Virginia," *The American Presidency Project*, July 3, 2018.

44 Donald J. Trump, "Remarks at a 'Make America Great Again' Rally in Evansville, Indiana," *The American Presidency Project*, August 30, 2018.

45 Donald J. Trump, "The President's News Conference with Prime Minister Giuseppe Conte of Italy," *The American Presidency Project*, July 30, 2018.

46 Ben Zimmer, "What Trump Talks About When He Talks About Infestations: The Frightening Political History of the World 'Infest'," *Politico*, July 29, 2019, https://www.politico.com/magazine/story/2019/07/29/trump-baltimore-infest-tweet-cummings-racist-227485/

47 Bianca Quilantan and David Cohen, "Trump Tells Dem Congresswomen: Go Back Where You Came From," *Politico*, July 14, 2019, https://www.politico.com/story/2019/07/14/trump-congress-go-back-where-they-came-from-1415692

48 DiMaggio, "Fascism by Gaslighting."

49 Donald J. Trump, "Remarks at a 'Make America Great Again' Rally in Johnson City, Tennessee," *The American Presidency Project*, October 1, 2018.

50 Rupert Neate and Jo Tuckman, "Donald Trump: Mexican Migrants Bring 'Tremendous Infectious Disease' to US," *The Guardian*, July 6, 2015, https://www.theguardian.com/us-news/2015/jul/06/donald-trump-mexican-immigrants-tremendous-infectious-disease

51 Randall L. Bytwerk, ed., *Landmark Speeches of National Socialism* (College Station: Texas A&M University Press, 2008); David Livingstone Smith, "'Less Than Human': The Psychology of Cruelty," *National Public Radio*, March 29, 2011, https://www.npr.org/2011/03/29/134956180/criminals-see-their-victims-as-less-than-human

Chapter 13

1 John Dewey, *The Public and Its Problems* (Athens, OH: Swallow Press, 1954).

2 Hannah Natanson, Lori Rozsa, and Susan Svrluga, "Florida Bills Would Ban Gender Studies, Limit Trans Pronouns, Erode Tenure," *The Washington Post*, March 5, 2023, https://www.washingtonpost.com/education/2023/03/05/florida-bills-would-ban-gender-studies-transgender-pronouns-tenure-perks/

3 Kathryn Joyce, "The Guy Who Brought Us CRT Panic Offers a New Far-Right Agenda: Destroy Public Education," *Salon*, April 8, 2022, https://www.salon.com/2022/04/08/the-guy-brought-us-crt-panic-offers-a-new-far-right-agenda-destroy-public-education/

4 Michelle Goldberg, "Florida Could Start Looking a Lot Like Hungary," *The New York Times*, February 27, 2023, https://www.nytimes.com/2023/02/27/opinion/desantis-higher-education-bill.html

5   Ibid.
6   Trevor Timm, "Ron DeSantis Has His Next Target in His Sights: Freedom of the Press," *The Guardian*, March 7, 2023, https://www.theguardian.com/commentisfree/2023/mar/07/ron-desantis-freedom-of-the-press-florida; Editorial Board, "Florida Is Trying to Take Away the American Right to Speak Freely," *The New York Times*, March 4, 2023, https://www.nytimes.com/2023/03/04/opinion/desantis-florida-free-speech-bill.html
7   On this issue, see the excellent series of articles by Kathryn Joyce: Kathryn Joyce, "Republicans Don't Want To Reform Public Education. They Want To End It," *The New Republic*, September 30, 2021, https://newrepublic.com/article/163817/desantis-republicans-end-public-education; Kathryn Joyce, "The Guy Who Brought Us CRT Panic"; Kathryn Joyce, "Fighting Back Against CRT Panic: Educators Organize Around the Threat to Academic Freedom," *Salon*, March 7, 2022, https://www.salon.com/2022/03/07/fighting-back-against-crt-panic-educators-organize-around-the-to-academic-freedom/
8   Henry A. Giroux, "Reclaiming the Radical Imagination: Challenging Casino Capitalism's Punishing Factories," *Truthout*, July 13, 2014, https://truthout.org/articles/disimagination-machines-and-punishing-factories-in-the-age-of-casino-capitalism/
9   Amiad Horowitz, "Loyalty Oaths for Teachers in Florida's New Red Scare," *People's World*, June 28, 2021, www.peoplesworld.org/article/loyalty-oaths-for-teachers-in-floridas-new-red-scare/
10 Anton Troianovski, "Putin's Mission to Indoctrinate Schoolchildren," *The New York Times*, July 17, 2022, pp. 1, 12.
11 Max Boot, "DeSantis Is Smarter Than Trump. That May Make Him More of a Threat," *The Washington Post*, July 6, 2022, https://www.washingtonpost.com/opinions/2022/07/06/desantis-starter-disciplined-trump-nixon-danger-democracy/
12 Hannah Natanson, "'Slavery was Wrong' and 5 Other Things Some Educators Won't Teach Anymore," *The Washington Post*, March 6, 2023, https://www.washingtonpost.com/education/2023/03/06/slavery-was-wrong-5-other-things-educators-wont-teach-anymore/
13 Hannah Natanson and Moriah Balingit, "Caught in the Culture Wars, Teachers Are Being Forced from Their Jobs," *The Washington Post*, June 16, 2022, https://www.washingtonpost.com/education/2022/06/16/teacher-resignations-firings-culture-wars/
14 Will Bunch, "GOP's Violent, Expanding War on LBGTQ Kids Should Make You Think About 1930s Germany," *The Philadelphia Inquirer*,

NOTES

June 16, 2022, https://www.inquirer.com/opinion/anti-lgbtq-violence-republican-rhetoric-20220616.html

15 Ruth Ben-Ghiat, "How Trump's Cultivation of Violence Contributed to Jan. 6," *Lucid*, July 7, 2022, https://lucid.substack.com/p/how-trumps-cultivation-of-violence?utm_source=substack&utm_medium=email

16 Paul Rosenberg, "Theocrats Are Coming for the School Board—But Parents Are Starting to Fight Back," *Salon*, December 19, 2021, https://www.salon.com/2021/12/19/theocrats-are-coming-for-the-school-board–but-parents-are-starting-to-fight-back/

17 Cited in Lina Buffington, Tamara Martinez, Pat McLaughlin, Jennifer Porter, and Nicole Puglia, "The Educational Theory of Adolph Hitler," *New Foundations*, August 18, 2011, https://www.newfoundations.com/GALLERY/Hitler.html

18 Ibid.

19 John Simkin, "Education in Nazi Germany," *Spartacus Educational*, January 2020, https://spartacus-educational.com/GEReducation.htm

20 Buffington et al., "The Educational Theory of Adolph Hitler."

21 Staff, "The Holocaust Explained," *The Wiener Holocaust Library*, March 2020, https://www.theholocaustexplained.org/life-in-nazi-occupied-europe/controlling-everyday-life/controlling-education/

22 See Richard J. Evans, *The Third Reich In Power* (New York: Penguin 2005), especially pp. 263–298.

23 Elizabeth A. Harris and Alexandra Alter, "With Rising Book Bans, Librarians Have Come Under Attack," *The New York Times*, July 8, 2022, https://www.nytimes.com/2022/07/06/books/book-ban-librarians.html

24 Evans, *The Third Reich In Power*; Lisa Pine, *Education in Nazi Germany* (Oxford: Berg, 2010); Danielle Appleby, "Controlling Information with Propaganda: Indoctrinating the Youth in Nazi Germany," *Dalhousie Journal of Interdisciplinary Management*, 9 (Spring 2013); Jacob Wilkins, "This Is What Children Learned at School in Nazi Germany," *Lessons from History*, February 2022, https://medium.com/lessons-from-history/this-is-what-children-learned-at-school-in-nazi-germany-6377a4eabd61

25 Talia Lavin, "Why Transphobia is at the Heart of the White Power Movement," *The Nation*, August 18, 2021, www.thenation.com/article/society/transphobia-white-supremacy.

26 Ibram X. Kendi, "The Danger More Republicans Should Be Talking About," *The Atlantic*, April 16, 2022, https://www.theatlantic.com/

ideas/archive/2022/04/white-supremacy-grooming-in-republican-party/629585/

27 Ibid.
28 I have written extensively on these issues. See more recently, Henry A. Giroux, *On Critical Pedagogy*, second edition (London: Bloomsbury, 2020); Henry A. Giroux, *Race, Politics, and Pandemic Pedagogy* (London: Bloomsbury, 2021), and Henry A. Giroux, *Pedagogy of Resistance* (London: Bloomsbury, 2022).
29 Kendi, "The Danger More Republicans Should Be Talking About."
30 Geoff Mann, "Is Fascism the Wave of the Future?" *The New Statesman*, February 11, 2022.
31 Jeffrey St. Clair, "When History Called on the General," *CounterPunch+*, July 10, 2022, https://www.counterpunch.org/2022/07/10/when-history-called-on-the-general/; see also, Ariel Dorfman, "Stumbling on Chilean Stones—and Chilean History," *The Nation*, January 27, 2022, https://www.thenation.com/article/world/chile-history-pinochet-boric/
32 Cathryn Stout and Thomas Wilburn, "CRT Map: Efforts To Restrict Teaching Racism And Bias Have Multiplied Across the U.S.," *Chalkbeat*, April 2021, https://www.chalkbeat.org/22525983/map-critical-race-theory-legislation-teaching-racism
33 Dimitris Kant, "A Letter from Hellen Keller to Nazi Youth," *Katiousa*, May 13, 2022, http://www.katiousa.gr/istoria/gegonota/mia-epistoli-tis-elen-keler-pros-ti-nazistiki-neolaia/
34 Ellen Willis, *Don't Think, Smile: Notes on a Decade of Denial* (Boston: Beacon Press, 1999), p. 45.

Chapter 14

1 Liz Hamel, Audrey Kearney, Ashley Kirzinger, Lunna Lopes, Cailey Munana, and Mollyann Brodie, "KFF Health Tracking Poll—June 2020," *Kaiser Family Foundation*, June 26, 2020, https://www.kff.org/racial-equity-and-health-policy/report/kff-health-tracking-poll-june-2020/
2 Larry Buchanan, Quoctrung Bui, and Jugal K. Patel, "Black Lives Matter May Be the Largest Movement in U.S. History," *The New York Times*, July 3, 2020, https://www.nytimes.com/interactive/2020/07/03/us/george-floyd-protests-crowd-size.html

NOTES

3 Martin Gilens and Benjamin I. Page, "Testing Theories of American Politics: Elites, Interest Groups, and Average Citizens," *Perspectives on Politics*, Vol. 12, No. 3 (2014), pp. 564–581.

4 Hart Research Associates/Public Opinion Strategies, "Study 18164: Social Trends Survey," *NBC/Wall Street Journal*, March 2018, https://www.wsj.com/public/resources/documents/wsjnbcpoll0314final.pdf

5 David Shepardson and Nandita Bose, "Biden Signs Bill to Block U.S. Railroad Strike," *Reuters*, December 2, 2022, https://www.reuters.com/world/us/biden-signs-bill-block-us-railroad-strike-2022-12-02/

6 The Intergovernmental Panel on Climate Change, "The Evidence Is Clear: The Time for Action Is Now. We Can Halve Emissions by 2030," *IPCC*, April 4, 2022, https://www.ipcc.ch/2022/04/04/ipcc-ar6-wgiii-pressrelease/; Jim Tankersley, "Biden Signs Climate, Health Bill into Law as Other Economic Goals Remain," *The New York Times*, August 16, 2022, https://www.nytimes.com/2022/08/16/us/politics/biden-climate-health-bill.html

7 Michael D. Shear and Liam Stack, "Obama Says Movements Like Black Lives Matter 'Can't Just Keep on Yelling'," *The New York Times*, April 23, 2016, https://www.nytimes.com/2016/04/24/us/obama-says-movements-like-black-lives-matter-cant-just-keep-on-yelling.html

8 Anthony DiMaggio, "Orwellian Hellscape v. Neoliberal Caretakers: American Politics in the 'Post-Trump' Era," *CounterPunch*, June 25, 2021, https://www.counterpunch.org/2021/06/25/orwellian-hellscape-v-neoliberal-caretakers-american-politics-in-the-post-trump-era/

9 Pew Research Center, "Amid Campaign Turmoil, Biden Holds Wide Leads on Coronavirus, Unifying the Country," *Pew Research Center*, October 9, 2020, https://www.pewresearch.org/politics/2020/10/09/the-trump-biden-presidential-contest/

10 Monmouth University, "More Americans Happy about Trump Loss than Biden Win," *Monmouth University*, November 18, 2020, https://www.monmouth.edu/polling-institute/reports/monmouthpoll_us_111820/

11 Fadel Hassan, "Poll: 62% of Trump Supporters Say Nothing He Could Do Would Change Opinion," *Axios*, November 5, 2019, https://www.axios.com/2019/11/05/monmouth-poll-trump-approval

12 Kim Reynolds, "House File 802," *Office of the Governor*, June 8, 2021, https://www.legis.iowa.gov/legislation/BillBook?ga=89&ba=hf802

13 Bill Lee, "Senate Bill No. 623," *State of Tennessee*, May 25, 2021, https://publications.tnsosfiles.com/acts/112/pub/pc0493.pdf

14 Legislature of the State of Idaho, "House of Representatives House Bill No. 377," *Ways and Means Committee*, 2021, https://legislature.idaho.gov/wp-content/uploads/sessioninfo/2021/legislation/H0377.pdf

15 Legislature of the State of Idaho, "House of Representatives House Bill No. 377," 2021.

16 Michael Crowley and Jennifer Schuessler, "Trump's 1776 Commission Critiques Liberalism in Report Derided by Historians," *The New York Times*, January 18, 2021, https://www.nytimes.com/2021/01/18/us/politics/trump-1776-commission-report.html; Gillian Brockell, "'A Hack Job,' 'Outright Lies': Trump Commission's '1776 Report' Outrages Historians," *Washington Post*, January 20, 2021, https://www.washingtonpost.com/history/2021/01/19/1776-report-historians-trump/

17 Andrew Solender, "Trump Launches 'Patriotic Education' Commission, Calls 1619 Project 'Ideological Poison'" *Forbes*, September 17, 2020, https://www.forbes.com/sites/andrewsolender/2020/09/17/trump-launches-patriotic-education-commission-calls-1619-project-ideological-poison/?sh=55488244155a

18 Donald J. Trump, "A Plan to Get Divisive & Radical Theories Out of Our Schools," *RealClear Politics*, June 18, 2021, https://www.realclearpolitics.com/articles/2021/06/18/a_plan_to_get_divisive__radical_theories_out_of_our_schools_145946.html

19 Jon Jackson, "Tucker Carlson Wants to Monitor Classrooms for CRT; Teacher Says, 'Let's Make it Happen'," *Newsweek*, July 9, 2021, https://www.newsweek.com/tucker-carlson-wants-monitor-classrooms-crt-teacher-says-lets-make-this-happen-1611207; Paul Blest, "The GOP Wants Cameras in Classrooms to Right Teachers' 'Sinister Agenda'," *Vice*, February 3, 2022, https://www.vice.com/en/article/bvnynd/gop-cameras-classrooms-iowa; Jonathan J. Cooper, "Trump Ally Kari Lake Wins GOP Primary for Arizona Governor," *The Associated Press*, November 27, 2021, https://www.azcentral.com/story/news/politics/arizona/2021/11/27/gop-gubernatorial-candidate-kari-lake-supports-cameras-classrooms/8768587002/

20 Gabriella Borter, Joseph Ax, and Joseph Tanfani, "School Boards Get Death Threats Amid Rage Over Race, Gender, Mask Policies," *Reuters*, February 15, 2022, https://www.reuters.com/investigates/special-report/usa-education-threats/

21 Trump, "A Plan to Get Divisive & Radical Theories Out of Our Schools."

22 Ibid.
23 Ibid.
24 Daniel De Vise, "DeSantis Wants a 'Core Curriculum.' That Idea Is College Kryptonite," *The Hill*, February 5, 2023, https://thehill.com/education/3843399-desantis-wants-a-core-curriculum-that-idea-is-college-kryptonite/; Stephanie Saul, Patricia Mazzei, and Trip Gabriel, "DeSantis Takes on the Education Establishment, and Builds His Brand," *The New York Times*, January 31, 2023, https://www.nytimes.com/2023/01/31/us/governor-desantis-higher-education-chris-rufo.html
25 Simone Carter, "Florida Voters Don't Understand Ron DeSantis' War on 'Woke': Analyst," *Newsweek*, January 12, 2023, https://www.newsweek.com/florida-voters-dont-understand-ron-desantis-war-woke-1773378
26 Saul et al., "DeSantis Takes on the Education Establishment, and Builds His Brand."
27 Julia Manchester, "Haley Criticizes US 'Self-Loathing': America Is Not a Racist Country," *The Hill*, February 15, 2023, https://thehill.com/homenews/campaign/3859490-haley-criticizes-us-self-loathing-america-is-not-a-racist-country/
28 Saul et al., "DeSantis Takes on the Education Establishment, and Builds His Brand."
29 Anemona Hartocollis and Eliza Fawcett, "The College Board Strips Down Its A.P. Curriculum for African American Studies," *The New York Times*, February 1, 2023, https://www.nytimes.com/2023/02/01/us/college-board-advanced-placement-african-american-studies.html
30 Paul Blest, "Florida Republicans Are Terrified of Gender Studies Majors: A New DeSantis-Backed Bill Would Ban Gender Studies, 'Intersectionality,' and 'Critical Race Theory' from the State's Public Colleges and Universities," *Vice*, February 27, 2023, https://www.vice.com/en/contributor/paul-blest
31 Marcon Institute, "America in Denial: Exposing the Religious, Racial, and Class Dimensions of Rightwing Extremism," *CounterPunch*, February 24, 2023, https://www.counterpunch.org/2023/02/24/america-in-denial-exposing-the-religious-racial-and-class-dimensions-of-rightwing-extremism/
32 Anthony DiMaggio, *Rebellion in America: Citizen Uprisings, the News Media, and the Politics of Plutocracy* (New York: Routledge, 2020), pp. 7–9.
33 Ibid., pp. 7–9.

Conclusion

1. Most clearly stated by one of the apostles of neoliberalism, Milton Friedman. See Milton Friedman, "The Social Responsibility of Business Is to Increase its Profits," *The New York Times Magazine*, September 13, 1970, http://umich.edu/~thecore/doc/Friedman.pdf
2. Prabhat Patnaik, "Why Neoliberalism Needs Neofascists," *Boston Review*, July 13, 2021, https://bostonreview.net/class-inequality-politics/prabhat-patnaik-why-neoliberalism-needs-neofascists
3. Ibid. Pankaj Mishra, "The New World Disorder: The Western Model Is Broken," *The Guardian*, October 14, 2014, https://www.theguardian.com/world/2014/oct/14/-sp-western-model-broken-pankaj-mishra
4. Pete Dolack, "When Does a Formal Democracy Degenerate into Fascism?" *CounterPunch*, June 11, 2023, https://www.counterpunch.org/2023/06/11/when-does-a-formal-democracy-degenerate-into-fascism/
5. Dahlia Lithwick, "What Will Come from This Indictment," *Slate*, June 13, 2023, https://slate.com/news-and-politics/2023/06/trump-indictment-reveals-two-americas.html
6. Peter Baker, "Justice System Is Put on Trial in Trump Case," *The New York Times*, June 11, 2023, p. 1.
7. Lithwick, "What Will Come from This Indictment."
8. Kira Lerner, "12m Americans Believe Violence Is Justified to Restore Trump to Power," *The Guardian*, June 9, 2023, https://www.theguardian.com/us-news/2023/jun/09/january-6-trump-political-violence-survey
9. See, for instance, Jeff Sharlet, *The Undertow: Scenes from a Slow Civil War* (New York: Norton, 2023). Also, see Sam Levine, "Fears that Republicans' Rhetoric After Trump Indictment Could Spark Violence," *The Guardian*, June 11, 2023, https://www.theguardian.com/us-news/2023/jun/11/trump-indictment-republicans-rhetoric-violence
10. Alan Singer, "The Culture Wars Against History and Education," *Daily Kos*, May 22, 2023, https://www.dailykos.com/stories/2023/5/22/2170670/-The-Culture-Wars-Against-History-and-Education?utm_campaign=recent&fbclid=-IwAR3nAP8nRkxWUbZUesM-h8xMGsadBTDIkFYJ3W5Zlva83vN94MXeftMcjOU

11 There are too many references to mention here, but important sources would include Jason Stanley, *How Fascism Works: The Politics of Us and Them* (New York: Random House, 2020); Ruth Ben-Ghiat, *Strongmen: Mussolini to the Present* (New York: W. W. Norton, 2021).
12 Singer, "The Culture Wars Against History and Education."
13 G. M. Tamás, "On Post-Fascism," *Boston Review*, June 1, 2000, https://bostonreview.net/articles/g-m-tamas-post-fascism/
14 Gary Olson and Lynn Worsham, "Staging the Politics of Difference: Homi Bhabha's Critical Literacy," *Journal of Advanced Composition*, Vol. 18, no. 3 (1999), pp. 361–391.
15 Henry A. Giroux, "Fascist Politics in the Age of Neoliberal Capitalism: Confronting the Domestication of the Unimaginable," *CounterPunch*, April 11, 2023, https://www.counterpunch.org/2023/04/11/fascist-politics-in-the-age-of-neoliberal-capitalismconfronting-the-domestication-of-the-unimaginable/
16 Ibid.
17 Cited in Will Bunch, "Real DeSantis Launch Glitch Was Its Fascism | Will Bunch Newsletter," *The Philadelphia Inquirer*, May 30, 2023, https://www.inquirer.com/columnists/attytood/desantis-twitter-campaign-announcement-kissinger-100-birthday-20230530.html
18 Martin Pengelly, "Ron DeSantis Says He Will 'Destroy Leftism' in US If Elected President," *The Guardian*, May 30, 2023, https://www.theguardian.com/us-news/2023/may/30/ron-desantis-fox-news-interview-destroy-leftism
19 Margaret Sullivan, "Now's the Time to Think About Just How Bad a DeSantis Presidency Would Be," *The Guardian*, May 25, 2023, https://www.theguardian.com/commentisfree/2023/may/25/ron-desantis-florida-record-presidential-campaign
20 Toni Morrison, ed., *James Baldwin, Collected Essays: No Name in the Street* (New York: Library of America, 1998), p. 371.
21 The Editors, "Ron DeSantis's Antiscience Agenda Is Dangerous," *Scientific American*, May 25, 2023, https://www.scientificamerican.com/article/ron-desantiss-anti-science-agenda-is-dangerous/
22 Moira Donegan, "Schools and Universities Are Ground Zero for America's Culture War," *The Guardian*, February 5, 2023, https://www.theguardian.com/commentisfree/2023/feb/05/schools-and-universities-are-ground-zero-for-americas-culture-war
23 Angela Y. Davis, *Freedom Is a Constant Struggle: Ferguson, Palestine and the Foundations of a Movement* (Chicago, IL: Haymarket Books, 2016), p. 88.

INDEX

Abbott, Greg 45
abortion, policies against 160
academics, abdication of responsibility by 206–7
Adams, Scott 18, 19
Adler-Bell, Sam 163
agency
 culture, power, politics and 140–1
 see also political agency, crisis of
Ali, Wajahat 133
anti-communist rhetoric 216
anti-intellectualism as form of redemption 80
anti-racism, attacks on 199–201, 204–6
anti-Semitism
 celebrities 18–19
 fear of violence as result 111
 Fuentes, Nick 110–11
 Neo-Nazi-groups 19
 QAnon 125
 threats on social media 19
 Ye (Kanye West) 108–10, 111
Arbery, Ahmaud, murder of 30–1
atomization of human beings 20–1, 25, 26, 112–13
authoritarianism
 decline in freedom 130
 global trend for authoritarian leaders 130
 historical memory, attacks on 139

 language, and conditions for 141
 resistance to 141–2
 slow violence of 135–6
 violence and 129, 135–7

Baldwin, James 26, 84, 106, 136
Balibar, Etienne 44
Balingit, Moriah 190
Ben-Ghiat, Ruth 159, 161
Berardi, Franco 170
Bergenruen, Vera 19
Biden, Joe 64, 65–6, 85
Biggs, Andy 211
Black Lives Matter (BLM)
 growth of movement 197–8
 Trump's attacks on 180, 201–2
Black youth, war on 159–60
book banning 118–19, 135
Boot, Max 45, 190
Bourdieu, Pierre 82
Bowers, Robert 161–2
Bruni, Frank 107
Buffington, Lina 191
Bunch, Will 59

Carlson, Tucker 63, 89, 90, 94, 150, 161
Chait, Jonathan 132
Charen, Monica 45
child labor laws 46
children, war on 46, 159–60
Christian nationalism *see* white Christian nationalism

citizen activism
  growth of 197–8
  vigilante violence as response to 30
  and vigilante violence, implications for 33
  see also Black Lives Matter (BLM)
Clarke, Colin P. 161
Cohen Stanley 110–11
collective responsibility, neoliberalism and 53
Collins, Ben 74
colonial fascism 1
communal bonds
  collapse of 49–50
  difficulty forming 24
  elimination of 80
competition as central to neoliberalism 54
connections, politics of 113–15
consciousness, collapse of 49–50
conspiracy theories 38
Constitutional law, white Christian nationalism and 121
court sanctioned violence 32
  Rittenhouse, Kyle, violence by and trial of 29–30, 32–3
COVID-19, neoliberalism and suffering during 73
Crary, Jonathan 21
Crimo, Robert 59, 65–8
critical agency and thinking
  attacks on 20, 79–80, 119, 130–1, 193
  education in 194
  pedagogical 217
  war on 152
critical race theory, attacks on 199–201, 204
Crosse, Jacob 110

cruelty
  children, war on 46
  collapse of consciousness, integrity and social bonds 49–50
  contempt for human rights, equality and justice 53–4
  cutting of safety nets and programs 46
  economic tyranny 48–9
  in fascist politics 43–4
  history of in America 44–5
  media and 47
  militarization of American society 55–6
  neoliberalism and 50–7
  as not connected with fascism 47
  Republican Party 45–7
  systemic power relations, lack of analysis of 47–8
  violence under neoliberal fascism 54–7
Crusius, Patrick 66
cultural apparatuses, role of 25–6
cultural politics 212
culture
  as educational force 82, 215
  power, politics, agency and 140–1
  as resistance site 82
  as war zone 78–9

Davis, Angela 131
Davis, Eric 89
death threats 74–5
democracy
  as being replaced with fascism 133
  denialism of fascism, implications of 144
  global capitalism sees as enemy 1–2

illiberal, in center of American politics 2
as under threat, polls on 36–9
Democratic Party
  denialism of fascism 61, 64
  disenchantment with 199
  fascism and 167
  neoliberal politics, embrace of 198–9
  Trump's attacks on in speeches 179, 180–1
democratic socialism, vision of 85
denialism of fascism
  academics 60–1
  after mass shootings 62–9
  democracy, implications for 144
  Democratic Party 64
  erasure of serious discussions 59, 144
  mass shootings 59–60
  in media discourse 59, 64–9
  past, fascism as belonging in 61–2
  in political culture 60
  by politicians and parties 61, 63–4, 65–6
DeSantis, Ron 18, 25, 45, 187–91, 193, 195, 215–17
  as a fascist 105–8
  white Christian nationalism 121
  white supremacy and 105–7
Dewey, John 187
digital culture
  fascist rhetoric on 19
  references to violence in online spaces 75–6
  toxic role of 21
disaster relief packages 160
disconnection of events and problems
  DeSantis, Ron, fascist actions of 105–8
  fascism as blossoming under 114
  Fuentes, Nick 110–11
  reclaiming social democracy 113–15
  as signalling fascism 102–3, 104
  Ye (Kanye West), anti-Semitic and white supremacist comments by 108–10, 111
disposability, politics of 45
  consequences of 69
  reappearance of fascism and 47
  violence against 'undesirable groups' 66
Dolack, Pete 210
Dominion Voting Systems' claim against Fox News 88–92
Douglass, Frederick 141–2
Dubois, W.E.B. 1

Eastman, David 25
Eco, Umberto 22–3
economic structures of domination, role of 25–6
economic tyranny 48–9
economics as fueling support for Trump 175–7
education
  attacks on historical memory and 131
  book banning 118–19
  as censorship and indoctrination tool 215
  collaboration with other agencies 171
  critical agency and thinking 194
  critical pedagogical practices 217
  critical thinking, efforts to silence 119
  culture as force for 82, 215
  in a democracy 213–14

for empowerment 217, 218
fascist model of 214–15
gangster capitalism 213
librarians, attacks on 193
in Nazi Germany 191–3
politics as force for 26
repression, pedagogies of 214–15
as resistance site 82
resistance to repressing and rewriting history 215
resistance, pedagogy of 213
right-wing wars against 212
role of in resistance 170–2
war on critical 153
see also Nazification of education
elections
　Americans' view of after voter fraud propaganda 90
　future, voter fraud claims and 92
　officials, threats against 22
　rigging 27
　seen as being perverted 34–5
　vigilante violence and 33–4, 36
　voter nullification 34
elimination, production for 44
eliminationist ideology and politics 126
eliminationist language, use of by Trump 178, 180–1
Ellis, Meaghan 106
equality and justice, contempt for under neoliberalism 53–4
erasure of serious discussions 59, 94
　January 6th insurrection 144–6
ethics, collapse of 48–9
ethnic diversity, seen as threat 34
evidence-based reasoning, respect for as deteriorating 153
exceptionalism, American 144

fascism
　America as nearly tipping into 129
　American society as saturated with 104
　characteristics of 4
　components and attributes of 23–4
　current form of 160–1
　DeSantis, Ron 105–8
　different forms of 3
　disconnected events and problems as signalling 101–3, 104
　erasure of serious discussions of 59
　expanded definition of 23
　as fix for neoliberalism 210
　global 169
　history of in America predating Europe 160
　mobilizing passions of 165
　as present at highest level of politics 112
　as present danger 103–4
　refusal to acknowledge scale of 3
　rhetoric of 18–19, 31–2
　silence as complicity and cooperation with 104
　similarities between 1930s Germany/Italy and US today 5–6
　symptoms of rise of in America 3
　women and 164
　see also language; lying; resistance; street fascism; violence
fast violence 136
Feuer, Alan 74
financial elite
　lust for power 22–3
　power of 21

Finchelstein, Federico 32, 92
First Amendment, white Christian nationalism and 121
Flynn, Michael 18, 162
Fox News, voter fraud claims and 88–92
Frankl, Viktor 134
freedom in right-wing discourse 51–2
freedom of speech, attacks on 188–9, 204
French, David 73, 76
Friedfeld, Alex 75–6
Fuentes, Nick 64, 110–11

Gaetz, Matt 64
gangster capitalism 209, 210, 213, 218
  see also neoliberalism
Garland, Merrick 76
Gendron, Payton 59–60, 62–3, 65
Ghansah, Rachel Kaadzi 49–50
Gillespie, Michael 133
Gilroy, Paul 3, 131, 132, 134
global capitalism, democracy seen as enemy by 1–2
Goebbels, Joseph 77
Goldberg, Michelle 188
Goodman, Amy 22
GOP (Grand Old Party) *see* Republican Party
Gosar, Paul 64, 161
Graeber, David 112
Graham, David 137
Graham, Lindsay 75
Greenblatt, Jonathan 111
Greenwald, Glenn 93
Griswold, Eliza 132
Grob, Leonard 168
gun violence *see* street fascism
guns, carrying of in public 138
Guthrie, Savannah 124

Hall, Stuart 50
Han, Byung-Chul 77
Hannity, Sean 89
Harvey, David 57
Hayes, Kelly 104
Hedges, Chris 21, 163, 165
Hillsdale College 120
historical conjuncture, new 50
history
  America's, refusal to tell the truth about 106–7
  fascism seen as 61–2
  learning from 6, 104
  repressing and rewriting 26–7, 130–1, 139, 149–50, 170, 215
  whitewashing of 117
Hitler, Adolf 191
homegrown extremists 56
House Bill 999 188
human rights, equality and justice, contempt for under neoliberalism 53–4
Hutchinson, Cassidy 137

Idaho, Bill 377 200
ideological domains as resistance sites 82
illiberal democracy in center of American politics 2
immigrants
  DeSantis's treatment of 105–6
  pain inflicted on 160
immigrants, Trump's attacks on 181–3
individualism 48, 49, 112–13
Ingraham, Laura 90
integrity, collapse of 49–50
intellectuals, abdication of responsibility by 206–7
Iowa, House Bill 802 199–200
irrationality as form of redemption 80

isolation 21, 24
Italiano, Laura 75

January 6th insurrection 91–2, 137–9
   alternative reality regarding 150
   erasure of serious discussions 144–6
   media on 164
   QAnon and 125–6
   Trump's withholding of presidential documents 149–50
   white supremacy and 132, 145
Johnson, Derrick 95
Johnson, Ron 64
Jones, Robert 123
justice, contempt for under neoliberalism 53–4

Keller, Helen 196
Kelley, Robin D.G. 135
Kendi, Ibram X. 194
Kent, Joe 74

Lake, Kari 74
language
   1930s fascism, Trump's as reminiscent of 218
   complicitous force, language as 77
   conditions for authoritarianism and 141
   degradation of 49
   global politics, understanding 169
   of hate and bigotry 162
   incendiary, used to provoke violence 211
   neoliberal logic as shaping 77
   new, for rethinking theory, politics and power 83, 85, 166, 213

   as part of repression 163
   of public life, need to reclaim 83
   Republican Party 77
   for resistance 167–8
   as structuring thought 109
   violent, upsurge in 73
   weaponized, language as 77, 79, 91
law and order as under threat 31
   see also violence
learned helplessness 78
Legum, Judd 105
Levi, Primo 62, 103, 212
librarians, attacks on 193
Limbaugh, Rush 150
Lindell, Mike 124
loneliness 21
Lorde, Audre 113
Lowenthal, Leo 20
Lusane, Clarence 111–12
Lyamlahy, Khalid 113
lying
   as central to fascism 87
   communities of color as targets of voter fraud propaganda 87–8
   extremist groups 157–8
   Rittenhouse trial, avoidance of fascism/white supremacy in coverage of 92–7
   suppression of discussion on racism and fascism 94
   voter fraud propaganda 88–92

Mann, Geoff 112
masculinity, veneration of 122–3
Mason, Paul 51
mass shootings 31
   denialism of fascism after 46, 59–60, 62–9
   frequency of 73
   lone wolf narrative 68–9
   media reporting on 62

Nazification of education and 195
right-wing pollination of 63
as warning signs 29
Masters, Blake 132, 163
Mastriano, Carl 132
Mastriano, Douglas 52
McElvaine, Robert 107
media
 cruelty as not connected with fascism 47
 denialism of street fascism 59–60, 64–9
 Fox News, voter fraud claims and 88–92
 history, war on 150
 increase in violence, analyses of 76
 on January 6th insurrection 164
 as misinformation engines 26
 official source bias 94
 Rittenhouse trial, avoidance of fascism/white supremacy in coverage 92–7
 silence on threat of fascism 163–4, 168
 white replacement theory, mainstreaming of 63
Meloni, Giorgia 164
mental illness, mass shootings and 66
microaggressions by Neo-Nazi-groups 19
migrants *see* immigrants
militarization of American society 55–7
miseducation 26
Mishra, Pankaj 51
Moms for Liberty 118–19
Morrison, Toni 32
Morrow, Paul 141
Moynihan, Denis 22

naïve realism 120
Natanson, Hannah 190
Nazification of American society
 deprivation and dehumanization, policies of 159–60
 education's role in resistance 170–2
 language needed to resist 166
 language of violence 163
 media silence on threat of fascism 163–4
 mobilizing passions of fascism 165
 neoliberal capitalism 166–7
 Republican Party updated form of fascism 164–5
 resistance, politics and language needed for 167–8
 right-wing social media discourses of hate 162
 Trump and 178, 181–3
 violence and threats as normalized 157–9
 white replacement theory, promotion of 161–2
 women, fascism and 164
Nazification of education
 critical agency and thinking, attacks on 194, 195–6
 critical race theory, attacks on 199–201, 202–3
 critical thinking, attacks on 189
 DeSantis's policies 187–91
 education in Nazi Germany 191–3
 House Bill 999 188
 librarians, attacks on 193
 marginalized youth, attacks on 190
 mass shootings and 195
 racism and 192

Russia, comparison with 189–90
  teachers, impact on 190
  violence, threats of 191
Neo-Nazi-groups,
  microaggressions by 19
neoliberalism 166
  collective responsibility and 53
  competition as central to 54
  contempt for human rights, equality and justice 53–4
  domination as internalized 79
  economic tyranny 48–9
  economics as fueling support for Trum 175–7
  fascism and 51, 133–4
  as freedom 52–3
  gangster capitalism and 209
  legitimization crisis of 50–1
  neofacism as fix for 209
  new ideology, need for 209
  pain and suffering as entertainment 24
  violence and 139
  white supremacy and 133–4
Nixon, Rob 135
No Left Turn for Education 119
normalization
  of fascist actions 19
  of violence 22, 46–7, 76, 157–9
  white replacement theory 63–4
Novikov, Sergei 189

Oath Keepers 84
Orbán, Viktor 188
Orwellian propaganda 199, 200, 202, 203, 204, 207
Ottman, Joe 191

Paladino, Carl 132
Pape, Robert 76
Patnaik, Prabhat 209
Pearsall, Sarah 106

Pendle, George 164
police brutality, racist 73, 123
political agency, crisis of 130
  culture, power, politics, agency and 140
  repressing and rewriting history 139
  suppression of historical memory 130–1, 135
political culture, denialism of fascism in 60
politicians
  denialism of fascism 63–4, 65–6
  lust for power 22–3
  Republican, fascist views of 18
  see also Democratic Party; Republican Party
politics
  culture, power, agency and 140–1
  as war zone 78–9
politics of disposability
  consequences of 69
  reappearance of fascism and 47
  Republican Party 45
  violence against 'undesirable groups' 66
populism, use of term 60
Posner, Sarah 27
Powell, Sydney 90, 124
power: culture, politics, agency and 140–1
privatization 24
production for elimination 44
protest, mainstreaming of 198
Proud Boys 84

QAnon 38, 123–6

racial diversity, seen as threat 34
racism

INDEX

anti-racism, attacks on 199–201, 204–6
anti-racist pedagogies 194
Black youth, war on 159–60
critical race theory, attacks on 199–201, 204
January 6th insurrection 144
lying and 87
Nazi Germany comparison 192–3
Nazification of education 192
Philadelphia and Detroit as focus for attacks 88
police brutality 73, 123
Republican Party as driven by 131–2
voter fraud propaganda, communities of color as targets of 87–8
white Christian nationalism and 123
whitewashing of history 117
Reich, Robert 18, 75
Reilly, Ryan J. 74
religious fundamentalists 27
see also white Christian nationalism
reproductive rights, policies against 158
Republican Party
 2024 elections 152
 alternative reality re. January 6th 150–1
 children, cruelty aimed at 159
 critical race theory, attacks on 199–201, 202–3, 204
 cruelty 45–7
 death threats by politicians 74–5
 denialism of fascism 61
 deputizing of vigilantes 129
 echoes of the past 132
 fascism and 132
 fascist views of politicians 17, 18
hateful rhetoric used by politicians 18–19
highest level of politics, fascism as present at 112
January 6th insurrection, attitudes towards 151
politics of disposability 45
racism as driving 131–2
repressing and rewriting of history 26–7, 130–1
as ushering in updated form of fascism 164
violence as means of bonding 77
violence as strategy 136–7
as welcoming white supremacists and anti-Semites 111
white Christian nationalism 120
white replacement theory 63–4
white supremacy 132, 143–4
working class, portrayed as savior of 173–4
resistance
 analysis of tools of authoritarian regimes 82–3
 education, ideology and culture as sites of 82
 education's role in 170–2
 language, need for knowledge of use 84
 politics and language needed for 167–8
 reclaiming social democracy 113–15
 social movements, uniting globally 170
 starting point for 141–2
rigging of elections 27
right-wing media platforms, fascist rhetoric on 19
Rittenhouse, Kyle, violence by and trial of 29–30, 32–3, 87, 92–7

INDEX

Roof, Dylann 62
Rosenberg, Paul 191

Sainato, Michael 46
Schell, Jonathan 47
scientific reasoning, respect for as deteriorating 153
self-interest 49
self-normalization 79
separation 24
Shapiro, Josh 52
silence as complicity and cooperation 104
slavery, DeSantis's reading of 106–7
slow violence of authoritarianism 135–6
Smith, Michelle R. 162
Soave, Robby 93
social bonds
  collapse of 49
  difficulty forming 24
social democracy
  need for 212
  reclaiming 113–15
social media
  fascist rhetoric on 19
  references to violence in 75–6
  right-wing discourses of hate 162
  toxic role of 21
social movements
  growth of 197–8
  vigilante violence as response to 30
  and vigilante violence, implications for 33
  see also Black Lives Matter (BLM)
social responsibility, neoliberalism and 53
social scientists, abdication of responsibility by 206–7
St. Clair, Jeffrey 195
Stancil, Kenny 74

Stanley, Jason 3
Stefanik, Elise 63–4, 161
Steppling, John 21
street fascism 31
  denialism of fascism after 59–60, 62–9
  lone wolf narrative 68–9
  media reporting on 62–9
  right-wing pollination of 63
  as warning signs 29
Street, Paul 60–1
symptoms of rise of fascism in America 3–4
systemic power relations, lack of analysis of 47–8

Taibbi, Matt 93
Tamas, G.M. 1–2, 158, 213
Tarrant, Brenton 62–3, 162
Taylor Greene, Marjorie 64, 74, 161
teachers, impact of Nazification of education 190
Tennessee, Senate Act 493 200
Thompson, Bennie 138
Timm, Trevor 188
Tlaib, Rashida 95
Tomasky, Michael 17, 51–2
toxic masculinity 122–3
transnational corporations, power of 21
Trump, Donald
  1930s fascism, language reminiscent of 218–19
  2024 elections 152
  alternative reality re. January 6th 150
  analysis of speeches 178–83
  on BLM as threat 180
  BLM, attacks on 201
  critical race theory, attacks on 202–3
  cruelty 45
  Democrat Party, attacks on 179, 180–1

economics as fueling support
for 175–7
efforts to overturn 2020
election 151
eliminationist language, use of
by 178–9, 180–1, 203
embrace of violence 75
hatred of dissent 84
immigrants, attacks on 181–3
January 6th insurrection 137–9
as legitimizing violence 158–9
militarization of protest
policing, call for 180
Nazification of American
society 178, 181–3
polling position 138
QAnon, links with 123–4, 125
rhetoric as fueling vigilante
violence 31–2
right-wing socio-cultural
political values, support for
and 177
as signpost of American
fascism 168
symptoms of rise of fascism in
America 3–4
threats of violence 75
violence as licensed and incited
83–4
as welcoming white
supremacists and anti-
Semites 111
white Christian nationalism 121
working class support as
doubtful 174–5
working class, Trump as savior
of 173–4

universal citizenship 212

values, call for new set of 85
vigilante violence
court sanctioned 29–30, 32
elections and 33, 36

law and order as under threat
31, 32
normalization of 29
racial/ethnic diversity seen as
threat 34
Republican Party as supporting
35–6
as response to citizen activism
30
right-wing rhetoric as fueling
31–2
self-defense as justification
30–1, 32
as sign of rising fascist culture 29
social movements, implications
for 33
violence
authoritarianism, American
135–6
avoidance of discussions
linking fascism to 59
in daily life 20
death threats 74–5
far-right extremists 22
fast 136
as habitualized 81
January 6th insurrection
137–9
lying and 87
Masters, Blake 163
as means of bonding 76
media analyses of increase in 76
Nazification of education 191
neoliberal capitalism and 166
under neoliberal fascism 54–6
neoliberalism and 139
normalization of 22, 46–7, 76,
157–9
as part of neoliberal fascist
order 165–6
references to in online spaces
75–6
slow violence of
authoritarianism 135

as spectacle 78
systemic causes not analysed 47
as threatening dissent 167
white supremacy and 158–9
see also vigilante violence
voter fraud propaganda
　Americans' view of elections after 90
　communities of color as targets of 87–8
　future elections, impact on 92, 152
　lying 88–92
voter nullification 34

Wallace, Henry 23
Wehner, Peter 138
West, Kanye *see* Ye (Kanye West), anti-Semitic and white supremacist comments by
white Christian nationalism
　as almost mundane 178
　Americans' views on 122
　book banning 118–19
　Constitutional law and 121
　discourses of hate 162
　Hillsdale College 120
　invocations of Christian savior politics 121
　masculinity, veneration of 122–3
　Moms for Liberty 118–19
　No Left Turn for Education 119
　other countries compared to US 121–2
　QAnon 123–6
　racism and 123
　white supremacy and 123
　whitewashing of history 117
white replacement theory 19
　conspiracy to replace white voters 88

media mainstreaming of 63
promotion of 161–2
Republican leaders as advocating 63–4
white supremacy
　critical agency and thinking 194
　DeSantis, Ron 105–7
　as fascism 1
　Fuentes, Nick 110–11
　indoctrination in education 194–5
　January 6th insurrection 145
　mainstreaming of by Republican Party 143–4
　neoliberalism and 133–4
　Philadelphia and Detroit as focus for attacks 88
　Republican Party 132
　Rittenhouse trial and, media avoidance of in coverage 92–7
　violence and 158–9
　white Christian nationalism and 123
　Ye (Kanye West) 108–10, 111
whiteness as form of redemption 80
Willis, Ellen 167, 196
Wilson, Tim 161
women, fascism and 164
working class
　Republican Party/Trump portrayed as savior of 173
　Trump support and 174–5
Wright Mills, C. 115

Yang, Maya 25
Yates, Micheal 48
Ye (Kanye West), anti-Semitic and white supremacist comments by 108–10, 111
youth, war on 46, 159–60

Printed in the USA
CPSIA information can be obtained
at www.ICGtesting.com
LVHW011558180524
780598LV00003B/222